INVESTOR BEWARE
Investigating Investments
and Scams

Henry H. Rothenberg

Wordware Publishing, Inc.
Dallas, Texas

Library of Congress Cataloging-in-Publication Data

Rothenberg, Henry H.
  Investor beware.

  Includes index.
  1. Investments.   I. Title.
  HG4521.R778   1988   332.6'78   88-10629
  ISBN 1-55622-055-3

© 1988 Wordware Publishing, Inc.

All Rights Reserved

1506 Capital Ave.
Plano, Texas 75074

No part of this book may be reproduced in any form or by any means
without permission in writing from Wordware Publishing, Inc.

Printed in the United States of America

ISBN 1-55622-055-3

10 9 8 7 6 5 4 3 2 1
8804

All inquiries for volume purchases of this book should be addressed to Wordware Publishing, Inc., at the above address. Telephone inquiries may be made by calling:

(214) 423-0090

Foreword

Prior to the black Monday of 1987, non-stock market investors had already lost billions of dollars, destroying retirement dreams and college plans for hundreds of thousands of people. *Investor Beware* restores those dreams and assures their fulfillment both in and out of the stock market. It introduces you to the world of potentially profitable, diversified investment opportunities as well as their attendant hazards—before you invest. It familiarizes you with a variety of investment opportunities and explains what you should know about each type of business or investment you encounter. Finally, it tells you when to seek professional advice—before you become seriously involved in any type of investment opportunity.

Contents

	Page
Foreword	iii
How This Book Can Help You	xv
How to Protect Yourself	xv
Introduction	1
Questions You Must Ask	1
The Importance of Investment Knowledge	2
The Importance of Economics	3
Index to Basic Sections	5

Section 1
Spotting Investment Con Games and Swindlers

Chapter 1 — How to Protect Your Assets and Credit	9
Judging Integrity of Promoters	11
Salesmen and Closers	12
Essence of a Sales Pitch	12
Written Agreements and Promises	14
Sales Tactics	15
Check the Deal with Professionals	17
Chapter 2 — Even Your Best Friend Can Con You!	19
Con Artists and White Collar Crimes	21
Preferred Inducements Used by Con Men	23
Tax Deduction Inducements	24
Friends for Fraud	24
Summary	27
Chapter 3 — Why Confidence Games and White Collar Crimes Flourish	29
Mobility of Hucksters	31
Enormous Profits	33
Little Jail Time	33
High Cost of Prosecution	33
Embarrassed Victims	35

Chapter 4 — Ponzi-Type and Pyramid Schemes 37
Ponzi-Type Schemes 39
Sophisticated Investors Also Get Trapped 41
Pyramid Schemes 42

Chapter 5 — Don't Trust Guarantees 45
Worthless Guaranteed Bonds 47
What is a Legal Guarantee? 48
Insurance Company Guarantees 48
Bank Guarantees 49
Checking a Guarantee 50

Chapter 6 — Creative and Imaginative Accounting 53
Tricky Accounting 55
Distortion by Banks 56
Qualified Statements 57
Capitalizing Expenses 57
Who Prepared the Financial Statement? 58

Chapter 7 — How the Swindlers Entice and Snare Their Prey 59
Vending Machines 62
The Bait 62
The Pitch 64
Protection 65

Chapter 8 — Watch Your Broker! 69
Self-Serving Brokers 72
Program Trading 73
Churning Accounts 73
Other Problems 74
R.E. and B.O. Brokers 75
Examples of Fraud 75
Insurance Brokers 77
The Broker's Frustration 78

vi

Section 2
Basic Investment Principles

Chapter 9 — Risk-Taking Versus Gambling 83
   Risks and Gambles 86
   Prudent Risk Takers 86
   Ultra-Conservative Investors 87
   Everybody Takes Risks 88
   Judicious Savers 89
   Intelligent Investors 91
   Can You Afford to Lose? 91

Chapter 10 — Analyze Your Investment Disposition 93
   Before You Invest 95
   Ambivalent Investors 96
   Analyzing Your Disposition 97
   Matching Your Investment with Your Disposition ... 99
   Consider Your Patience Quotient 101

Chapter 11 — Establishing Your Investment Goals 103
   Why People Invest 105
   What are Your Investment Goals? 105
   Consider Your Age 106
   Consider Your Spouse 107
   Margins 108
   Protecting Your Assets 109

Chapter 12 — Using Debt to Increase Your Wealth 111
   Leverage 113
   Non-Recourse Instruments 115
   Margin Accounts 116
      Benefits of Using Margin Accounts 117

Chapter 13 — Selecting the Correct Legal Operating Entity 119
   Fictitious Firm Names 121
   Sole Proprietorships 122
   Trusts 123
   Joint-Tenancies 124

General Partnerships 124
    Advantages and Disadvantages of General
        Partnerships 125
    Criteria for Selecting a Business Partner 125
    The Partnership Agreement 126
Limited Partnerships 127
    Examples of Limited Partnerships 127
    The Limited Partnership Agreement 130
Corporations 131
    Forming a Corporation 132
    What are the Disadvantages of a Corporation? .. 133
Subchapter S Corporations 134
Concluding Comments 135

Section 3
What You Should Know About Finances

Chapter 14 — What is Economics and Who Uses It? 139
    Importance of Economics 141
    Economics Defined 141
    Economic Contradictions 142
        Keynesians 144
        Monetarists 144
        Supply-Side Economics 145
        Minor Economic Theories 146
    Important Economic Indicators 146
        Foreign Exchange 147
        Balance of International Trade 148
        Gross National Product and Gross Domestic
            Product 148

Chapter 15 — How to Interpret the Investment Climate .. 151
    Timing the Economic Climate 153
    Interpreting the Indicators 154
    Twelve Leading Economic Indicators 155
    Sensitive Economic Factors 156

Chapter 16 — Who Regulates the Money Supply? 159
    The Treasury Department 161
    The Federal Reserve System 162
    Money Supply 163

Monetary Indexes	164
History of M-1 and Black Monday	165
Controling the Availability of Money	167
A Fed Dilemma	168
A Review	169

Chapter 17 — Forecasting Inflation, Deflation, Recession, and Depression ... 171

Definitions	173
Statistics	174
Conflicting Beliefs and Forecasts	175
Inflation	176
Major Causes of Inflation	178
Deflation	179
Recession	180
Depression	182
Recent Lessons	183

Chapter 18 — How the Federal Budget Affects You ... 187

Investors are Affected by the Budget	189
Surplus or Deficit	189
The Budget Deficit	190
Not a Fiscal Policy	190
Not a Trade Deficit	191
Pump Priming	193
Effects of GNP	193
Deficit-Reduction Theories	195

Chapter 19 — The Import/Export Balance of Trade Quandary ... 197

The Trade Deficit	199
Economic Signal	199
The Balance of Trade	200
Protectionist Bills and Tariffs	203
Tariffs	204
The Quandary	205
Canadian Lumber and U.S. Wheat	208
Look for Signals	212

Chapter 20 — Interest Rates and the Value of the Dollar 213
   How Interest Rates Affect You 215
   Who Controls Interest Rates? 216
   Affect of Interest Rates on Spending 216
   Affect of Interest Rates on Debtor Nations 217
   Affect on Dollar Value 217
      Influence of Federal Reserve 218
      How Foreign Investors React 218
   Corporations and Equity Financing 219
   Bonds and Other Securities 220
   Inflation and Economic Cycles 223

Chapter 21 — Income Shelters and Tax Traps 225
   Abuses 228
   Tax Audits 228
   Legal Tax Shelters 229
      Capital Gains 230
      Interest 230
      Depreciation 231
      Securities 232
      Installment Sales 232
      Short Term Losses 233
   Tax Shelters or Tax Traps 234
   Unusual Tax Breaks 235
   A Few Suggestions 236
   A Final Word 239

Section 4
X-Raying a Business

Chapter 22 — How to Understand Financial Statements . 243
   Protective Clauses 246
   Request Important Financial Documents 247
   Determine Their Accuracy 248
   The Balance Sheet 251
   Earnings 252
   The 56-Question Test 254
      A Quick Preview of the 56 Questions That You
         Should Ask 255

Ratios—Their Importance and How to Create and
  Understand Them 260
The Explanations of the 56 Questions and Answers . 261
About the Investment Analysis Chart 299

Section 5
The Different Types of Investments

Chapter 23 — Syndications 307
  Six Kinds of Ownership 309
  Evaluating Investments in Syndications 312
  Conservative and Speculative Syndication 314
  The Meaning of Insured 315
  What to Look For: Advantages and Disadvantages .. 316

Chapter 24 — Franchises 319
  Benefits of Franchises 322
  Areas to Investigate 323
  Termination 327
  Questions to Ask 327

**Chapter 25 — The Lure and Risks of Venture Capital
Opportunities** 331
  High Risk—High Reward 333
  S.B.I.C.s and Limited Partnerships 334
  What Venture Capital Buys 335
  The Operation 335
  Risks and Problems 336
  What to Look for 337
  New Opportunities 338

Chapter 26 — Real Estate as an Investment 339
  Fundamentals of Property Ownership 342
    Function of Escrow Companies 343
    Types of Ownership 343
    Equity Sharing 344
    Mistakes to Avoid When Purchasing Real Estate 345
    Before You Give a Deposit 348
    Buying Undeveloped Land 349
  About Taxes 351

xi

Chapter 27 — Stocks, Bonds, and Commodities 353
   What are Securities? 355
      Classes of Stock 356
      Quality Rating 357
      Listing on the Stock Exchanges 357
      Buy Low—Sell High 359
      Market Price 360
      Price Determined by Supply and Demand 361
   Sophisticated Trading Techniques 362
   Mutual Funds 364
   Advisors and Planners 368
   Margin Accounts 369
   Convertible Securities 372
   Municipal Bonds 374
   Zero Coupon Bonds 377
   Commodities 378
   Investment Tips 379

Chapter 28 — Buying or Starting a Business 383
   Business-Related Statistics 386
   Ingredients Required for a Successful Business 387
   Why Some Fail 388
      Lack of Planning 388
      Lack of Capitalization 388
      Lack of Experience 389
      Unanticipated Events or Circumstances 389
      A Lack of Continued Planning and
        Management 390
      The Inability to Maintain Adequate Records 390
   Where to Get Assistance 390
   Should I Buy an Established Business or Start
    My Own? 391
   How Much Should I Pay for the Business? 392
   Selecting the Correct Operating Entity 393
   Franchising 394
   How to Find a Business 394
   What to Look for When Buying a Business 396

  The Sophisticated Way to Buy or Sell a Business 397
  Professional Advice 398
  Location 399
  Competition and Promotion 400
  Goodwill 402
  General Business Tips and Guidelines 402

Chapter 29 — Investing in Gold 409
  The Cost of Gold 411
  Ways to Invest in Gold 412
    Mining Company Stocks 415
    Gold Coins 415
  Factors Affecting the Price of Gold 417
  Investor Alerts 418
  Conclusion 419

Chapter 30 — Oil and Gas Exploration and
  Development 421
  Exploration and Development Projects and
    Procedures 424
  Fraudulent Practices 425
  Not Fraudulent but Risky 426
  Imaginative Accounting 427
  Importance of Distribution Facilities and Contacts ... 427
  How to Investigate a Venture 428
  The Agreement, Requests for Addional Funds,
    and Up-Front Fees 428
  Economic and Political Risks—Who Profits and
    Who Loses 429
  Tax Advantages 430
  Economic Considerations 430
  The Value of Reserves 432

Conclusion 435

Index 437

How This Book Can Help You

Swindlers thrive at the expense of every investor that they are able to seduce. Investors who are unable to recognize their "pitch" will always be at their mercy.

Too many investors and would-be business people, because of a lack of knowledge or experience on their part, go broke before their money gets a chance to work for them. Few situations are sadder than when people become victims of bankruptcy because they have never had a fair chance to succeed—and especially so if their loss has involved their retirement or pension funds.

How to Protect Yourself

Obviously, these conditions require immediate solutions. Fortunately, help is available. As an investor you can protect yourself if:

- You constantly remind yourself that your first obligation, to yourself and your family, is to PROTECT your investment capital, credit, and assets from swindlers and bad deals. Uncertain and risky deals must be avoided by the average investor.
- You become aware of certain investment principles before you invest.
- You become familiar with the business, economic, and financial climates in which your money can function and work for you.
- You learn how to screen and evaluate promoters, businesses, and investments.
- You learn how to interpret and understand a financial statement, as well as how to make comparisons with similar ventures.
- You become acquainted with the many types of potentially profitable businesses and diversified investment opportunities that are available to you.
- You consider all of these factors in conjunction with the pertinent provisions of The Tax Reform Act of 1986.
- You seek professional assistance when it is required.

Fortunately, this book addresses the technicalities of all these suggestions. *Investor Beware* is designed as a guide to help you select profitable investment or business ventures that are tailored to your available funds, investment needs, and temperament.

Introduction

Nearly everyone aspires to find a profitable, risk-free venture or investment that guarantees them a sizable income with a minimum contribution of money, time, or work on their part. Unfortunately, most easy-money offers usually expose interested investors to a multitude of seemingly logical but impractical "get-rich-quick" schemes that only benefit the promoters.

As the cost of living has risen, so too has the gullibility of many potential investors. This is particularly true since they became aware that even double paychecks can't provide future financial security without the aid of sound investment. Many people sense that their economic salvation lies in becoming involved either in a business or some form of investment.

Questions You Must Ask

Potential investors seeking investment guidance usually ask their advisers the following basic questions, all of which are fully explored and answered in the following pages.

- What type of investments do you recommend for me?
- Is this the right time for me to invest?
- Can I really get started in investments or buy real estate, like the ads say, without making any down payment?
- Should I consider buying a franchise of a thriving business or start a new business?

But, when they consider an actual business or investment, they forget these equally important questions:

- Is this investment really legitimate or could it be a scam?
- What risks are involved, and can I afford them?
- How will my investment money be protected?
- How long will my money have to be tied up before I get it back?

- How long will I be tied up in this deal if it goes sour?
- Does this investment offer any special tax advantages?
- What is the amount of profit that I can expect, for how long a period of time, and does that profit warrant the risks that are involved? (For example, by comparison, if you could secure a reasonably safe return of 10 percent on your investment, an exploratory oil-well investment with a potential return of 15 percent would be too risky.)

Unfortunately, too many of the answers provided by professional investment counselors are either biased, self-serving, or based upon an incomplete understanding of the entire investment opportunity spectrum. Furthermore, too many professionals specialize in only one investment field and cannot provide you with a comprehensive picture of the variety of opportunities that are available in other investment fields.

Even when investors have an unbiased source of good opportunities to investing, most do not possess the basic background information required to analyze and act upon them intelligently.

Thus, if you are entertaining the idea of becoming a well-informed, successful investor, it is essential that you read this book before you invest. It attempts to protect you from making unnecessary mistakes and also from being swindled by sophisticated frauds and con games.

The Importance of Investment Knowledge

Most investors are unaware of how easily they can be misled by well-meaning friends or professional crooks and misadvised by uninformed brokers, insincere and careless investment advisers, or poorly trained and unsophisticated banking personnel. Even though both investors and borrowers have lost millions of dollars in Ponzi-type mortgage schemes, very few states have regulations that properly control firms that originate first and second mortgages. Too many investors are still being duped by phony guarantees. They cannot believe that the world is saturated with companies, investment advisers, and brokers who unconscionably and illegally concentrate on separating people from their money.

For example, are you aware that in most American jurisdictions any person can become an investment adviser by merely saying or declaring that he or she is one? The law does not prevent an unqualified person from advertising as an investment counselor, and many do.

Even though the Securities & Exchange Commission registers Investment Advisers who are involved in the sale of securities and willingly furnishes important background and financial information about its registered advisers, reportedly, very few investors request this type of information. Although most registered advisers are honest, some have caused investors to be victimized by their misleading information and even theft. Fortunately, the SEC attempts to revoke registrations whenever justified, but such revocation comes too late to help the victim.

When it comes to selecting a timely, suitable investment, potential investors are often misdirected by the media. Even when only seeking news or entertainment on radio or television, they are bombarded by a blitz of hyped, conflicting, and controversial investment messages, as well as inflexible, one-viewpoint-only economists who are constantly quoted by the press. One alleged authority says, "Buy gold!" Another insists, "Buy real estate!" Another says, "Trust deeds!" A fourth advises, "Tax-free bonds!" Another touts "Stocks!" Another says, "Business!" Meanwhile, banks and Savings & Loans on the verge of going broke say, "Trust us!"

There is no limit to the types or scope of illegal investment schemes that are employed to swindle unsophisticated and sophisticated investors alike. Banks and even government entities are not immune, for they too are constantly being defrauded.

The best protection against financial disaster is to acquire investment knowledge—especially about the important factors that influence and control the economic environment in which you, your money, and your business or investment will thrive and function. Far too many investors are unfamiliar with, or overlook, the important effect interrelated economic factors have on their investments.

In addition to emphasizing the same economic information used by business and economic analysts, you can create your own economic forecasts, or at least understand the economic climate in which your investments will work for you.

The Importance of Economics

Because I recognize that most people are adverse to economics, only the important factors that could affect your investments are discussed. Thus, the Gross National Product (GNP), interest rates, the strength of the dollar against foreign currencies, money supply and credit, housing starts, inflationary and deflationary tendencies, and prevailing tax philosophies are made interesting and are explained in simple, understandable terms.

Many people require help in selecting and managing their IRA or Keogh Plan funds. In this book, they are treated as tax shelters and their intricacies are briefly explained.

Financial statements are another subject that plagues many investors. Whether experienced or inexperienced, very few would-be investors know the importance of, much less how to read, a financial statement. Fewer still know the difference in the exact meaning of net earnings as compared to "Net, Net, Net."

You and I will explore the many different types of financial statements. I define the accounting jargon, demonstrate how to interpret them, and evaluate the answers. Moreover, with the aid of a Sample Comparison Chart and 56 explanatory questions and answers in Chapter 22, you learn how to make intelligent comparisons. You also learn how to compare the financial structure and efficiency of businesses and corporations by examining their financial statements before investing in them.

If you have any doubts as to whether or not you require the information contained in this book, you may test yourself with the following example:

Suppose that a few years ago, four people that you knew formed a business venture that you assumed was successful. One day you meet one of the partners on the street, and after greeting and exchanging pleasantries, he says, "One of our partners wants to retire. Would you like to take over his quarter interest in the business for $25,000?"

Before you can make an intelligent decision about involving either, or both, your money and yourself in that investment, there are certain questions that you should ask. Here is the test: Do you know the specific questions that must be asked before you say Yes? When the questions are answered, will you know the meanings of the answers? If you ask at least 56 questions and understand the answers, then you only need this book as a reminder.

The key questions are all here, and I explain their importance and show you how to interpret and evaluate the answers. Also, the key questions will help you understand and evaluate the worthiness of any business proposition or investment—from a small deal or franchise to a large corporation—including sophisticated stock market activities. Without this information, you are a handicapped investor without the tools that are required to properly check out and evaluate opportunities such as franchises, gold, independent businesses, many types of real estate, oil and gas exploration and development, various types of syndications, and a variety of venture capital opportunities.

Index to Basic Sections

This book is divided into five sections:

The First section, *Spotting Investment Con Games and Swindlers*, contains eight chapters about fraudulent practices. It was designed to alert you to misleading advertising, fraudulent schemes, "imaginative accounting," and just plain bad advice.

The Second section, *Basic Investment Principles*, contains five chapters. These discuss important, fundamental investment concepts that people usually ask about, including the use of leverage and margin. It introduces you to the different legal entities under which they may own, lease, operate, or manage property, businesses, and investments.

The Third section, *What You Should Know About Finances*, provides the background for understanding conflicting economic forecasts, and then helps you create your own. It explains money, the functions of the Federal Reserve Bank, the importance of interest rates, budget deficits, import/export trade deficits, and the relationship of all of those factors to both domestic and international economics.

The Fourth section, *X-raying a Business*, explains the importance of financial statements and then introduces and explains sample balance sheets, profit and loss statements, and retained earnings statements. It then provides 56 key questions and answers together with the necessary definitions that you may require to understand and properly evaluate any venture. An Investment Analysis Chart has also been included to help you compare the value and efficiency of investments, businesses, or corporations, on the basis of the answers that you receive to the 56 questions.

The Fifth section, *The Different Types of Investments*, contains eight chapters that provide constructive, practical information about the major types of current business opportunities and investments, including the stock market.

Throughout the book, The Tax Reform Act of 1986 is referred to whenever applicable; and special emphasis has been placed on self employment, tax shelters, tax traps, and write-offs.

Preferably, this mass of helpful information should be blended with a tested business philosophy and this is mine in a nutshell: Investments and business are similar to a lottery—you can't win if you don't take a chance and buy a ticket. Even in the non-speculative areas of real estate, the only people who have profited from real estate during the different real estate booms were the people who bought and controlled some of it. Ordinarily, there is no way that those who sit on the sidelines can get lucky or make a profit.

Hopefully, *Investor Beware* will provide you with the type of knowledge and judicious confidence that will enable you to begin a successful investment program, instead of just continuing to sit on the sidelines repeating, "I could have. . . I should have. . ."

Henry H. Rothenberg

Section 1: Spotting Investment Con Games and Swindlers

Chapter 1: How to Protect Your Assets and Credit

How to Protect Your Assets and Credit

When you respond to an advertisement that offers to send you investment information—whether for free or for a charge—you usually get more than you bargained for. This is because the people who offered to send you the information may sell your name to other promotional-minded people who would also like to contact you. Those name buyers believe that if you respond to one investment ad without knowing too much about it, you are likely to respond to their direct mail or personal telephone solicitations. As a result, it is very likely that your name may eventually appear on what is commonly referred to as a "sucker list."

Thus, by answering just one ad, you may expose yourself to a variety of similar offers. Some may be legitimate but others, despite their legitimate appearance, may come to you from dishonest people who think you might be a soft touch for their pitch. To avoid being overly exposed to these solicitations, you should never send money through the mail to anyone with whom you are not familiar.

Judging Integrity of Promotors

Even when you come face to face with people who want you to invest with them, you should never forget that you cannot judge their integrity by their appearance, charm, or surroundings. Con artists, both men and women, come in every size and shape. They may seem charming, educated, well-spoken, religious, sincere, and full of confidence. Or they may be poorly dressed, crude, shifty-looking, poorly educated, ill at ease, even unreasonably audacious. However, none of these attributes or lack of them, gives you any foolproof clue as to their innate integrity because there is no easy way to spot dishonest salespeople or con artists. Swindlers think differently because they do not mind your risk; they want your money, and they usually know how to get it with pleasant conversation and charming persuasion. Instead of using force, they will attempt to separate you from your money by depending on your gullibility, greed, or laziness. If you say yes to a swindler, you have only yourself to blame.

While honest people can be cheated, it is more difficult to swindle honest people, because they do not want, or expect, something for nothing. On the other hand, an intelligent person can be swindled if he or she is inclined to be gullible, or to want something for nothing, or to look for special deals that other people cannot get. Despite their intelligence, they are too lazy to investigate the principals and otherwise check out the deal.

Preying on their victim's gullibility, swindlers come prepared to tell an interesting, time-tested story (their pitch). A *pitch* is a well-rehearsed, frequently repeated, high-pressure sales talk that is calculated to make a sale. The pitchman knows from experience that his spiel may get you to part with your money. This is how hordes of illegitimate siding salesmen are trained. Their pitch, with variations that best suit the product being sold, has been adapted by many other industries and people.

Salesmen and Closers

In order to protect yourself from these cheats, it is essential for you to distinguish between "salesmen" and "closers." Most salesmen know their product and a little about selling, but they are not considered closers. At best, they are good salesmen, and they may be honest or dishonest. Closers, on the other hand, are a different, more sophisticated type of salesperson. They are not likely to ferret out or qualify buyers (salesmen or others do that for them). In fact, salesmen frequently arrange the closer's appointments with prospects, after qualifying them. Good closers are like experienced, amateur psychologists; they know people, what makes them tick, and how to push the buttons that get them to sign on the dotted line.

Closers prefer to visit you at your home, preferably in the evening, when your mind is not too fresh and when your spouse is around. That way they eliminate your chance to say that you cannot buy now because you must discuss everything with your spouse. They will not want to come to your office because they know there may be too many distractions.

Essence of a Sales Pitch

The essence of the siding or "sample home" pitch, as it is called, is that the homeowner can earn a lot of money while living in a beautified, weather-proof house with all of its attendant benefits. Essentially, the siding (roofing or investment company) has been looking for one "sample house in the area that they can beautify and insulate against the heat and cold, and that will never have to be painted again." From experience, they point out, this is the type of area in which, if the neighbors see the modernized exterior, many of them will want the same job. Naturally, the neighbors will ask who did the work. If you tell them, or just supply their name to the salesman, and they subsequently sign up for the job, you will be paid a large bonus for each referral. The company can afford to pay the bonus, they say, because it is in lieu of normal advertising costs. Further, they explain, "from our experience, we know that a sample house like yours will give us so many extra jobs that we will give you an especially low price with exceptionally low financing. Of course, that low price with good financing will be less than the commissions you will earn from regular referrals."

The whole pitch is designed to overcome your resistance, for how can you resist signing up for all these features:

1. A beautified, temperature-controlled house that will give you low fuel bills.
2. A house that will never require painting.
3. A house that will be worth more when you sell it.
4. Will cost you nothing because you will be paying for it from referrals.
5. Your referrals can exceed the price of the installation, earning surplus money without work.
6. All of this is yours free with just a little down payment and easy financing that they will arrange for you.
7. The monthly payments will be adjusted to your needs so that you can make the payments out of the referrals.

In fact, if you say yes and your credit is approved, you will get the siding and financing as promised. Unfortunately, you will receive few, if any, of the other promised benefits. The price is much higher than normal; you will seldom, if ever, make a referral that they can sell; and you are stuck for many years of monthly payments. You were sucked in by your gullibility that you could get something for nothing as well as your failure to investigate the deal and its principals before taking a contractual step that would put you in debt for many years.

Conscientious, honest salesmen may be inclined to employ unusual sales tactics, or even promise referral fees, but they do not make referral fees the basis for the sale; they do not intend to fool or cheat you. When you say no to a basically honest salesmen, he will not try to high pressure you to change your mind. He will want to change your mind, of course, and he may use some extra, gentle persuasion. But, usually, there is not enough profit in the average deal to allow him to spend too much time with you or be induced to cheat you. He will try to make the sale as quickly as he can; but, at your request, he will give you an opportunity to "think it over."

It is incumbent upon you to take the time to ascertain all the facts. Before you part with your money, you should always investigate the salesperson as well as his firm. When looking over the firm's attractive sales literature, don't be taken in by the glitz of self-serving, attractive pictures or unverified remarks and statements of other people, which can be quite appealing at first glance.

Inexperienced people cannot always be faulted for their gullibility when confronted by experienced confidence men. But they can be faulted for expecting something for nothing, which frequently is the case. Furthermore, the Better Business Bureau is available to help you ascertain the facts.

Investment fraud can also be avoided by making sure that you have a clearly written agreement detailing what you are going to acquire and when. Unfortunately, even in legitimate deals, the most carefully drawn agreement may not protect you when you need it. Chapter 5 *Don't Trust Guarantees* explores this topic in greater depth.

Written Agreements and Promises

If you sign the agreement and part with your money, how do you know that the salesman is authorized by the company to sign the contract? In many fraud cases the contracts are stolen, forged, or specially prepared by the swindlers themselves.

Hard-nosed swindlers will promise, print, write, or sign anything that prompts you to give them your money. Until they are caught, that is how they make their living. Even when the agreement is presented in a properly written and signed form, you may want your lawyer to check the document before you sign it. During the period your lawyer will take to examine the paperwork, you will be giving yourself a cooling-off period to think things over and check with either one or more of the following entities: the Better Business Bureau, the police department, or the district attorney's office. If the deal does turn out to be a scam (a slang expression that refers to a preplanned swindle), the swindler may become fearful that you may not be the fool he took you for, and his fear of being caught may cause him to take his proposition elsewhere.

Sales Tactics

Experienced confidence men, with their constant exposure to danger, are not dismayed by your first refusal to sign a contract and give them your money, nor by your expressed intent to check with your lawyer. Sometimes, they graciously agree to the delay, repack their sales paraphanalia, shake your hand, and proceed toward the door. The swindler knows that these departing tactics will usually place your mind at rest and allay your suspicions, and that at that stage you may be more vulnerable than you were before. Even when they do not use the departing-ploy technique, they feel that while you continue to talk to them, they are continuing to build your confidence in them. They also know from past experience and similar situations that, by employing any of the following tactics, they can instill enough confidence in you to get you to give them a check or cash.

1. Remaining cool, friendly, and seemingly understanding about any resistance you have.
2. Asking you for a drink of water, trying to follow you in the kitchen, and attempting to get you and your spouse to sit down together at the kitchen table with the pretense that they are just easy-going, friendly people.
3. Finding out (from clues around the house) whether you have a hobby, asking you about it, hoping that they can identify with it.

Successful salesmen are usually well informed about many popular hobbies. They can chat with you about it, even compliment you for the picture or trophy that you are likely to show them. They may swap unusual stories, helping you to feel a kinship. They will want you to feel that you have found an understanding friend. If you do not have a common hobby, they may either refer to what you do for a living, a fact that they would have established at the beginning, or they will try to sense some other point with which they can establish a closer relationship that will lead to your trusting them. Usually, their manner and the time and attention they give you will convince you of their sincerity.

Take the hobby of fishing, always a pleasant topic that appeals to many people. The swindlers may tell you about the boat they own and how they invite guests to go fishing with them. Major sports are also a favorite topic that enables them to drop the names of stars athletes as people they know or with whom they do business. They will try to discover at least one of your achievements, preferences, or hobbies so that they can soften you up to trust what they say. These types of conversations are referred to as "confidence builders."

4. Reemphasizing the benefits of the product or service in question and enumerating what you lose if you do not agree NOW to buy the special deal that you are being offered. The benefits will include: how much you need the product or service, how much money it can make or save you, and how much time it will save you.
5. Showing you valid-looking but phony and exaggerated documentation concerning the merits and low price of their service or product.
6. Working on your greed factor (your desire to become rich quickly) by offering you a special discount or an unusual deal, because they don't have extra time, and it will cost them time and money to come back. (On a phony deal, they will offer you anything that sounds reasonable, because you won't get it anyway.) Whatever they can get from you is a profit to them.

If you are dealing with swindlers, their only investment is time, so it makes sense to them to stick with you instead of finding a new "pigeon" and starting all over with an unknown potential victim. Not all swindlers will use the same techniques, but aside from trying to hustle you into signing on the spot by using the "I'm leaving the area to work in another area" routine, most of them will seem to respect your decision to wait and will proceed to offer you more bait.

Even if you and the seller are completely honest, a written agreement is mandatory, because at a future date there is a possibility that either you or the seller will honestly believe that some of the terms of the agreement were different from what they actually are.

Check the Deal with Professionals

To safeguard the loss of your money and to avoid future law suits, before signing any deal or transferring your money, you should check every transaction with both your attorney and your accountant. No matter how trustworthy the other parties to the transaction seem to be, there is never a business-like reason not to use professional assistance. Sometimes, it is wise to use an attorney as an escrow, or to use an escrow company to hold your money until the agreement is fulfilled. Above all, you should only use the services of an attorney or escrow company that you know or that has been recommended to you by someone you trust.

Chapter 2: Even Your Best Friend Can Con You!

Even Your Best Friend Can Con You!

If you are planning to become an investor, you will have to learn to spot and avoid confidence people and the games they play. You must be able to spot investment scams, swindlers, and phony friends and acquaintances. If you do not assume this responsibility, the odds are quite high that you will be ensnared by them. You must always remember, too, that a stranger cannot hurt you as much as a friend or acquaintance, because the stranger cannot get as close to you as your friends and acquaintances.

Con Artists and White Collar Crimes

A con artist with a plan needs someone to fleece. If he has a plan but no way of getting strangers to invest in his scam, wouldn't it be easier for him to contact his friends and acquaintances (even relatives) and get them to contact their friends? That is why, even though you must be loyal to your friends, you must always be careful that you have the correct perspective on the friendship.

I have known people who, when asked for a sizable loan by a friend, have volunteered the requested money as a gift rather than as a loan. Their philosophy was that if the friend was a worthy one, he would repay it if he could. If the friend was not worthy, they would not get it back whether it was donated or loaned. Moreover, they felt that by offering and giving the gift, they would not have to worry about getting it back or destroying a friendship in the event that the friend was sincere and honest but could not afford to repay the loan.

Even if you become familiar with the hundreds of prevalent types of "white collar" crimes, you still may be snared by the new kinds of cunning swindles that constantly victimize the innocent. Both the new and the old swindles will continue to victimize thousands of people every year.

In short, even though you are alerted to many cunning schemes, there is no end to the ways that any investor can be misled, swindled, and financially ruined for life by what the police call white collar frauds. The acknowledged fact is that there just are not enough police and investigators to pursue the perpetrators or enough jail cells to hold them.

No crime is legally classified as a white collar crime, per se, nor is there punishment specified for such crime. The best working definition of *white collar crime* is that it is any type of crime, usually non-violent, committed by a member of a class of people whose normal duties permit them to wear white collars. A few of the actual crimes encompassed by the term include: bribery, embezzlement, theft, fraud, and tax evasion. Other recent types of crimes include computer data tampering and accounting stealth.

Who are these con men and women who rely on these schemes to make a living and, perhaps, someday defraud you? It is your personal responsibility to find out who they are and how they may affect you. They may come from well-respected backgrounds and be college educated. Psychiatrists refer to them as high achievers. They can be bankers, lawyers, accountants, brokers, appraisers, a close relative, a spouse, or one of your best friends who has permitted his greed or ego to affect his ethical conduct.

Some of these schemers get more fun out of outfoxing you or making you look dumb than they do from spending your money. They are the schemers who must constantly gratify their egos by proving they are smarter than the people they are going to fleece. They fulfill their desire by separating someone from his money, without force, simply by illegally defrauding him. They usually are well-educated and can devise and execute their schemes with regularity and success. They are aware that if they are caught, prosecuted, and convicted, their punishment will not be as severe as it would be for the commission of a violent crime. Moreover, they also know that their victims frequently will not admit that they have been fleeced and will not prosecute them.

Unfortunately, when looking for culprits in fraud cases, one is frequently reminded of the old axiom, "You can't cheat an honest man." Though that axiom is not always true, it suggests that there would be fewer victims of fraud if more investors tried to be more ethical, less greedy, and did not depend on other people to protect them. White collar crime could not affect as many victims if more people were not in such a hurry to earn "big bucks" without working for them.

Potential white collar victims unknowingly set themselves up to be plucked by con men, whose major talent is that they know how to read human beings. Through experience and association with other white collar schemers, they know how to find the easiest people to victimize. They need merely attract any of the following types of people:

1. Inexperienced types who trust everybody
2. Those who believe that they can make money easily
3. Those who don't mind getting an edge to take advantage of someone else, even their friends and acquaintances.

Con men love to pursue deals when their intended victims seem to have a little bit of larceny of their own. It makes the con men feel that they have something in common with their victims and it helps—if their conscience ever needs it—to justify their actions.

Preferred Inducements Used by Con Men

It is much easier to swindle a person who has a touch of larceny in his own heart than it is to swindle an honest person. The reason is that honest people, compared to those looking for an easy buck, are more inclined to evaluate the merits of any proposition or the character of the people who introduced them to it. They do not mind working for what they earn. They likely abide by the Golden Rule—that is—they do not want to take advantage of anyone else.

The preferred inducement to invest used by con men or women is an expressed or implied promise "to get rich quick" by getting in on the ground floor of any of the following:

1. A business or venture with special tax-breaks
2. A loan that promises a usurious return on the principle investment
3. A life of ease with little work because other people do the managing or the work (such as in multilevel marketing scams, which are variations of pyramid schemes)
4. Any type of easy-to-get, easy-to-start part-time business

The desire to acquire other people's money without working for it seems to be one of the strongest motivators for inducing people to act dishonestly. As an investor, your only defense against predators who want to take your money is to remain constantly aware of their presence and your own concupiscence. If a friend has a dishonest, minimum-risk plan to avoid taxes that could benefit both of you, it might not seem unusual to you that he would want to give you the chance to share in the plan with him. But, be sensitive to your propensity to make a quick profit or save tax dollars by getting involved in dubious schemes with questionable associates. All investors who try to save on taxes through suspect tax shelters are not guilty of criminal wrongdoing. But they do expose themselves to civil suits by both the federal and state authorities for back taxes, interest, and penalties. Even if it's not a tax shelter that your friend wants to get you involved in, its legality should be uppermost in your mind.

Tax Deduction Inducements

In one fraud case a federal grand jury indicted a Charles Atkins and others in March of 1987. The *Wall Street Journal* reported, "According to government officials, Mr. Atkins promised investors $4 in tax deductions for each dollar invested in the limited partnerships." Because Atkins was well known, many prominent people became limited partners. Their combined deductions exceeded $10 million. All the deductions were eventually disallowed.

One of the techniques used in schemes like this is to secure tax deductions by having the limited partnership establish year-end trading and interest losses on their books. Then, through securities trades made solely for the purpose of establishing a book profit in the following year, the securities would be reacquired in the new year. Accordingly, they share in the limited partnership's profits although it is frequently understood, and sometimes agreed upon by the general partners, that the partnership was not created to make a profit.

As strange as it may seem, those who become limited partners in some partnerships believe they are already in too high a tax bracket to want to make more money. Many investors, depending on their tax bracket, would have more spendable money if they could show legitimate tax losses. Remember, however, that if fraud is involved in such losses, the investment could be lost.

Friends for Fraud

A few words about friends. Assume that you have the greatest friends in the world, and that you would have no hesitancy in selecting any one of them to become the executor of your estate.

Unfortunately, history does not support your blind confidence; it indicates instead that you should not be surprised if one of them disappoints you or even tries to con you while you are still alive.

Consider the "friends" of the run-away San Diego con man who allegedly fleeced several neighborhood wives, their mutual friends, their relatives, and other trusting souls. When he was caught, he faced a federal indictment listing 120 counts of criminal activity. His career, when it began, was spectacular.

It started in 1947 when he went to Sing Sing Prison at the age of 27 for persuading his family and friends to invest a few hundred thousand dollars to buy steel that was so scarce it did not exist! After his release, he frequently changed identities, locations, wives, and employers. No matter where he was or who he purported to be, his business consisted of embezzling from or conning his friends, acquaintances, and employers. Then he would disappear.

In the mid-70s he moved to San Diego where he worked as an accountant and the manager of a commodities pool involving money from hundreds of investors. He married yet again and became an exemplary husband and devoted stepfather. However, in March of 1984, a day before the U.S. Futures Trading Commission was scheduled to inspect his books, he told his wife that he did not feel well and was going to see a doctor. At this point, he simply disappeared.

In January 1985, he resurfaced in Cincinnati, Ohio, where he was looking for employment as an accountant. He was spotted by an employee of an employment agency who had been alerted by an FBI Wanted circular bearing his picture. He was jailed without bail.

At the time, the FBI believed that he had collected more than $2 million from investors. In June of 1985 the government charged him with bilking some 800 investors out of $16.4 million, and he pled guilty to some of the charges. He claimed that his assets were less than $20,000. The fact was that his commodities pools were bankrupt. When the newspapers published the story revealing that he had been married eight times, more people seemed interested in his personal life than in his financial swindles. Some of the reports were that he had eight identities in eight states with six wives. Nonetheless, you can be sure that the 800 people he swindled were interested in more than his bigamy.

In another case involving friendship, members of the famous

Osmond family were allegedly defrauded by a Mormon bishop, J. Gary Sheets, who was considered a friend of the family. In the 70s the popular Osmonds became famous and wealthy through their recordings and television appearances. Thereafter, as happens to many wealthy, theatrical celebrities, they were exposed to promoters, many of whom consistently managed to reduce their capital. Apparently, those sad experiences did not affect them when they met Sheets in 1983 because they developed a close friendship. The Osmonds were not solicited for investments until 1985.

Until the collapse of his company, CFS Financial Corp., in 1985, Sheets was considered a financial genius as well as being a respected member of the Mormon Church. He was not a fly-by-night, having formed his company in 1971. He and a large sales force sold many interests in partnerships, and his earnings were estimated to be $600,000 a year from commissions plus an annual salary of $72,000. However, sometime prior to his company's insolvency, many of the partnerships sold by him and his high-commission salesmen ran into financial difficulties. Customarily, these are the cases in which the promoters find it necessary to borrow from Peter to pay Paul.

CFS became insolvent in 1985. Many of its defunct, limited partnership properties were seized by banks and creditors. Of the 1,500 investors who had invested $1.5 million, only a few will recover just a portion of their original investment.

According to a suit filed by Osmond in 1986 in the Salt Lake City Federal Court, Sheets began to invite Osmond to participate after he became aware of his financial difficulties. Based on a promise from Sheets that he would invest one-half his funds in a real estate syndication, Osmond gave him $30,000 of his pension money.

Although the examples of swindling in this book are designed to keep you constantly conscious of how easy it is to be cheated, you must not overlook the many other ways that you can sustain heavy financial losses. Fortunes have been lost because of honest, well-meaning but financially uninformed friends, who think of themselves as financial wizards. Many of them seem to know more about gaining your confidence and persuading you to invest than they know about conducting financial or business matters legitimately.

A story entitled "Designer-home Fraud Ends in 26 Months in Prison" that appeared on July 18, 1986, in *The Vancouver Sun*, a Canadian newspaper, sketchily revealed yet another unique scam. It was used by one Edmund Wilson to defraud his friend, Art Moloney, out of $125,000.

In 1980, using a "residential retreats" concept that involved a plan for low-cost designer homes, Wilson interested his friend in investing $125,000. Wilson claimed that he had 40 to 50 designs for houses from seven top architects. Actually, he only had a few preliminary sketches and no contracts. In addition to investing the $125,000 with Wilson, Moloney was to use his real estate expertise to help market Wilson's "residential retreats" concept as the 1981 prize home of the Pacific National Exhibition. In early 1981, Wilson did secure a contract with the Exhibition to build its prize home, using a design by one of the top architects. In 1986 Wilson pleaded guilty to defrauding his friend Moloney as well as others in various fraudulent schemes and received a 26-month sentence.

The greatest abuse of friendship occurs when a friend approaches you to become an investor in one of the variations of the Ponzi or pyramid schemes. Chapter 4 describes these types of schemes in detail.

Summary

The thrust of this chapter has been primarily to:

1. Explain and alert you to who the culprits might be so that you can avoid their enticements.
2. Make you consider, before investing, whether you are greedy, expecting too much, or investing with responsible people of good character.
3. Make you aware that when friends recommend a business to you, that you exercise more than the ordinary amount of care before you entrust your money to them.

Even if friends have very high character, under the pressure of severe financial reverses, their desperation may cause them to defraud their best friends. Frequently, by promising to pay a high rate of interest, they induce their friends to give them urgently needed funds which they have no intention of repaying. They can even justify not paying the funds back. A common self-serving excuse is that the friend who loaned them the money was wrong to charge them such a high rate of interest.

If you do know a trustworthy, experienced person with a successful track record for making money in a specific business, by all means consider investing your money with that person. But remember, no business venture is absolutely risk-free. You have to eliminate as much risk as you can. The easiest way to do this is by keeping in mind that you—not your friends or their acquaintances—are responsible for your money. The Roman Law *caveat emptor* means "buyer beware" and applies to your investments.

Chapter 3: Why Confidence Games and White Collar Crimes Flourish

Why Confidence Games and White Collar Crimes Flourish

If you have ever wondered why the authorities permit the continuing number of fraudulent schemes to persist year after year when the toll of victims and their financial losses continue to increase, the answer is simple: Investigating and prosecuting fraud cases is very expensive and crime-fighting budgets are usually limited. On top of this, most jails are already full. Many fraud cases require years of investigation as well as years of sparring in court during trials and appeals. The costs in terms of manpower and money are extremely high. To make matters even more frustrating, most convicted white collar criminals spend less than a year in jail, according to a November 1986 government study.

Mobility of Husksters

Contributing to the high and mounting crime rate are increasing numbers of telephone and telemarketing frauds and the mobility of these hucksters, who move to different cities or states at will. According to Federal Trade Commission Chairman Daniel Oliver, "These hucksters hustle the public for an estimated $3 million a year." Besides trying to sell goods and services, these telephone pitchmen also use their high-pressure sales techniques to sell dubious oil and gas leases, gemstones, and other rare stones. Once victimized, the victim's name and telephone number become a valuable asset that can be sold to other hucksters. The elderly, especially those who are confined to their homes and frequently lonely, are anxious for conversation and are very susceptible when confronted by an experienced con man. Worried about keeping up with inflation, they respond to offers of a chance to participate in high-yield investments without first checking them out. It has been reported that they have even given money to help colonize the moon.

Pitchmen use inexpensive long distance telephone services. They use the phone with the ease of an experienced carpenter hitting a large nail. They procure some of their leads from names of honest but possibly greedy, susceptible people, frequently referred to as moochers—from responses they make to appealing advertisements on radio and television or in newspapers and magazines. The individual hustlers and the companies they represent are "fly-by-nights" who visit all states, seldom staying in one place long enough to get caught.

Fortunately, federal government fraud agencies and the National Association of Attorneys General in a joint effort have agreed to keep each other informed about the whereabouts and techniques of recognized con men.

Nevertheless, securities fraud cases continue to proliferate. Proving allegations against brokers or other miscreants is expensive and time consuming. In an effort to relieve court congestion and secure quicker justice, many court officials are urging investors to use arbitrators to bypass the courts.

Violent crimes, such as murder, robbery, and assault usually get priority treatment over non-violent crimes like fraud. Under such conditions, too many prosecutors feel that the remedy for the victim might be a civil action to recover regular or punitive damages for fraud and deceit. Unfortunately, in most cases of criminal fraud, the perpetrators either disappear, hide their assets, or go bankrupt, thus preventing any remedy through civil law.

Based on the concept that many frauds could be treated as civil cases, many swindlers receive special consideration when they promise to help prosecuting attorneys secure convictions against co-conspirators or perpetrators of similar scams. But, this lenient practice is of little value to those victims who have already been swindled out of their hard-earned money.

The Securities & Exchange Commission and the Commodity Futures Trading Commission also have tended to settle alleged fraud cases by imposing fines and/or restricting similar activities in the future. In one case, an alleged defendant—Conti Commodity Services—paid a record fine of $1.5 million.

The allegations stemmed from an alleged silver manipulation in 1979 and 1980 that was settled about seven years after the crime. An undisclosed portion of the $1.5 million fine was for alleged slipshod supervision of a multimillion-dollar sugar and cocoa futures trading program.

Enormous Profits

Another important factor in the proliferation of white collar crime is that the profits are enormous because the commodity that the swindlers sell is usually limited to their own inexpensive hot air. Of course, those high profits enable the swindlers, when caught, to employ talented defense attorneys. For white collar criminals, high legal fees are a contemplated risk which is part of their normal cost of doing business.

The size of their illegal profits induce most swindlers to continue their trade even after they are caught and punished. First, their expensive, experienced criminal lawyers know how to delay the trials for long periods of time. While awaiting trial, the swindlers are usually out on bail free to raise legal fees through more of the same kind of nefarious activities that brought them to court in the first place. Second, if the swindlers are convicted, they frequently find legal grounds for immediate appeal of their conviction and are often released on bail. This permits them to continue their criminal activities until they lose their last appeal.

Little Jail Time

In November 1987, the *Wall Street Journal* reported that Robert Bonner, a U.S. attorney in Los Angeles, complained that almost 60 percent of the people he has convicted of bank fraud or embezzlement since January 1986 haven't done a day of jail time.

High Cost of Prosecution

A prime example of the cost of conducting an investigation and prosecuting a criminal fraud action against a notorious swindler recently occurred in Canada. There, the Mounties and prosecutors don't seem to believe in permitting swindlers to profit and prosper without just punishment. The Canadian government's investigation of one man's swindling several banks of an estimated $1 million, is reported to have cost the government nearly $1 million to prosecute. Nonetheless, their efforts eventually resulted in the man's conviction and incarceration in 1984.

The swindler's *modus operandi* was to con car dealers into loaning him cars on consignment. Then, using the cars as security, he conned an individual into loaning him $300,000. Thereafter, he borrowed $900,000 from the Continental Bank of Canada, giving them as security a combination of non-existent property, a false financial statement, and forged telexes that referred to a large line of credit from a Detroit bank. He paid off that loan with money he borrowed from the Bank of Montreal by using the same type of credit statements. If you were to analyze this prosecution from a return on investment point of view, the conviction would hardly seem worthwhile since it cost almost as much to convict the criminal as he ended up taking through his illegal acts. However, the proper perspective regarding such expenses is the benefit gained by society in having this man behind bars.

In a different case in Washington, D.C., it took nearly two years of litigation before a federal judge enjoined an investment managing firm from misleading its 15,000 subscribers. The firm was accused of misrepresenting the source of some feature articles that spotlighted certain companies. The alleged problem was that the articles were written by public relations agents for one of the spotlighted companies.

From that case, the investor should learn to check the source of the information that is inducing him to invest. Is it press agent puffery or substantial facts on which a prudent person may base an intelligent investment decision?

Long investigations and costly trials are not limited to North America. In Paris, France, after the collapse of the Boussac textile group in 1981 and the subsequent bankruptcy of its holding company, it took four years of intensive investigation, producing 10,000 pages of testimony and 60 hours of hearings, to secure convictions against three brothers. A fourth brother was acquitted. The brothers were charged with illegally transferring money for their own use, abuse of corporate assets, and presenting inaccurate balance sheets, etc. It is these types of lengthy trials that enable confidence games and white collar crimes to flourish throughout the world.

With respect to the difficulties encountered in curbing alleged frauds, the foreign press has criticized the inequality of the punishment meted out by U.S. stock exchanges to the sales representatives of their member firms for their alleged frauds. It has been suggested that the punishment given to sales representatives (mistakenly referred to as brokers) is more severe than that received by their employing brokers. For example, in the options case (a very tricky field), many investors feel too many brokers undertrain their options salesmen. However, the main objection by the press is that the brokers are given more leniency than their representatives when a fraud occurs because the member firms own the exchanges.

Embarrassed Victims

Another reason why white collar crimes flourish is that too frequently the victims, including top-level government officials and prominent, influential, and wealthy people, are ashamed to admit that they had been swindled out of large sums of money. Many such victims would rather suffer a heavy financial loss than admit that they acted unwisely. There is a chance for you to spare yourself that type of grief, provided you observe three basic rules:

1. Be responsible for your own investment investigations and actions. Do not depend on the recommendations of even your most trusted friends, because their investigations may not be deep enough to uncover all of the impending, dangerous facts. The other person might even be in a better financial position than you and better able to afford a loss.
2. Know the character of the person making the offer and other principals with whom you become involved, along with their business backgrounds. Arrange to contact a disinterested party who knows them.
3. Assuming that you have checked and are satisfied with all of the important facts and principles involved in a transaction, **do not give anybody any earnest money**. If you decide to participate in the venture, first secure a good commercial attorney. Ask him to draw up the necessary papers, including escrow instructions to be signed by all parties, with the purpose of opening an escrow transaction with his agreement. After the escrow is opened, subject to your lawyers' agreement, you may deposit your earnest money into the escrow account. You can never be too careful.

Chapter 4: Ponzi-Type and Pyramid Schemes

Ponzi-Type and Pyramid Schemes

Most people are unaware that their minds are being constantly bombarded by an endless variety of fraudulent schemes that were specifically designed to allay their deep-rooted suspicions and then to snare their money. Foremost among the schemes that help to swindle gullible victims out of millions of dollars in short periods of time each year are the ubiquitous Ponzi-type and pyramid schemes.

Ponzi-Type Schemes

Ponzi schemes derive their name from Charles A. Ponzi one of the best known and most successful swindlers of the early 20th Century. However, famous as he was, he merely followed an old tested formula for stealing money from innumerable investors. These investors were attracted to the scheme because they saw so many other people—without experience and doing little work—getting paid high profits simply for the use of their money. These schemes today offer unsophisticated investors a much higher return than most other investments, and sometimes even more than the phony "get-rich-quick" type of businesses that may suggest that some work or experience is required.

The original Ponzi-type scheme was very basic. Subsequent operators created an aura of wealth using a swanky office, fine clothes, and expensive cars (sometimes even a plane). They disseminated hints or suggestions that they had a very profitable venture that distributed very large profits to lenders. This is the kind of come-on that makes most investors perk up their ears and ask for a piece of the action. Ponzi-type schemes are usually very profitable for their operators—until they get caught!

The *modus operandi* for current Ponzi-type schemes is still the same, except that many of the new breed of swindlers also use the media extensively. Frequently, variations of Ponzi schemes are combined with pyramid schemes in which the unsuspecting victims are induced to solicit additional victims for which they receive financial rewards.

Usually, the Ponzi operator does not possess a tangible venture, but when investors meet or hear about other investors who are receiving unusually large interest payments or loan repayments when requested, their strong desire for part of the action causes them to become careless about investigating.

Frequently, many of the investors reinvest their interest payments. The reinvested interest payments that are reloaned to the Ponzi operators, together with the money from newly acquired loans, are then used to pay for personal and office expenses and to continue to pay earned interest.

These types of schemes have become so popular that the Securities & Exchange Commission issued a brochure with the following example of how the Ponzi scheme pays off "old investors with money coming in from new investors."

Investor A gives promoter (P) $1,000 on P's promise to repay $1,000 plus $100 interest in 90 days.

During the 90 days, P makes similar promises to investors B and C, receiving $1,000 from each of them. At the end of the first 90-day period, P may offer to pay A the $100 "interest" and to return his original $1,000. More likely, he will invite A to reinvest the $1,000 plus the $100 "interest" for a similar or higher return at the end of another 90 days. Thereafter, A, believing he can continue to receive an excellent return on his investment, is likely to bring other potential investors to P.

The principal activity of the Ponzi operator is to create a prestigious front. He must maintain a busy-looking office, keep meticulous records, and try to pay off all obligations on time or when requested. Originally, he depended on word-of-mouth advertising, but now he also uses all forms of media advertising and often issues fancy brochures filled with untruths.

These schemes flourish as long as new investors continue to contribute fresh investment funds. However, when too many people ask for the return of their money at the same time or when the operator cannot continue to pay back the earned interest on time, the authorities step in, and inevitably the scheme fails.

Usually, however, the authorities do not come into the picture until long afterwards because when the operator senses that there is not enough new money coming in to continue the scheme, he either disappears with all the money or reveals the bad news that the investments went sour. Thus, when the blow-up occurs, the lenders are out both their interest and principal. When interest rates are low, Ponzi-type schemes last longer before they are detected because they require less capital to operate.

Sophisticated Investors Also Get Trapped

Even sophisticated investors get taken in by Ponzi-type schemes. The bait is very tempting: for a loan of any size for a short period—with the operator's personal guarantee, if requested—lenders will receive a much larger return on their investment than they can obtain anywhere else. Sometimes the original investors believe that they have actually doubled their money. That's why they reinvest; and that's why even sophisticated investors are anxious to invest without investigating.

All Ponzi and pyramid schemes fail because there are not enough people in the world to make them work. Sometimes the schemes benefit the early-joiners, but they are only profiting from the losses incurred by other subsequent joiners.

The following scenario, detailed in the Securities & Exchange Commission's brochure on Ponzi schemes, ought to give you pause.

> Robert Dale Johnson, operating as Ridge Associates, promoted a purported wine import business involving the purchase and sale of "industrial wine," ostensibly for use in the manufacture of salad dressing and other by-products. In fact, there is no such thing as "industrial wine."
>
> Investors were sold short-term promissory notes in amounts ranging from $2,500 to $250,000 and were promised a return of the amount borrowed plus profit ranging from 30 percent to 100 percent within six to nine months, depending upon the maturity date.
>
> In this case, there was no wine import business. The promoter used the borrowed money for his own stock market purchases and other personal uses. The operation kept going because many investors, instead of cashing their promissory notes upon maturity, agreed to new ones that they thought would allow their capital and profit to accumulate. Those investors who did not want to continue were paid off with funds from new and present investors.

By now, you should be able to guess how the scheme ended.

Pyramid Schemes

Pyramid schemes continue to proliferate for three reasons:

1. There are many gullible people in the population who do not want to think for themselves.
2. When disguised as business opportunities, which they frequently are, they may not be recognized as pyramid-type schemes.
3. The scheme is very attractive to unsophisticated non-business people who want to invest or who see a way to improve their financial position without exerting any great effort.

Hopefully, these people eventually learn that only they have the responsibility of protecting their money from fraudulent investments. Instead of their believing that the law protects them, that most people are honest, and that the plan cannot fail, they should learn, before they put up any money, that it is their responsibility to protect themselves by investigating any propositions that are advanced to them which sound too good to be true.

Aware of the magnitude of pyramid-style frauds, and attempting to fulfill its statutory duty to prevent them, the SEC has provided the following example of a pyramid scheme. It is essentially a business variation of the familiar chain letter. It works this way.

> Promoter (P) offers A and B the chance to invest by purchasing "distributorships" at $1,000 each. The distributorships give A and B the "exclusive" right to sell "distributorships" to others for $1,000 each and to sell certain products to the public. However, each $1,000 that A and B receive from the sale of their distributorships must be divided with P, say 50-50. Thus A and B can theoretically realize $500 on each distributorship they sell, and can completely recover their $1,000 investment by selling only two distributorships each. P, however, has received not only A's and B's $1,000 each, but also will receive $500 for each distributorship that A and B sell.
>
> Initially, it would appear that this can go on forever with no one getting hurt and everyone making money. But the

following chart shows that the number of investors needed to keep the pyramid scheme working quickly exceeds the population of the United States. The chart assumes that P initially sells distributorships to six persons, each of whom brings in an additional six purchasers per month.

Months	Participants
1	6
2	36
3	216
4	1,296
5	7,776
6	46,556
7	279,936
8	1,679,616
9	10,077,966
10	60,466,166
11	362,796,056
12	2,176,782,336
13	13,060,694,016

World population is under 4 billion. U.S. population is approximately 220 million.

The chart also shows why such a scheme is called a "pyramid." The promoters are at the top of a pyramid-shaped flow of money. Money coming from later investors flows upward to the top. Being at the top may result in your receiving a lot of money quickly, but it is virtually impossible to determine at the beginning where in the pyramid you stand.

The Securities & Exchange Commission recently brought action against Koscot Interplanetary, Inc. and other similar organizations to bar them from marketing products through a program characterized as a pyramid selling scheme.

Koscot was alleged to have operated what it termed a "multilevel distributorship." The chart below depicts the alleged distribution setup of Koscot.

Profit from Sponsoring an Investor

	Cosmetic Discount	Required Investment	Investor	Koscot
Level 3 Distributer	65%	$5,000	$3,000	$2,000
Level 2 Supervisor/Retail Manager	55%	$1,000	$600	$400
Level 1 Beauty Advisor	45%	None	None	None

As you can see, at Level 1 is the Beauty Advisor whose income is derived solely from retail sales of Koscot products made available to him or her at a 45 percent discount. At Level 2 is the Supervisor or Retail Manager. To become a Supervisor, a $1,000 investment was required. In return, a Supervisor received cosmetics at a 55 percent discount, to be sold either to the public directly or to be held for wholesale distribution to Beauty Advisors. In addition, the Supervisor who recruited another Supervisor for the program received another $600 from the $1,000 investment paid to Koscot. At Level 3 is the position of Distributor, which required an investment of $5,000. A Distributor was entitled to purchase cosmetics at a 65 percent discount for distribution to Supervisors and Beauty Advisors. For sponsoring a Supervisor, the Distributor would receive $600 and for sponsoring another Distributor, he would receive $3,000.

The investment promotion was made at "Opportunity Meetings" conducted by Koscot employees in conformity with scripts specially prepared for them. Employees were instructed to drive to meetings in expensive cars—preferably Cadillacs—to dress expensively and to flaunt large amounts of money. Koscot employees apprised prospects of the "virtues" of enlisting in the Koscot plan. It was intended that prospects would be enticed into signing a contract by these ostentatious displays in the evangelical atmosphere of the meetings. While these promotions emphasized the money to be made from becoming a Supervisor or Distributor and then recruiting other "investors," little effort was made to sell cosmetics to the public. Consequently, one's "investment" could be recouped only by a never-ending increase in the number of new "investors" at all levels.

When the bubble finally burst, the insubstantial structure of the corporation and its virtual lack of assets was exposed. Widespread publicity resulted in the drying up of new investors. Thus, the company's many investors found their hard-earned savings lost forever.

Chapter 5: Don't Trust Guarantees

Don't Trust Guarantees

It is a sad, shocking experience to learn that the guaranteed investment you depended upon to take care of you in the future may be worthless. Even a guarantee issued in good faith by municipalities or those issued by insurance companies to banks or thrift organizations can turn out to be worthless.

Worthless Guaranteed Bonds

Imagine the consternation of some 4,500 investors, who had bought $2.2 billion of guaranteed public utility bonds, when the bonds became practically worthless. The guaranteed bonds were issued prior to 1981 by the state of Washington's Public Power Supply System (WPPSS) to finance its nuclear power plants 4 and 5. The bonds were guaranteed by 28 municipalities in the form of "take or pay" contracts in which the municipalities would receive the energy and the WPPSS would pay the bonds with the funds received from the municipalities.

A "take or pay" contract obligates the promisor to pay whether or not the promisor actually receives the product, which in this instance was electrical power. A New York law firm rendered an opinion that the contracts with the municipalities were valid.

After the WPPSS defaulted on the bonds in 1983, the Chemical Bank and Trust Company in New York sued the municipalities to recover their losses under the guarantees. Unfortunately for the bondholders, the Washington State Supreme Court, in a decision that was later upheld by the U.S. Supreme Court, declared that the guarantees were invalid because the municipalities did not have the authority to sign "take or pay" contracts. The reasoning of the Washington Court was that it considered the "take or pay" contracts to be guarantees of the bonds if the nuclear plant failed. Under their charters, the municipalities did not possess the authority to issue such a guarantee.

The Court's reasoning as to the effect of the "take or pay" contract was unexpected in most legal circles, but the basic principle that was reinforced was the elementary legal principle that for a guaranty to be effective, the guarantor must have the *authority* and *capacity* to issue a guaranty. The word capacity here refers to being legally qualified to perform the act.

In 1984, the Court expanded its ruling and released from liability 60 additional guarantors of the project. Naturally, the case was appealed to the U.S. Supreme Court, which refused to alter the non-liability ruling of the Washington Court.

What is a Legal Guarantee?

Through common usage, most people think of a *guarantee* as a promise to rectify a mistake, fulfill a contract, or pay off a debt. That definition is not incorrect. Technically, the word "guarantee" refers to the person to whom a guaranty is made by a guarantor (the promisor). Legally, a guaranty "is a promise to answer for the payment of some debt, or the performance of some duty, in the case of failure of another person who, in the first instance, is liable for such payment or performance." A guaranty may differ in its scope and intent and may be termed either general, absolute, conditional, limited, or special. Regardless of the name or intent of the guaranty, to be legally enforceable, it must contain all of the elements that validate any legal contract.

A bond is a certificate in which a person, corporation, or government guarantees to pay a specified sum of money on or before a specific date. The conventional method for governments, municipalities, and large corporations to borrow money is to issue and sell bonds. These bonds contain specified dates for both the payment of interest and repayment of the principal.

Insurance Company Guarantees

Consider for a moment guarantees issued by insurance companies. What would you think about buying a trust deed or mortgage that paid the prevalent rate of interest and was backed by an insurance company that met the requirements of the BankAmerica Corporation in their capacity as a trustee? By now, you should think twice before answering, otherwise, you might get stung in the same manner that befell the BankAmerica Corporation. In the first quarter of 1985 the bank wrote off $94 million in losses for the fourth quarter of 1984. The losses arose because a pool of insured mortgage securities defaulted, and the insurance companies that had guaranteed the mortgages could not pay off after the default.

The ascertainable facts are that the bank acted as both an escrow and a trustee for pools of mortgage loans. They were packaged by another company that used them as collateral for mortgage-backed certificates that were sold to Eastern thrift (a form of bank) associations. By purchasing these insured certificates, the thrifts avoided the high costs attached to originating individual mortgage loans.

The market value of mortgage certificates is usually based on the appraisal value of the underlying property and the guarantee of an insurance company. In this case, serious allegations were made that the appraisals were faulty, meaning the properties were over-appraised or had faulty titles. Furthermore, the two insurance companies—Pacific America Insurance Company of Wilmington, Delaware, and Glacier General Assurance Company with offices in California—were allegedly in financial difficulty. To prevent the involved thrifts from suffering financial losses, BankAmerica aggressively made satisfactory arrangements with them.

This case points out that aside from the other potential problems that can arise from real estate loans, it is also important to verify the financial ability of any insurance company that is involved in issuing guarantees in a transaction. Further, investors must also be aware that even large financial institutions may overlook the essential requirement of double-checking the insurance companies with whom they are dealing.

Standard & Poor, an organization that is highly regarded for its ability to rate corporations, recently lowered the claims-paying rating of two insurance companies because they did not have the capital to support the amount of insurance they had issued. Again, the lesson is do not automatically rely on a guarantee just because it is backed by an insurance company. If you are depending on the guarantee to protect yourself in the event of a default, then check the rating of the company with your State Insurance Commission or in one of the established books that rate companies.

Bank Guarantees

Many people mistakenly believe that their bank and savings deposits are insured by the full faith and credit of the U.S. government. They are not.

The Federal Deposit Insurance Corporation (FDIC) tries to

protect commercial bank depositors, and the Federal Savings and Loan Insurance Corporation (FSLIC) tries to protect savings and loan depositors. However, depositors should be aware that even though both corporations are federal, their financial liability to pay-off claims is limited because they function as corporations. The limited liability protection that inures to the benefit of corporations is one of the main reasons that so many firms operate as corporate entities.

The solvency of the aforementioned FDIC and the FSLIC depends upon arrangements made with the Federal Home Loan Bank Board or Boards. For example, in September 1985 news sources reported that the Federal Home Loan Bank in San Francisco was being petitioned to form a quasi-governmental agency to help relieve the embattled FSLIC. The *Wall Street Journal* stated, "The FSLIC has allowed hundreds of essentially insolvent S&Ls to continue to operate because it doesn't have the resources to pay for their liquidation or merger into healthy institutions."

Checking a Guarantee

Too many people rely on their interpretation of the guarantee instead of concentrating on its validity, the actual net worth of the guarantor (the total amount of liabilities, including guarantees, subtracted from gross assets), and merits of the proposition being guaranteed.

The Washington State utility case should alert you to the necessity of obtaining a valid guaranty contract, checking the legal capacity of the guarantor to enter into a contract, and verifying the authority and capacity of the guarantor to enter into and sign the legal contract that contains the guarantee. The other basic elements of an enforceable contract are that a legal consideration be paid, and the purpose of the transaction must be lawful and not against public policy.

Here are some examples of how to protect yourself when you are involved with a guaranty.

1. Make sure that the organization that signs the document is an organization with assets. It should not be merely a shell corporation without assets that is being used by the company from which you want the guaranty.

2. Make sure that the guarantor and party being guaranteed have a legal existence that is recognized by the state. For example, it cannot be a legal corporation without first being incorporated, which is the equivalent of possessing a charter from the state to operate within its borders. Moreover, the guarantor corporation and the party being guaranteed should have been incorporated before they sign the guaranty.
3. Make sure that the organization and all of the signatories have the authority to issue the guaranty in question. In this regard, it is not uncommon to insist upon receiving a copy of an authorizing resolution of its board of directors.
4. Make sure that all responsible parties and necessary officers and directors of the company sign the document, and that the corporate seal is affixed. In some areas it is important that the individual percentage of ownership of each of the signatories is designated alongside their respective signatures.
5. The document should contain the words that the guarantors are "jointly and severally" liable. This means that any one of them may be held responsible to pay for the entire debt.
6. Uphold your part of the contract to the letter of the law and do not permit any variation from the terms. Permitting late payments or extending time for payment or granting other indulgences can void a guarantee.
7. Give prompt written notice to the guarantor if a default occurs. Failure to do so promptly may void the guarantee.

This chapter was written to give you a better understanding of how to "guarantee" a guaranty by giving you the working knowledge of what constitutes a valid guaranty. The truth is that you are responsible for protecting your own assets; thus, you must be responsible for obtaining enforceable guarantees. If you are basing your investment decision on the validity of the guarantee, and you are not satisfied that it is enforceable, do not invest. There are hundreds of other legitimate opportunities.

Chapter 6: Creative and Imaginative Accounting

Creative and Imaginative Accounting

Tricky, creative, imaginative, and non-uniform accounting procedures constantly mislead investors and cause huge financial losses. For instance, a difference in gains and losses of millions of dollars can occur between two similar companies—one domestic and the other foreign—due to their different accounting systems and wildly fluctuating exchange rates. Investors can also be misled by financial statements that list inflated assets, promissory notes that will never be paid, and an imagined or overpriced inventory.

Tricky Accounting

An excellent example of the type of creative accounting that can hide a company's insolvency for years was revealed by the FBI in Fort Lauderdale, Florida, in 1986, when two founders of the ESM Government Securities, Inc. and an outside auditor pleaded guilty to conspiracy and fraud charges.

ESM was organized in 1976. By 1978, it had lost $3 million. When the SEC closed ESM in 1985, the firm owed its customers $300 million. The technique that was allegedly used to defraud investors was not new and is used frequently to fool the unwary. It involves forming many companies, all controlled by the same group. According to the FBI, in the ESM case there were three companies: the parent company, ESM Group, Inc.; a second company, ESM Government Securities Inc.; and a shell company, ESM Financial Group, Inc. Each played an important role in the scheme.

Actually, ESM Group, Inc. engaged in two separate types of financial transactions. One involved *repurchase agreements*; the other dealt with *reverse purchase agreements*. The former type of transaction involves the sale of government securities accompanied by an agreement that the securities will be repurchased at a price that includes accrued interest. Reverse purchase agreements involve lending money to financial institutions, such as Saving & Loan Associations, in exchange for government securities.

The modus operandi for the fraud was that the executives of ESM transferred their losses to their parent company, ESM Group, Inc., who covered their losses by having their books falsely reflect a large and fictitious accounts receivable from ESM Financial Group, Inc.

Allegedly, ESM, owing more in government securities than it actually possessed—about $320 million—kept the securities in a pool instead of in individual accounts and were able to pledge the same securities to different customers. It was also alleged that an outside auditor, one of the defendants, found the undisclosed losses in 1980. However, he agreed to take payoffs for his silence.

Knowing the modus operandi of this case should make you aware that the same accounting tricks, depending upon the swindler you deal with, can be used to defraud you whenever you do not probe deeply enough.

When defendants in these types of accounting cases plead guilty, they get punished and the government saves the costs of a long prosecution. However, the public is the double loser. A small portion of the public suffers from the fraud, but the majority of the public suffers an irretrievable information loss. This is because many of these trials could disclose the many other nuances of creative and imaginative accounting that might be taking place in corporations in which they, the investors, may be investing their hard earned funds.

Distortion by Banks

Even banks distort their true picture. Unfortunately, the government seems to shy away from giving banks a bad time, possibly because the government itself is so dependent on the banking system. When too many banks get into trouble, too much publicity can result in the termination of foreign capital deposits or the withdrawal of foreign investments in this country.

Here is an example of the government protecting the banks.

In 1984 when the U.S. Controller of the Currency warned six banks about "window dressing," the banks were unidentified. "Window dressing" is a practice in which banks use temporary transactions to distort their true status before they issue their quarterly reports. For example, the transaction could involve the transfer of federal funds from affiliated and correspondent banks in return for a return deposit after the report is issued. This could also include an increase in discretionary accounts (these are usually trust type accounts, managed by a bank, in which they have unhampered authority to use their judgment and discretion to determine where, and for what period, the funds might be safely stored or deposited, including Eurodollar deposits). This kind of "window dressing" by a bank is only a portion of what is meant by this chapter's title, "Creative and Imaginative Accounting."

In 1984 the press reported that one of America's largest accounting firms paid millions of dollars to settle lawsuits that alleged the firm was "recklessly negligent" in failing to detect such abuses as the bribing of major U.S. defense contractors, chronically overstating earnings, concealing losses, and flagrantly misusing federal funds. Moreover, two of the firm's officers accepted kickbacks as well as embezzled funds. Consequently, any person who depended on the balance sheet to invest in the company's stock was misled due to the alleged negligence of the accountants (if that is what it actually was).

Qualified Statements

Always be careful not to depend on any statement that contains the word "unaudited." In one multimillion-dollar San Diego swindle that had sophisticated people relying on unaudited statements, the excuse was that by keeping the statements unaudited they could prevent competitors from learning their invaluable business secrets.

Also, when you begin to depend on other people's accountants and their financial statements, you must check the entire statement down to the last paragraph to see if the accountants have added a "qualified statement" clause in their report. If the statement bears a qualified clause, find out why. It may be a signal that something is wrong.

Capitalizing Expenses

Another legal but creative accounting maneuver that could mislead unwary investors occurs when corporations capitalize certain development costs that other companies in similar businesses treat as expenses. For instance, whenever a company capitalizes its development expenses, their earnings and assets appear to be increased. This enables them to lose more money if they have to without the losses being discernible to the average investor. This is because capitalized investment costs spread the cost over many years, whereas when those same costs are expensed, the cost is deducted for the year in which the cost occurs. This does not make the expensing company's balance sheet look as good as that of the company that capitalized the costs as assets.

For example, the members of the Securities & Exchange Commission are split on the subject of which accounting procedure should be used for the oil and gas industry. Small and mid-sized companies use the full-cost method, and some companies even capitalize dry wells. Large companies seem to prefer the "successful efforts" method and expense their dry wells.

Who Prepared the Financial Statement?

Whenever you receive a prospectus or financial statement that is printed with different sizes of print, one large and the other small, beware! It pays to remember the old adage, "The large print giveth, and the small print taketh away." If you read the document, make sure that you understand the small print. Ask questions about what you do not understand, and try to get answers in writing.

Don't get involved in any type of established business without reviewing a financial statement that has been prepared for it by the equivalent of a certified public accountant. Make sure that it has been prepared without written qualifications that make you uncomfortable. If you do not understand how the qualifications will affect your investment, get your own accountant to review it *before* you invest.

Always insist on financial statements, but be wary of them. Chapter 22 addresses how to evaluate them.

If you don't understand all of the deceptive maneuvers described in this chapter, don't become too concerned. This chapter is not intended to be a short course in accounting; its sole function is to alert you to accounting abuses that might affect your investments.

Chapter 7: How the Swindlers Entice and Snare Their Prey

How the Swindlers Entice and Snare Their Prey

Any book about protecting you from fraudulent practices would be remiss if it omitted some of the tricks that crooks use to dupe sophisticated and unsophisticated investors alike. Though professional merchandisers insist that all business starts with a sale, the sale cannot be effected without a buyer. Or in our situation, the swindle cannot occur until the crook first finds and then fools a trusting, gullible investor.

Professional swindlers know all the ways to ferret out their "marks," qualify them, and then fleece them. Most prospects are secured through *boiler room* telephone solicitations or through one or more forms of misleading advertising. A boiler room refers to any space that houses telephone pitchmen (a type of super salesperson who is both persuasive and knowledgeable about human behavior). After they phone prospective investors, their usual pitch is that they can offer the investor a fantastic proposition that will make them a bundle of money in a hurry.

The master swindlers—those who concoct or copy successful, established scams and then promote them with the aid of their selected pitchmen—know what you want to hear to induce you to invest with them. Many of them have criminal records but avoid rearrest by constantly changing locations. Accordingly, they or their agents will lie to the hilt and tell you anything they sense will allay your fears and induce you to fork over your hard-earned cash. Even though their companies may only have been formed a week before they contact you, they may tell you that they have been with the company for 15 years.

They may tell you that they are arranging a special deal just for you and that your profits will be "fantastic." They will offer you larger returns than you can get anywhere else. Contracts to purchase precious gems and metals have been very popular with them in recent years.

Vending Machines

Vending machine routes offer an excellent example of a business opportunity you should approach with extreme caution. Placed in strategic locations, vending machines dispense products ranging from soup to nuts—even insurance policies. As such, they hold a great fascination for prospective investors who want to own their own businesses with little work involved. And who can blame them? After all, who wouldn't like to have a machine collect money for you, while you sleep, take short vacations, or do whatever else pleases you? One scam gives people the opportunity to own a route of vending machines all set up to collect a tidy little sum of money for them. Inexperienced people would find it hard to turn down such an offer.

I would point out to you here that there are many legitimate manufacturers, distributors, and salespeople associated with the vending machine business. But certain types of swindlers use vending machines as the focal point of their scams with newspaper ads that contain many of the following phrases.

BE YOUR OWN BOSS. NO EXPERIENCE REQUIRED. ESTABLISHED COMPANY OFFERS SPECTACULAR PROFITS FROM YOUR SPARE TIME. NO EXPERIENCE REQUIRED. MODERATE INVESTMENT.
PLEASE REPLY TO BOX AOK, C/O TRUSTY NEWSPAPER

These ads might also include any of the following extra inducements: "Established routes," "Guaranteed Income," "Cash Business," "No bookkeeping," "Just two hours a week."

By itself, the ad will attract a number of inquiries but does not snare anyone. A potential investor is not considered snared until he parts with his money or signs an enforceable contract.

The Bait

Each ad was carefully composed to perform several specific functions. The first function is to act as bait in order to attract the attention of potential victims. The second function is to induce a large flow of inquiries. The third function is to find people with money who, by answering a blind newspaper ad, usually qualify themselves as being the type of people who could easily be susceptible to a professional sales pitch. In other words, when people respond to this type of blind advertisement, they are transmitting a signal that they are not too sophisticated about business deals or making investments. Why? Because they're not only providing their name and address they're also providing information that they have money to invest. Inexperienced people who let themselves be taken in this way automatically set themselves up to be snared.

After the victim has been snared (forked over some cash or signed a contract), he might not want to use all of his cash or may not have enough, so he agrees to sign a chattel mortgage or note obligating him to make large monthly payments—all of this for the right to purchase a vending machine route and the machines that go with it which could easily turn out to be profitless and obligate him to make payments out of his regular salary or bank accounts for many years.

Variations of the sucker bait type of ad discussed here appear in the media regularly because this type of advertising has snared countless victims ever since legitimate coin-operated machines became popular. One of the reasons that so many people have fallen victim to these ploys is that they have yet to learn a basic lesson in life, to wit: There are very few people in this world who are able to buy and operate a profitable, legal business in their spare time with a moderate amount of cash.

Moreover, even when the prospective investor becomes skeptical, the con artist persists because he knows that ordinarily experienced investors do not answer these types of ads.

For example, the ad said, "Established Company." Factually, in scam situations, only the manufacturer of the coin vending machines is established. Its distributor—usually the promoter who placed the ad and who sells the routes and machines—is usually an independent entrepreneur who, if not legitimate, will not remain in the same location too long.

Up to now, the investor has been attracted by the bait of the ad. But he is not caught until he signs a contract and money changes hands as has been pointed out previously. The typical scenario used to make the actual catch goes like this:

After the ad is answered, the distributor's representative will usually arrange to meet the investor in a posh hotel room which is used as a "front." Ordinarily, the investor will be greeted in the hotel room by an affable, sincere-looking salesperson and one or more attractive-looking vending machines. Originally, there were gum ball, peanut, candy, and prize machines. Then came cigarette, newspaper, music, and all types of sundry dispensers. Now they have added insurance, soft drinks, hot drinks, ice cream, sandwiches, pizza, and everything you can think of.

The Pitch

The usual pitch sounds quite plausible: "The distributor's route man has been checking out some good money-making locations. The machines are now ready to be placed in these locations and we want a few people who qualify for their own part-time business to service the machines and collect the money, which will only require a few hours a day." Further elaboration will reveal that the owner of each new location will receive a certain percentage of the money picked up from his machine and that the machines will be restocked from supply sources—more often than not the distributor. Ordinarily, it will be specified, for example, that "we have already set up locations for three routes and have already selected two people to buy the machines and service two of the routes. One route is left and you (the prospective sucker) look like the right type of person to take it on. It will involve about ten machines."

The sales representative, who is actually a "closer," may then apply a little negative psychology: "You look like the type of person we're looking for. However, before the deal can be finalized," he cautions, "you will have to be approved by the board of directors. If you're approved by them, you will then receive a guaranteed minimum return on your investment if the machines do not produce the profit we think they will."

In sales parlance, the term "closer" refers to a proven top-notch salesperson extremely adept at getting prospects to consummate a deal by signing a contract and paying the money. Frequently, the closer only sees the prospect after a salesman has done the preparatory shakedown work.

The importance of the story I have related here is enhanced if one remembers that when the advertisement was answered, the "victim" had already proven that he had money, was naive, possibly lazy, and wanted to earn money the easy way with a minimum amount of work.

I can tell you that these bait schemes proliferate by the thousands because many of the victims don't like to admit that they were duped. However, in Canada, hundreds of people did complain which resulted in two men being convicted in 1984 of fraud and conspiracy for selling $1 million worth of vending machines and market territories to about 250 people. They were told that the locations available to them were market-tested, profit-guaranteed, and that each person had been approved by the Board of Directors. (Sound familiar?) The court subsequently found that no board existed, no investor was turned down, the territories were not market-tested, and no one collected on his guarantee.

Telling the victims that they have to be approved by a board of directors serves two purposes: First, it is a proven way of indicating to the victim that the salesman represents a large organization that has a board of directors that supervises what transpires. Second, it is considered negative psychology because it infers that even though the salesman would approve you and wants you to sign the deal, you do not have the deal until the board approves you. It has been established that this type of negative psychology transfers the thoughts of the victim away from the merits of the deal and causes him to be concerned with whether he has the necessary qualifications and reputation to be accepted.

Any advice about how to avoid being swindled is not going to be foolproof because too many people are not yet aware of how hard most successful people have worked to become successful. They do not realize (perhaps because they believe that successful people are smarter) that most people who become successful do so through their own efforts and very hard work; that without inheritances or luck they found it necessary to combine their innate or learned skills, mental powers, and sense of economic timing with long hours of tedious, hard work. These people accepted responsibility and were aware that making a buck was never easy. Many curtailed their recreation time and were not able to enjoy their families to the fullest. Although it can be done, it is still very difficult to swindle that type of person. From experience, most of them are aware already of the warnings that must be heeded by naive investors.

Protection

The best protection that any investor can secure is to investigate before he invests. This means: investigate the principals as well as the investment vehicle. If possible, try to secure the names of other investors and check with them. If you cannot get the names of other investors, try contacting local people in the same type of business. They may be glad to help you. They might even offer you their established business at a lower price.

Consider how you became involved in the deal. Was it through a reliable source? Check both your source and the proposition with the Better Business Bureau. The BBB may have some pamphlets describing the plan that has been proposed to you.

Secure the services of a recommended commercial lawyer. If you do not have one, contact your local bar association. They will provide you with a few names. If the transaction involves many figures or tax avoidance, then definitely contact a Certified Public Accountant.

Always ask yourself, if something happened to the deal, what practical recourse would you have? Anybody can sue if they have any money remaining. Winning the suit, however, and then collecting is another matter. Therefore, it is better to spend the time in the beginning before you spend the money later. Don't permit yourself to get rushed into any deal for fear that someone else will snap it up before you do.

While pursuing an investment, be realistic. Don't respond to ads that offer guaranteed profits on a part-time basis with a small investment and no experience. It's a pipe dream!

Spotting Investment Con Games and Swindlers

13 Quick Tips on What to Watch for

- Any "get-rich-quick" proposition, regardless of the source.
- Any proposition that you cannot check out, regardless of the reason.
- No permanent office address or listing in the telephone book.
- Any contact started with an unsolicited phone call.
- Propositions that require unjustified trust on your part.
- Where *you* finance the major part of the transaction.
- When you do not know the promoters or the principals.
- Plans that make you a salesman or that pay you for referrals.
- "We only have a few deals available in this area, and the others are already taken, and there is only this one deal left."
- Special deals on gems, strategic metals, oil, government real estate, futures contracts, unusually high interest rates for your money, and deals that promise to get you financing on a mortgage that has been hard to finance.
- No audited financial statement from the offeror.
- Vending machine routes—you've been through this before!
- The proposition or agreement regarding what you get is not stated in writing.

Any of the above propositions may be legitimate, but experience dictates that they should be thoroughly investigated by professionals before you put up your money or credit. Remember that these tips are only a partial list, the purpose of which is to make you conscious of the innumerable swindlers to whom we all are constantly exposed.

Chapter 8: Watch Your Broker!

Watch Your Broker!

A broker is an agent who represents his or her principals—buyers or sellers—in their efforts to negotiate and consummate a transaction. Brokers are usually licensed and regulated by the regulatory bodies of the states in which they work or the federal government. For instance, stockbrokers are registered and regulated by the National Association of Securities Dealers. People that we refer to as stockbrokers are in fact registered representatives; they are employed by broker-dealers whose firms are members of a stock exchange. In fields such as real estate and business opportunities, the broker is usually permitted to employ licensed salesmen for whom the employing broker is responsible.

All brokers and salesmen owe their clients the highest degree of care and ethical conduct. They cannot make secret profits and must reveal to their respective clients any significant information that might affect the transaction. All brokers owe their clients their best efforts.

Brokers are compensated by either a set fee or a specified percentage of the total sales price. The percentage of commission that will be charged for a sale is negotiable at the time the brokerage agreement is entered into.

The average stockbroker's most prevalent complaint is this: "If I give my clients a recommendation on which they make a huge profit they consider me a financial genius. But if they lose money, then I'm considered a lousy broker." While this may be a valid complaint, it obscures the large number of investors who have lost fortunes because of being misled by various types of brokers. Some of the brokers might have been well-meaning, but many were self-serving, inept, uninformed, or negligent.

Sometimes it seem as if stockbrokers have a license to help people lose their money legally. Similar to some doctors who like to play God, too many stockbrokers try to make their clients believe that they possess money-making expertise in all aspects of the market.

The truth is, a stockbroker is the exception if he is up-to-date in even one type of investment. Unfortunately, stockbrokers are authorized to give advice and sell more types of investments than they know or understand the salient details about. They are not alone in this: The same criticism applies to many real estate, insurance and other types of brokers. They would prefer to earn their living as honestly and as ethically as possible, but they can do more business if they pose as experts in as many facets of their trade as their conscience will permit. Brokers tend to puff their knowledge because the average client has more confidence in a broker who professes to be an expert than one who admits to knowing very little about a subject.

Self-Serving Brokers

The majority of stockbrokers usually earn their living from commissions derived from fulfilling buy and sell orders. With some exceptions, unless their clients buy and sell some type of security, they receive no commissions for giving advice. Consequently, commissioned brokers are under pressure to execute orders and make a profit for their employers who, contrary to their advertising, are not to be confused with charitable institutions. They are more interested in their own profits than in those of their clients.

Don't be impressed by fancy brokerage offices. They were specially designed to inspire you with confidence. Some of the largest and most important stock brokerage offices in the country have admitted or been found guilty of improper and even fraudulent conduct. One major brokerage company recently paid an $8 million fine for a felony conspiracy involving the manipulation of checks. This practice resulted in the victimization of many banks.

Although some brokers carelessly cause client losses by self-serving, commission-inspired investment advice, the average client is not fault-free when it comes to being guilty of ignorance and laziness. Too many investors do not want to do their own investment homework; they just want someone to give them a bottom line figure, without their having to check out how it was established. These investors tend to trust anyone who poses as having financial experience and who will do their financial thinking for them.

When they meet a broker who inspires this type of confidence, and who apparently will assume the responsibility, they are happy to let that broker do their financial planning for them. But even if their brokers are conscientious, who do you think gets most of their time? The small investor or the investor who trades daily and provides large commissions?

Program Trading

Investors in the stockmarket should be aware of a relatively new investment tool called Program Trading. It has become a very important part of the market, used primarily by mutual funds, management firms, and very large traders of stocks to buy or sell automatically and almost instantaneously when predetermined events occur. Each event is determined by conclusions drawn by the computers from their use of various methods of reviewing past stockmarket actions, statistics, economic signs, and various stock indices.

When these signals reach a level that has been preset by the computer programmers, the prearranged programmed trading is immediately set into action. Heeding the interpretations, the programmed computers automatically place orders with their broker owners to buy or sell stocks when they reach a certain price level.

Critics suggest that if the broker engages in program trading, the smaller (average) investor is buying stocks that are not subject to the regular principles of supply and demand that usually set market prices. The mutual funds or big stock investors believe that their programs can be interpreted to indicate when to buy or sell large blocks of stocks at a profit without creating dramatic price fluctuations. Thus, the critics feel that brokers, who possess this type of inside information about the date that a large volume or group of stocks will be bought and sold, are in a good position to take advantage of self-serving, money-making manipulations before the average investors can manage to have their buy or sell orders executed.

Churning Accounts

In 1984 a federal judge froze the assets of a futures broker for allegedly "churning" a clients account, a charge that is difficult to prove in futures market transactions. The futures market offers investors the opportunity to speculate in sales or purchases of commodities (items such as coffee, sugar, butter, and grains) for delivery at a future date.

Here's an example of how the futures market operates and how churning occurs.

Assume that the investor purchases a contract to receive a specified quantity of a commodity—say sugar—for delivery at a future date at a certain price. Then assume that when the delivery date arrives, the price of sugar is much higher than the price he contracted to pay for it. The investor is now able to sell his contract for sugar at a higher price and make a profit.

Churning occurs when a busy or trusting client gives the broker the discretionary power to buy and/or sell securities for the client's account, without receiving special instructions for each purchase and sale. The broker churns the account by executing many buy/sell orders that produce tidy commissions for the broker, but give the client few gains and mostly losses. In the case being cited, the churner's commissions exceeded 90 percent of the total of the customer's equity in three brokerage accounts and 70 percent in eight other accounts. Allegedly, trading in the customer's $22,450 account generated commissions of $14,000 in 34 trading days.

Other Problems

In another 1984 case, the Vancouver Stock Exchange in Canada was reluctant to publicize a violation by one of its brokers who was allegedly involved in "high sailing." This term refers to manipulating the closing price of a stock to reflect a higher closing price than the price that is warranted by the actual supply and demand. The Exchange is less secretive today.

In another case in the United States, the Securities & Exchange Commission alleged that a broker appropriated $800,000 from various clients' accounts by forging their signatures to checks and then deposited some of the misappropriated funds into accounts he controlled. He concealed the fraud by instructing a subordinate to falsify the company's records.

All stock brokers are charged by the brokerage firms that employ them with the fundamental responsibility of "knowing their clients." This means that if the client costs the firm money by an improper act, such as causing them to sell stolen bonds unknowingly, the individual broker is considered to be at fault.

If brokers should know their clients, shouldn't their clients take time to learn something about the character and financial knowledge of their broker?

Congress became aware of the problems caused by dishonest, self-serving brokers. In 1934, the Securities & Exchange Commission was established to protect investors from misrepresentation and fraud. Although many of the problems have been curtailed, they still have not been fully eliminated.

R.E. and B.O. Brokers

The fields of real estate and business opportunities are also subject to many brokerage problems that emanate from dishonest practices. Real estate and business opportunity brokerage laws vary from state to state. A license to act as a broker is not necessary in all 50 states. Thus, some states permit real estate to be sold by an unlicensed broker. More distressing is the fact that some states permit unlicensed brokers to list and sell business opportunities, a field which, if their inexperienced clients are to be protected, requires much expertise and diversified knowledge.

Another serious real estate problem, causing clients much unhappiness and sometimes heavy financial losses, is that most clients assume that the real estate or business opportunity broker is always acting as that client's agent. Actually, the broker is usually the agent of the owner from whom he procured the listing. However, in many cases investigated by state authorities, many brokers secretly represented and financially benefited and protected the interests of other parties, or even themselves.

Recently, California passed legislation that compels brokers, who represent a buyer, to disclose whatever relationship they may have with the buyer. Hopefully, other states will follow this example.

Examples of Fraud

In response to the proliferation of major fraud cases "characterized by fraud, misrepresentation and embezzlement," the California Department of Real Estate, which licenses both real estate and business opportunity brokers, selected five of its most experienced investigators to form a special team, which is now referred to as a Crisis Response Team or CRT. In the summer of 1986 the Department revealed "that while the CRT has been in existence only since 1985, at this writing it is investigating more than 80 cases."

A thumbnail description of a few CRT cases are listed below.

1. The sale of an apartment complex from which buyer and broker walk away with over a million dollars at the seller's expense.
2. A Savings & Loan failure results in a take over by the Federal Home Loan Bank Board. Failure was caused by defaulted loans to licensees that exceeded the value of the securing real property. Evidence that straw buyers, inflated appraisals, and misrepresentation were used.
3. A Savings & Loan audits a mortgage loan broker brokerage firm which claims their records have been stolen. In reconstructing the records, a trust account shortage of over $2 million is discovered.
4. A group of licensees is estimated to have purchased over 100 homes from long-time owners. Homes are free and clear or nearly paid for. Owners were to receive a cash down payment and carry back a note secured by the first trust deed; actually they got an unsecured note. Buyers get maximum financing from a lender, default, and lender forecloses. Buyers walk away with the money and sellers are left with worthless paper. The CRT is cooperating with the local police departments.
5. A broker assists buyers and sellers in obtaining fraudulently inflated appraisals that are packaged with phony income tax statements, employment verifications, and loan applications. The lenders fund loans in the $300,000 to $500,000 range. After existing liens are paid off through broker's escrow company, brokers and accomplices split the excess funds. The district attorney is interested in this case.
6. A broker services real estate loans for some 600 investors. CRT finds $1.3 million in trust funds are missing. Evidence indicates the funds were used for covering the payroll and operating expenses of the broker's business.

The concluding paragraph in the Bulletin contained a reminder to the profession that "all except a small minority of California's real estate licensees conduct business in an honest and ethical way." Although the author agrees with this statement, potential investors should pay particular attention to the modus operandi of the examples.

Special emphasis must be placed on case number 4 because the scheme contains at least one important technique that could crop up to defraud you, as a seller, in commercial transactions. The technique is used in a sale transaction that involves financing by the seller, with the buyer promising the seller a secured note for the balance of the purchase price. A secured note differs from an unsecured note in that the secured note is a security device, which, when properly recorded, becomes an enforceable lien against the property and enables the seller to foreclose on the property if the note is unpaid. The unsecured note only permits the holder to *try* to recover the money from the buyer. If the buyer sells the property without honoring the note and either spends or hides his money and has no other assets, the noteholder has a worthless note.

It should also be noted that in case 4, the seller was promised a secured note but, perhaps unknowingly, received and accepted an unsecured note. That is another trap that you must avoid whenever you agree to accept a secured note. Seek and pay for the advice necessary to cover yourself in this situation.

Insurance Brokers

Logically, a book like this should discuss insurance companies rather than their brokers, but because the subject is brokers—and many investments require dealing with insurance brokers—a few words about them are in order.

Although insurance brokers and their salesmen are usually licensed, they seldom reveal that insurance rates can vary greatly for the same coverage. For a long time, Great Britain has been in the forefront of trying to correct two aspects of brokerage inequities. First, their concern is that the broker who just writes insurance for one company cannot offer the competitive rates that could be offered by a broker who writes insurance for several companies. Second, because commissions vary greatly and in some instances may amount to the first year's premium, some officials want legislation that would compel the brokers to reveal, without being asked, the amount of the commissions that they will receive from the different policies.

The moral is this: when you shop for insurance, do not just depend upon one broker or your regular broker. Ask questions and compare the strengths of the various companies and their reputation for service and paying off when required.

In January 1985 a large stock brokerage firm was sued by a group of Detroit physicians who alleged that they had been charged excessive mark-ups on zero coupon bonds. The mark-ups were supposed to be less than the conventional five percent commission for stocks, but some dealers charged a 15 percent mark-up. (Zero coupon bonds get their name from the fact they do not pay any interest until they mature.)

These types of cases, like the fraud cases, could be cited many times over, but by now you should be sufficiently alert to paying closer attention to what your broker does for you. While your broker, or his licensed or registered representative, may work out of an impressive looking office, you never know how long he will be there.

Most of the salespeople that you will be exposed to are generally referred to as brokers. But actually, the stock brokerage firm that employs them is the broker, and the person who will take charge of your account, in addition to the bookkeeper, is called a registered representative, who will be registered with the National Association of Securities Dealers.

There are many fine, outstanding, conscientious brokers and representatives, but that does not make them good advisers, nor are they paid to be advisers. Brokers joke about the fact that what really makes people consider them to be good is whether they can help them to buy low and sell high.

Unfortunately, as might be expected, many outstanding brokers have so many large accounts that they may not have the time or the profit motive to take on and properly service new, small accounts.

The Broker's Frustration

The main function of a broker is to politely take and execute your orders. This means he is authorized to buy or sell the specified amount of stocks you request, at a stipulated price when your order arrives at the floor of the exchange in which the stock is traded, and as soon as possible.

It is frequently difficult for brokers to give advice because not all clients want it. Furthermore, if the advice is wrong, the broker will be blamed. If stockbrokers had the knowledge and expertise that their new clients believe they have, they would not be taking your orders; they would be giving their own. There may be exceptions and, if so, I sincerely hope you find them and that your optimistic expectations are fulfilled.

Meanwhile, for the average person, a good broker would be one who is geared to:

1. Open his account graciously
2. Find out his investment goals
3. Inform him of appropriate investment vehicles that the firm handles or in which it specializes
4. Keep him abreast about what is happening to the general economy and businesses in which the investor wants to invest or is invested
5. Offer to make constructive suggestions
6. Hold the client's hand in times of stress.

If you need a stockbroker, first talk to the people you know who invest in the market and whose opinions you respect. Ask them if they would recommend a broker to you. Then visit the broker at his office; have a chat, exchange views, sift through what you are told, and evaluate for yourself if this is the person with whom you would like to deal. If not, get another recommendation. When you do not use a recommended broker, you may be assigned to one who may not possess either the personality that agrees with yours or the diversified experience that your temperament may require. When you find the right broker, open an account with him, and when you find the type of investment you like, discuss it with him. He may know about the stocks of similar but stronger companies that are priced lower. The average small investor may not follow his broker's advice when given, but he may still like to receive and evaluate it.

Therefore, judge your new broker by his character and reputation as well as the amount and quality of helpful service that he offers and renders to you. But don't forget, brokers earn their living from people like you. Ideally, you should complement one another.

Section 2:
Basic Investment Principles

Chapter 9: Risk-Taking Versus Gambling

Risk-Taking Versus Gambling

There are many reasons for people, who can afford to, to avoid investing. Some do not feel that they have sufficient knowledge to make safe investments. Others do not know where or how to get started. They may not possess sufficient drive or enthusiasm to do what is necessary to learn about investing. Meanwhile, others, aside from not wanting to lose money, do not want to gamble it away either. Then there are those who may have religious restrictions regarding gambling. Some of these people might benefit from a clarification of the difference between prudent risk-taking and gambling.

Assuming that most understand that the field of investing is a legal, necessary, economic part of our domestic and international trade, I share my views about the difference between prudent risk-taking and outright gambling. Hopefully, these ideas will help you to become a successful, prudent investor.

Whether we like it or not, life is full of uncertainties. Many people wager on these uncertainties. Some do it for pleasure; others become professional odds makers. The amateur gambler may take his money to a bookmaker. The professional bookmaker takes wagers from people who have different opinions about the outcome of an event. He does not charge them a fee to take their bet. Instead, he gives them odds like $7 to $5.

For a large event, the odds are usually determined by what the majority of the bookmakers in key locations across the country determine the odds should be on each of the contestants or teams. In formulating the opening odds, they use past performances, present physical condition, age, the weather, home field, and numerous other factors. An important factor is the percentage of money the public is willing to place on each side. If too much money is bet on one side, the odds are adjusted to help equalize the amount of money that must be paid. If they happen to get overbooked on one side, they *lay off* the excessive bets. To lay off a bet is to distribute it to one or more other bookmakers. The aim is to set the odds so, no matter who wins, the given odds will average out in their favor to ensure a profit. In other words, even though they are professional gamblers called bookmakers, they never take more wagers than they can comfortably handle and that will yield a profit, regardless of who wins or loses.

Risks and Gambles

The purpose of this example is to demonstrate the difference between prudent risk-taking and gambling. The individual bet maker is the gambler. The bookmaker is the prudent risk-taker. He uses many assets, including:

- A reputation for honesty
- The ability to pay
- The ability to secure the wagers
- Demonstrated skill
- A knowledge of mathematical percentages
- The ability to lay off bets as necessary

The bookmaker knows from experience that he is running a business that makes a profit, even if he makes an occasional mistake. He works to reduce the amount of risk to which *his business* is exposed. He could be called a prudent risk-taker.

In contrast, the individual bet makers, regardless of the odds, first have to win to benefit from the odds. But, whether they win or lose their respective wagers, it could be fairly said that they "gambled away their money." This contrasts the precautions taken by the professional bookmaker.

Prudent Risk Takers

Similarly, investments for the average investor should be viewed in the same light. In today's world, prudent investors are not gamblers, even though they take risks. They can justify their actions as being prudent risks and not gambling. For instance, they may have solid information and statistics about a certain industry. They may know about the raw materials and finished supplies, the market demand, the tenor of the times, and vital statistics that back up their investment opinions. They can consider the odds against their success, the price that they are willing the pay, and the profit potential, dividends, and the percentage of money (or *yield*) that will be returned on their investment.

They may invest in any of the fields discussed in this book. Their investments may be in real estate, oil wells, franchises, gold mines, or stocks and bonds. And they may select their area of investment based upon solid information and desired yields, thereby being prudent risk-takers, not gamblers.

Even in the oil business, it is possible to make prudent risk investments rather than taking the wild gambles that many people assume oil wells to be. In this business, if you put up the money and agree to drill very deep in one location to find a tremendous gusher, you may become wealthy overnight. However, this is gambling because the odds are against striking oil in a single try. Moreover, the deeper you go, the more expensive it gets.

On the other hand, if you want to invest in the oil business by drilling ten exploratory holes to a limited depth in tested areas, your chance for success improves considerably. This approach makes you a more prudent investor or risk-taker. Taking this approach one step further, you could combine forces with a few other investors and spread your risk by drilling 100 holes instead of 10. Using this approach, even if you strike oil in only 70 places, you are ahead. Your increased prudence minimized your chance for financial failure.

Unfortunately, risk cannot be totally eliminated. Even if you decide in favor of buying newly issued government bonds that pay the prevailing rate of interest, you take a risk. Once issued, the price of a bond fluctuates according to the rise and fall in interest rates. When interest rates rise, bond prices decline. Conversely, when interest rates decline, bond prices increase. On the other hand, non-government bonds are affected by additional risk factors, including the relative financial strength of the maker.

Nearly everyone wants to increase their income with a minimum personal expenditure of money, time, or effort. To achieve that goal, some investors willingly accept risk-taking as a normal part of investing. Others only invest in what they believe to be risk-free investments.

Ultra-Conservative Investors

Unfortunately, the ultra-conservative investor does not understand that there are no risk-free investments. As a result, many unsophisticated, ultra-conservative investors, while trying to avoid investment risks, also avoid legitimate financial opportunities. By making legitimate investments accompanied by moderate risk, they might have experienced dramatic improvements in their earnings and life style.

Actually, only wealthy people having already earned all they need should be ultra-conservative investors. Their major goal should be to preserve what they possess. Yet, too frequently, the financial vision of working ultra-conservatives is restricted to his or her job or savings account. While aware that others increase their earnings and improve their life style through various types of investments, they abstain from investing. Many unsophisticated wage-earners deny themselves the opportunity of increasing their earnings through investments due to some of the following reasons.

- They do not believe they have enough money to invest.
- They may be unfamiliar with leverage, borrowing, or buying on margin.
- They never take any risks.
- If they are ready to accept a risk, they do not know how to get started.
- They believe that investing is a form of gambling, and either they abhor gambling from a moral or religious standpoint or they, "Do not want to gamble away their hard-earned money."

Everybody Takes Risks

The dictionaries define gambling as "taking or risking money on anything of value or something involving chance." Many of those people who are afraid of the word "gambling" seldom realize that simply trying to live a normal life involves constant risk or chance-taking. Every time they cross a street, ride in a car, train, bus, boat, or airplane, or deposit money in a bank, they are taking a chance. Accidents happen unexpectedly, banks fail unexpectedly, and even the most careful people constantly lose their hard-earned money in unexpected ways.

Yet, many people constantly penalize themselves by avoiding intelligent investment choices that could favorably change their lives. They possess a phobia of gambling. Their usual excuse is, "I worked too hard for my money and I don't want to gamble it away."

These same people are unaware that when they put their money in a bank, they are also gambling. First, they are betting on the future liquidity of the bank and the ability of the Federal Deposit Insurance Company to pay a loss if there is a default. They are also gambling that inflation will not erode the value of their capital and that a bank deposit is a better investment than government bonds, real estate, or some other solid investment that may not erode their capital.

In other words, every time they make a decision about preserving their money, they are making the equivalent of a bet that the value of their money will be preserved better than if they had done something else with it. And as often as not they are in error. The point is that no one can avoid taking risks.

Unfortunately, the money of the smartest and most cautious savers is exposed to many hazards. Even when interest rates on bank deposits are high, the rate of inflation and taxes can exceed earned interest rates. Hence, one should not save more money than is necessary for ordinary living expenses when a bank pays lower interest rates than the overall rate of inflation.

Judicious Savers

Judicious savers have also been disappointed by bank and savings and loan mismanagement and fraud. Moreover, in cases where the Federal Deposit Insurance Corporation or the Federal Savings and Loan Insurance Corporation eventually pays off the losses, they do not pay lost interest.

As described in Chapter 5, investors who bought triple-A, guaranteed Municipal Bonds because of their safety factor, have also lost their individual, total investments, despite specific guarantees.

Even though U.S. government bonds and real estate—the basis of all wealth—can and do lose some of their value, some conservative investors believe that risk-free investments actually exist and that they can find them. They frequently penalize themselves by not considering superior investments that contain an acknowledged amount of risk (even if minimal) but which could actually be less risky than their theoretical risk-free investments.

If you believe the U.S. economy is not risky, consider why on July 29, 1986, Federal Reserve Board Chairman Paul Volcker warned the House of Representatives Banking Committee, "We live in a much more complex world than even a few years ago" . . . The giant trade deficit had put the U.S. in a "difficult and dangerous situation." He warned a recession could result if the situation were not corrected.

Repeating the thought for emphasis, risk-free decisions are a mirage that only exist in people's minds. In fact, there are no risk-free decisions or investments. That, however, should not be construed as an invitation to throw caution to the winds. It is only an invitation to consider the differences between gambling, speculating, and investing.

While no one should invest more than they can reasonably afford to lose, it is good planning to invest a certain affordable percentage of one's net income. The investment choice should offer an opportunity that can improve one's life style or increase one's investment portfolio.

Speculators are people who invest in projects even though they are fully aware of the involved risks. Even when people evaluate and understand investment risks, everyone does not possess either the temperament or finances to be a speculator.

As a rule, older people with limited income and who cannot easily replace lost capital should not be speculators. This is true regardless of the amount of potential profit anticipated. Ordinarily, even if the proposed project seems reasonably worthwhile and safe, the only people who should speculate in such projects are those who, if they lost, would have enough money left to try other investments.

Investor candidates include young people. They should have both the ability to earn and save additional investment capital. In particular, bright young people with limited capital but with guaranteed future earning prospects are in a position to invest. These people, with one important proviso, should give serious consideration to getting into promising deals that are patently meritorious. The proviso: they must not acquire additional liability if the project fails. This outcome is far from prudent risk-taking.

There are intelligent, informed, good gamblers and there are uninformed, unwise, rash, or compulsive gamblers. Unwise gamblers like to take chances without trying to eliminate risks. The thrill is the risk, not the winning. On the other hand, smart gamblers acquire facts and other necessary information to help them eliminate as many risks as possible. This is done before they put up their money. Aside from seeking favorable odds, their main concerns are trying to minimize their chances of losing their capital and maximizing their chances of successfully making a profit. Even if they take an occasional, unpredictable loss, they know that their overall performance will net them a worthwhile profit. They know that the bottom line in investing is not just the result of one investment but the total results of one's overall investment performance (net profits).

Intelligent Investors

Intelligent investors know that they cannot eliminate all risks. Like the good gamblers, they try to eliminate as many unnecessary risks as possible. After all, even banks make bad investment decisions. Intelligent investors are aware that unforeseen contingencies can unexpectedly make their well-planned investment decisions look like stupid mistakes, but they attempt to minimize the number of their mistakes and to profit from them in the future. Fortunately, *Investor Beware* tries to help you avoid or minimize your investment mistakes and financial losses without compromising your acquisition of experience and knowledge.

Recently, many mortgage-free homeowners or those with large equity positions in their homes (owning a larger percentage than they owe) have been urged by some investment advisers to borrow against their homes for speculating or investing. Although some people in certain circumstances might profit from mortgaging their homes, using one's home as investment collateral is not a recommended procedure for the average person.

Unless the homeowner has a guaranteed source of income with which to repay the loan if the project fails, the potential cash value in the home is better kept as a reserve in case of an emergency. People who depend upon the equity in their home to provide the cash for an investment are often unproven investors. Frequently, they do not have an investment track record and are not the type of people who should be speculating, investing, or taking risks that they cannot afford.

Can You Afford to Lose?

The bottom-line philosophy is this: As desirable and necessary as investments are, do not invest if you cannot afford to lose. However, if you can afford to lose but do not like the risks that are involved in all investments, first minimize risk-taking by educating yourself about the various types of investments that are available. When you consider a particular investment, secure a complete story including the personal and business history of the principals and participants. If you are in doubt about any of the answers, check the proposition and the principals with any of the following:

- Your attorney
- Your accountant
- The Better Business Bureau
- The police department
- The district attorney.

Hopefully, you can combine what you learn with what you glean from this book as a springboard to success.

Chapter 10: Analyze Your Investment Disposition

Analyze Your Investment Disposition

Before You Invest

Before making your first investment, it is important that you understand some things about yourself. Much of your success as an investor depends upon your learning some basic facts about your investment disposition combined with your investment goals. This chapter concentrates on your investment disposition (or personality). The next chapter concentrates on your investment goals.

Everyone would like to make money from his or her investments. This is true for all kinds of investors ranging from high-risk speculators to ultra-conservative investors. There are some major distinctions between speculators and investors.

The speculator is like the gambler—always looking for favorable odds. If the odds are favorable he takes a risk. A speculator jumps in and out of investments for quick profit. He is not as interested in investment basics as he is in fast money. On the other hand, he is mentally prepared to take a loss. By having favorable odds in most of his deals, he can suffer a few losses and still come out ahead. Of course, there are varying degrees of risk in speculation.

A true investor is considered to be more careful than a speculator. The investor wants to minimize risk. He seeks out long-term investment opportunities. He takes the time to investigate the business and financial soundness of a transaction. He understands the value of time and the long-term benefits derived from population growth and inflation. And he checks the character and reputation of the principals connected with a potential transaction. Of course, like speculators, the investor will always accept a quick profit.

The investor may be classified into three categories: moderate, conservative, and ultra-conservative. As the names imply, each category usually seeks investments that match their investment disposition.

The moderate investor seeks out more speculative investments that offer high rates of return. This classification of investor knows that high-return investments offer higher risks. But his disposition lets him accept the risk for the potential return. However, not being a true speculator, the moderate investor spreads his risks across several individual investments in a calculated manner. In this way, a failure in one investment area can be offset with a success in another.

The conservative investor is willing to take less risk. This classification of investor places more weight on security than on a high return. Some risk is acceptable for high-yield investments as long as the majority of his or her investment portfolio is considered secure.

The ultra-conservative investor minimizes risks even when potential investment returns may be high. The risk moves the ultra-conservative to highly stable investments that may offer low returns. But the security is the primary attraction; return is secondary.

Experienced speculators and the three categories of investors have a significant advantage over the new investor. The new investor rarely understands his investment disposition and is unsure of his goals. By not understanding his disposition or goals, he has difficulty in knowing where to find opportunities. When opportunities are encountered, he has difficulty in evaluating them.

Ambivalent Investors

Of course, nothing prevents a person from being ambivalent. He may try to make money both as a speculator and as an investor. However, the odds are against those who make investments that are not compatible with their investment disposition.

The purpose of this chapter is to help you better understand different investment personalities. This should help you categorize yourself and determine what your disposition actually is, not what you think it is. Armed with this information and using it for guidance, you stand a much better chance of making investments that better fit your individual needs.

Many speculators and investors are known as happy winners but poor losers. Their dispositions seem to change with the rise or decline in the value of their investments.

Although no one likes to lose money, short-term losses should not affect the health or demeanor of an investor. People who suffer for long periods of time over short-term losses should not be investors or speculators. Even before considering the effects of winning or losing, just worrying about a potential loss could be as devastating to some as the occurrence of a real, hard-dollar loss.

To some, the effect of a bad investment takes a toll on physical health, mental outlook, and the quality of investment decisions. If you possess a tendency to worry a lot about your investments, you are likely to make too many costly investment mistakes. Under stressful conditions, you might buy at the wrong time and overpay. Or you might sell at the wrong time, ensuring a loss on an investment that might have been profitable had it been held just a little longer.

Chapter 9 establishes that elements of risk are present in even the safest investments. Thus, before you try to select your investment preference, you should ignore the profit motive in favor of selecting what you feel is a comfortable type of investment. Of course, you must consider the comfort levels of your spouse and/or partners.

Too many people base their investment decisions on the opinions of friends or neighbors. Often, these are people who have common interests and goals. However, this does not ensure that their investment disposition coincides with yours. The type of investment that might not bother others might be a constant worry to you. Before investing, aside from evaluating your financial position and goals, you should separately evaluate yourself and those closely associated with you. Analyze the mental level of tolerance that each of you possesses. Determine your ability to cope with any unanticipated, distressing events.

Analyzing Your Disposition

In order to analyze your investment disposition, you should ask yourself and your associates the following questions. Carefully evaluate your answers:

1. Are you unable to cope with investment situations that experts in the field contradict each other about?
2. Are you the type of person who panics at the first signs of bad news, a recession, or a depression?
3. In times of uncertainty, do you follow what the crowd is doing, even if your considered opinion is different than theirs?

If you answered all three questions in the affirmative, you are most likely a conservative investor. You should avoid known risks. If you answered yes to the last question, then according to the economic laws of supply and demand, you are probably buying at a high price and selling at a low price. This is because when the crowd buys, their demand lowers the supply. This influences price increases. Conversely, when the crowd sells, the lower demand reduces prices.

If you cannot forecast how you or those involved with you would behave under stressful conditions, psychologists predict that you will follow your usual behavioral patterns.

As an investor, can you cope with constant changes in interest rates?

Assume for a moment that you invested a sizable amount of your available investment capital into a basically sound investment. This investment has given you a fair return for a period of two or three years. But, in the interim, inflationary pressures reduced the purchasing power of your yields while interest rates accelerated to new high levels. The money that you used to purchase your investment now yield a much higher rate of return. If it were available, you could loan it out at the new, high interest rates. The question is:

Would you sell your tested investment in order to use the proceeds to make a loan that would draw the new, high interest rates?

If the answer is yes! you might be sharp. And neither your current investment disposition nor your future investment-behavioral pattern is inclined towards conservative action.

Here is another example. You have an opportunity to invest in a venture that has the potential for extraordinarily high returns. However, it is possible that you might lose the entire amount of money after a few years. Now for the question.

What percentage of your reserve funds (which are not easily replaced) would you invest in this high-return, high-risk venture?

Would your answer be the same if a potential exists for a

liability from a deficiency judgment for more money than you invested? (This can happen if you do not legally limit your liability in advance.)

A young person with assured future earnings could invest 20 percent and still be considered conservative. If he followed the same pattern as a middle aged person, he might be classified as a speculative investor.

Matching Your Investment with Your Disposition

Consider the following two questions.

> Do you love to shoot craps or play poker or black jack?
>
> When you lose, are you still happy, particularly if you had a good time while losing?

If the answer to these questions is yes, then you possess the characteristics of a happy gambler. You have the makings of a speculator.

Here is another situation. You have made an investment where every conceivable risk has been eliminated. Now for the question.

> Are you satisfied to receive a smaller yield for your money than you can get elsewhere?

A yes answer makes you an ultraconservative investor. Even would-be investment counselors must understand their own investment dispositions, as illustrated in the following true story.

A few years ago, a successful investment counselor employed professional investment counselors as salesmen on a commission basis. Some of the salesmen earned more than $100,000 a year. The size of their earnings became common knowledge. As a result, the owner of the business was regularly solicited by inexperienced, would-be sales people. They wanted a chance at the large earnings. The owner could quickly tell that most of the the applicants were not ''sales-closers.'' They did not qualify for the job, and he knew they would starve if he hired them.

Not wanting to hurt their feelings, he never told them that they would not qualify. Instead, he patiently explained that the compensation was strictly on a commission basis. He told them that during the one- to two-month learning period, there would be no income. And after that, he continued, it might take many weeks or even months before a salesman could earn a commission.

Then he continued, "I want you to be honest with yourself. If you are single, do you have enough money to own and drive a prestigious car for a few months without earning any money? And when you do earn money, can you wait to receive it in long-term payments?"

Now we come to the crux of the story. "If you are married," he added, "I want you to ask yourself if you have the kind of wife who wants a regular paycheck she can depend upon weekly? Or can she go for a few months with the constant uncertainty of how much you will earn and when you will receive it? Also, during this time you will not be working regular hours, and she will be alone most evenings."

Needless to say, in every instance the unqualified, even including some good closers, disqualified themselves. Like everyone else, they would have liked a large paycheck, but neither they nor their wives had the financial waiting power or, more importantly, the required disposition for this type of position.

These same principles are applicable to you personally and to your family. The question then is:

> Can you or your spouse take a financial loss from an investment that goes temporarily or permanently sour without unduly disturbing your current or anticipated life-style?

and

> Can you forego the steady interest payments from bonds or savings accounts for the opportunity to greatly increase your earnings from a non-guaranteed, possibly non-dividend-paying investment, with the possibility of losing your capital?

If the answer is yes, you are showing the earmarks of a speculator.

Here is another similar situation. You are attracted to the benefits derived from income property.

Could you take the risks of purchasing income property with a small down payment that is subject to a large trust deed or mortgage?

How do feel about the concomitant risk of losing both your investment and the property? If the tenants vacate the premises, and you cannot replace them with new ones, your fears could materialize.

Are you more comfortable paying cash without any trust deeds or mortgages?

In this situation, if a vacancy problem arises, you have no fear of losing the property or your investment as long as you continue to pay the upkeep and taxes.

By now you should be able to classify yourself. Aside from considering investment dispositions, investors with a steady flow of income can take more risks than those who depend upon their weekly paychecks.

Thus, before you expose yourself to any type of investment, it is extremely important, in addition to considering the merits of the investment, that you also consider the various contingencies that can arise. Then, analyze your investment disposition and evaluate how well you can handle the total risks.

Consider Your Patience Quotient

Finally, become familiar with your patience quotient. Are you psychologically geared to wait for a long-term investment to mature? Or do you need quick results, regardless of how promising the future can be for a long-term investment? Ask yourself the questions in this chapter; give yourself an honest answer. Then find investments that correspond to your investment disposition.

Chapter 11: Establishing Your Investment Goals

Establishing Your Investment Goals

It may seem to many investors that investment reasons and investment goals are the same. Although both reasons and goals influence the types of investments made by many investors, there is an important difference. This chapter describes investment reasons, investment goals, and the difference.

Why People Invest
There are many reasons for people to invest their time, money, and credit. These include:

- Satisfying the need for power
- Recognition by others as an astute or shrewd investor
- The desire to retire comfortably
- Securing tax breaks
- Preservation of the value of one's wealth from taxes and inflation
- Increasing the value of one's funds to offset tax and inflation losses
- Augmenting one's income and capital for the "good life" when they can no longer be productive
- Concern for the future education of their children or grandchildren

One wise investor that I know says, "If you keep your money unemployed, you are a poor money manager. I treat every dollar that I own like a soldier that I send out to do battle for me and bring me more dollars."

This man's reason for investing is to utilize his accumulated capital as a working tool to increase his capital. This is a philosophy that you should adopt.

What are Your Investment Goals?
Let's assume that you have already determined your investment

disposition as discussed in Chapter 10. Further, assume that you have an idea of the types of investments with which you are comfortable. Finally, you have determined some of the basic reasons for investing. Now consider investment goals.

- Determine the amount of money you want to earn from your investment. This should be expressed as a percentage of the amount invested.
- Determine the amount of time it takes.
- Determine which investment vehicles you will use to satisfy your reasons for investing.

The last goal raises an important question. Do you have the knowledge and expertise to properly evaluate the type of investment that appeals to you and that could help you fulfill your goals? Hopefully, this book helps you answer this question.

- Determine if your goals are realistic.

After you establish your goals but before you invest, consider some personal characteristics:

> Age
> Marital status
> Present and anticipated socio-economic status
> Regular earnings
> Money or property expected from inheritances or trust funds
> Assets that are convertible into cash
> Short- and long-term obligations and debts
> Educational requirements and goals
> Present and future cost-of-living requirements.

Consider Your Age

Your age is an important characteristic because it is related to "time." This is one of the most important factors to consider in all investments. Time has many aspects. Time should not be confused with timing, which is another important investment factor. (Timing deals with fluctuations in sales prices as influenced by economic and market conditions that prevail at the time an investment is made.)

In considering the importance of time, assume that you live in a southwestern state that contains desert areas. One day you hear a radio program that reports certain facts. These include:

- The population of local urban areas is increasing.
- These areas are becoming congested.
- Many homes become unaffordable to the average working person.
- Rental properties are becoming expensive.
- Many people are thinking about moving to less congested areas, such as nearby desert areas.

You decide that your investment goal will be to make money by taking advantage of the population growth.

You then learn about an investment opportunity in vacant desert property near available drinking water. The investment does not require as much money as would be required to invest in vacant urban property. Upon further investigation, you determine that you can afford to buy and pay taxes on this ideal parcel of desert land. You know that it is directly in the path of growth. You are confident that the growth will increase the value. You believe that inflation and population growth, combined with the effect of the economic laws of supply and demand, will increase the value of the land.

If you follow your instincts and purchase the parcel of land, the profit that you will make from that investment, without improving it in any way, will depend upon one most important factor—the length of time you can hold the property before selling it. This is where the time factor becomes important.

Under normal circumstances, a 25-year old investor will usually derive more personal benefit from the use of time to increase the value of the land than will a 65-year old investor. Up to the point in the future where the land suffers from blight, the longer the property is held, the more expensive it becomes. In addition to the population growth and inflationary factors, there is an increase in land value due to improvements on the surrounding properties. For example, the completion of new roads, utilities, and adjoining homesites.

Consider Your Spouse

The second personal characteristic in the list dealt with your marital status. This is important for two reasons. First, a spouse is also a partner. In order for both of you to achieve or maintain a good relationship, your spouse must agree with your plans. He or she must be prepared to make whatever personal sacrifices are necessary to make or maintain the investment plan.

Two other personal characteristics are anticipated earnings and debt. Both must be considered before you establish your goals. If you forget to anticipate unexpected contingencies, you may experience difficulty in achieving your goals. You may be preoccupied with trying to keep pace with your current and future cost-of-living requirements.

If you are a young investor or an investment counselor, you should know that a young couple with limited assets can undertake greater risks than an older couple with substantial assets. If the investment goes sour, the people with greater assets may be legally liable and lose their assets. In contrast, the younger couple with limited assets has very little to lose when required to settle an incurred indebtedness.

Regardless of the goals they select, investors should attempt to keep sufficient financial reserves available. This is to prevent the need to dispose of investments that have not yet reached their maximum profit potential in the event of a shortage in funds. Many investors are compelled to sell their investments to meet unexpected, short-term financial problems that require immediate cash. If you fall within those financial parameters, select another goal, preferably based on what you can afford.

Margin

Many sound, potentially profitable stocks are bought on margin and then sold too soon. If the investor could afford to hold the stock just a few more weeks, a considerable profit could be realized. The tragedy is that the stocks are often sold because the purchaser's financial reserves are insufficient to meet a margin called because of a short term aberration in the market. Buying on margin means that a brokerage office finances a portion of a client's stock purchase. The brokerage firm holds the stock in trust as security, with "power to sell" the stock if the buyer does not maintain an adequate cash balance in his or her margin account. Again, if you think that you might have difficulty in meeting a margin call, do not buy stocks on margin. However, if you are prepared to be a speculator, you may decide to disregard this advice.

If you can afford the risk, possess readily available cash in reserve, and decide that it is your goal to make money via stocks or bonds, then learn about corporate and government financing. This is a must before you invest. If you learn about a sound, promising stock from reliable sources and interest rates on the balance that you will owe are low, then you should consider buying on margin. When interest on margin is tax deductible, many affluent investors do not mind paying high interest rates for the use of credit that can earn additional profits. This is particularly true for investors who have made large profits during the tax year.

If you decide that your goal is to speculate in real estate, your interest will be heightened by learning about the different fortunes that have been made by sharp buyers. These buyers, expecting to make a profit on a quick resale, used small deposits (earnest money) to tie up property in fast-moving areas. However, many deposits have been forfeited due to the sudden emergence of unforeseen financial contingencies. Prospective purchasers are sometime prevented from consummating what could have been a profitable transaction.

Protecting Your Assets

While trying to achieve your investment goals, you must always consider the importance of protecting what you already own and what you earn from other sources. Regardless of which types of investments you prefer, intelligent investment procedures mandate that you diversify your investments into more than one field. If a single investment field is preferred, diversify your investments within that field.

For example, if you prefer to invest in real estate, do not concentrate all of your funds into residential income property. Diversify by including commercial or industrial properties in your portfolio. In this way you can better weather the bad business cycles that are endemic to all types of investments. Or, if you insist on residential only, diversify into residential properties that are located in different socio-economic areas. If you prefer to invest in stocks, do not concentrate in one industry. This is true even when you understand one industry better than others. If you follow this advice, you will be balancing out your investments. This should always be a part of your investment goals.

To achieve your investment goals most easily, always try to keep your reserve funds in liquid, interest-bearing funds or accounts. This prepares you for the opportunities that a lack of available funds would cause you to miss. In addition, find a friendly banker and apprise him or her about your goals. See what is necessary to set up a credit line. Then, when you need money in a hurry, it will be available. The answers that you receive, in addition to the information in Chapter 12 about using leverage and margin as investment tools, are part of investment know-how. Armed with this know-how, you are prepared to establish and fulfill your investment goals.

As a review, reread the three determinants to the establishment of sound investment goals. Combine this with your investment disposition. You are now prepared to establish your investment goals.

Chapter 12: Using Debt to Increase Your Wealth

Using Debt to Increase Your Wealth

To illustrate the importance of debt, consider the following statement by Mr. Ted Turner, the internationally known business and sports entrepreneur. Quoted in the *Wall Street Journal*, he said, "By the end of this month, I'll owe $2 billion. . . .I'm pretty proud of that. Today it is not how much you earn, but how much you owe."

Lest you be misled, this type of debt only refers to investment debt, not debt that is accumulated by living beyond your means.

Investment professionals analyze investment results by considering the percentage of profit that is made from the amounts of cash or assets invested and the corresponding or risk of loss. Thus, a $100 profit from a $1,000 investment is much better than a $100 profit from a $10,000 investment. This is particularly true if the involved risk equals that of the $1000 investment.

Similarly, the profit from a no-down-payment investment, without risk—if that can be arranged—is better than the same investment requiring a cash down payment. This example should not be interpreted as a recommendation for the no-down-payment real estate deals that are being advertised in the media. I have a single objection to the no-down-payment real estate deals. If the people who have the intelligence to make a successful career out of no-down-payment real estate transactions used the same amount of time, effort, and energy in other ventures, they would achieve equal success.

Leverage

To become familiar with the intelligent methods of incurring indebtedness, look at the following examples of leverage, margin, and non-recourse instruments.

John Adams had a good income and wanted to invest in California acreage. His thinking was that if he invested in land now, in the future he would have the following options. In addition to protecting his money from inflation, he could:

- Sell all or a portion of the land for a profit.
- Build a house and live on it.
- Farm the land.
- Subdivide and sell the land.
- Subdivide and build houses for sale or rent.

When Adams found an area that looked as if it were in the path of early growth, he learned of two farmers were each willing to sell their 40-acre parcels of comparable land. Each wanted $40,000. However, there was a difference in the two deals. One farmer wanted all cash; he was also willing to sell ten acres for $10,000 cash. The other farmer wanted a 25 percent down payment for his 40 acres; he would carry the balance at 12 percent interest for a period of ten years. The monthly payments amounted to $430.42 per month including interest. John had the $40,000 in the bank. After careful consideration, John bought the 40 acres that he could buy with $10,000 down.

This decision used leverage. John borrowed $30,000 to increase his percentage of profit. For example, by being in the path of growth, there was a potential appreciation in land value of 10 to 15 percent in a single year.

The reason for using leverage to purchase the property was to earn a larger yield on the initial investment when compared to paying the entire amount using his available cash. If John paid the full $40,000, and if he sold it one year later, he would realize an increase in value of 10 percent, for a $4,000 profit. Considering that he would lose interest on the $40,000 withdrawn from the bank (or invested somewhere else with leverage) the $4,000 or a 10 percent yield was not a good profit.

Before you compare how John will fare if he employs leverage to make the purchase, you should remember that the increase in property value is the same whether it is purchased for cash or on terms. However, the percentage of profit, or the yield, usually increases with the use of leverage.

The financial benefits that accrue from buying the land on terms are easily derived. If John sells his property at the end of the first year, as assumed in our example, the gross yield on his $10,000 investment is 40 percent before deducting the 12 monthly payments. However, he did make 12 monthly payments amounting to $5165 (12 × $430.42). But, out of that $5165, only $3600 was interest; the balance of $1565 was like a saving, because it reduced the size of the loan to $28,435. Being a form of savings, it should not be charged as an expense. Therefore to secure the theoretical yield, divide the estimated sales profit of $4000 by $13,600 ($10,000 down payment + $3600 interest) for a 27 percent net yield from profits. This figure does not deduct taxes and sales expenses, which would apply in both situations.

Actually, the yield is higher because we have not calculated the amount of money earned by John's $30,000 bank deposit. Properly invested, his earnings could far exceed the $3600 paid in interest which could greatly increase the yield of his leveraged investment.

The advantages gained through the use of leverage in the purchase of land or for other investments should be clear. You should consider using leverage in your own investments.

Non-Recourse Instruments

Continuing the purpose of this chapter, i.e., explaining how to use debt to increase your wealth, any device that preserves your wealth deserves consideration. One such device is called *non-recourse paper*. Non-recourse paper refers to documents used in financing property. This document protects a debtor from being sued for additional funds if property is foreclosed by a seller.

Non-recourse papers are used by astute buyers in many real estate transactions. It can also be used by an investor in non-real estate transactions provided the investor specifies non-recourse during negotiations. For example, in California if, for whatever emergency or reason, John had been unable to make the payments on his $30,000 note, and if the farmer had to foreclose on the property to get it back, then the farmer could not have collected a *deficiency judgment* from John.

A deficiency judgment is a legal term that refers to the balance you owe if something you bought is legally foreclosed or repossessed. It includes the amount for which it is judiciously sold to satisfy the debt, the amount that is insufficient to satisfy the debt, plus the cost of legal proceedings. In some jurisdictions, the balance due that was not collected is still considered to be a valid legal debt, even though the debtor has already given back the property and has lost whatever payments were made. In California it only pertains to purchase-money trust deeds and mortgages, not to money that is subsequently borrowed from a non-owner lender.

Therefore, if you use the principles of leverage, avoid any

investment in which you cannot drop the investment by returning it to the creditor. Avoid being responsible for more money than you were obligated to pay up to the time that your ownership and possession ceased.

Margin Accounts

The stock market offers these types of opportunities. They are referred to as *margin accounts*. The term "margin" usually applies to stock purchases in which the buyer borrows a portion of the purchase money from a brokerage house, subject to the changeable margin rules set by The Federal Reserve Board. Margin rates can change whenever the Fed wants to use the rates as a tool to help them loosen or tighten the availability of credit.

For example, for a few years up to 1987, the margin rate was set at 50 percent. In comparison, when interest rates were lower in 1967, the margin rate was 70 percent.

The broker holds the margined stocks with the authority to sell them in the event that a sharp drop in their price impairs the value of the security. Once the stock is bought, Federal Reserve Board regulations require that the value of the account not drop below a specified margin rate. If it does, the broker issues a *margin call* to the investor. This requires the investor to put up sufficient cash or an equivalent value in stocks or recognized equities to comply with minimum margin requirements. The interest rates are usually above the prime rate and may vary according to the size of the margin account.

In a margin account, the investor's money is considered to be leveraged. This means that his money is being used to gain special benefits or extra profits. For example, assume that you desire to purchase 100 shares of a stock that is selling for $100 per share. After you place an order to purchase the stock in your regular account, you have five working days after the stock purchase to give your broker $10,000 plus commission. The payment is required even if you already have $100,000 worth of stock in your account. However, if, at the time of placing the order for the $100 shares of stock, you only wanted to use about $5,500 of your money, you could instruct your broker to buy 1,100 shares of stock on margin for $100 a share. If you do not already have a margin account, he will open one for you subject to the existing rules of the Federal Reserve Board. He will then try to buy the stock for you at your price. If he is successful, you have five working days after the purchase date to give him your $5,500 plus the normal commission fees. The broker's office will finance the balance for you, again, subject to the requirements of the Federal Reserve Board.

In 1987 the Federal Reserve Board required that the cash value of stocks in a margin account at the time of a purchase be at least 50 percent of the value of the stocks. If the investor does not have stocks in his account, he must put up 50 percent of the price of the stocks that he orders for his margin account. Once the account is active, the value of the stocks in the margin account is permitted to drop as low as 25 percent in some brokerage houses and 30 percent in others. If these levels are reached, a margin call is issued. The call requires that you deposit sufficient funds or equities to bring your stock to at least a 35 percent margin rate.

You should possess a speculatively inclined disposition to be comfortable with margin accounts. And never use a margin account unless you have access to sufficient cash funds to meet a potential margin call. This can and does happen when severe, sudden drops in stock prices occur. If you cannot meet the demands of a margin call, you can lose your entire investment in the event of a severe drop in the market. This is true even if the stock rebounds within a few days.

Under normal circumstances (and this is subject to change when market conditions become unstable) if your margin rate drops below 30 percent, some brokerage houses give you five working days to comply with the minimum requirements before selling your stocks. Remember, they must sell your stock to protect themselves. After all, they do want to hold, finance, and speculate with stocks selected by you. However, when days like Black Monday occur, brokerage firms may not give you more than a day to bring in enough funds or equities to cover your account. If the market heats up too much, the Federal Reserve Board can increase margin requirements to any amount that they believe is necessary to help cool off excessive buying on credit.

Benefits of Using Margin Accounts

The benefit derived from using margin is that, with a 50 percent margin rate, you can purchase approximately twice the amount of stock that you could normally afford to buy with cash. Consequently, the use of margin lets you nearly double your percentage of profit on the amount of money invested in the event of stock appreciation. Conversely, you lose twice as much if the stocks decline.

Another benefit derived from purchasing on margin is that if the stock pays a meaningful dividend, you receive the same dividends with a $5,000 investment as you do with $10,000.

If you do experience investment losses, there may be a severe tax consequence. Subject to future revisions and interpretations of the Tax Reform Act of 1986, the amount of investment interest that you are permitted to deduct is generally limited to the amount of your net investment income.

There are many ways to leverage investments. Margin accounts are only one. You should consider another leveraging alternative—your credit rating. Although the use of margin is an excellent investment tool, check your credit rating. If it is good enough to secure financing at a rate lower than that offered by your brokerage firm, you may prefer to leverage by using a bank loan or personal note.

Do you have an investment disposition that lets you live comfortably with ownership of a sound, non-stock market investment with heavy indebtedness? If so, strongly consider leveraging with margin. You can maximize your profits while minimizing your investment. However, as you read above, the use of margin is a double-edged sword. It is recommended as a wonderful investment tool; but it can be devastating if you become exposed to a demand for more money than you can raise—or afford to lose. Plan for the contingency of your investment turning sour. Unless you possess special knowledge concerning either a business or stock market investment, the excessive use of margin or too much leverage during troubled times is dangerous for the inexperienced investor and should be avoided.

Chapter 13: Selecting the Correct Legal Operating Entity

Selecting the Correct Legal Operating Entity

It is not necessary for a person to conduct his investments as a sole proprietor. Entrepreneurs and individual investors can also operate as joint tenants, as a trust, a partnership, a limited partnership, a stock corporation, or as a Subchapter S Corporation. Of course, all of these entities must be subject to and comply with applicable laws.

This chapter explains the differences between each of these legal entities. It emphasizes:

- The tax benefits
- The costs of establishing and conducting each form of business
- The avoidance of unnecessary liabilities germane to each type of entity

If you intend to operate any type of venture, it is advisable to first consult a good business attorney and a tax consultant or tax attorney. They will guide you toward the type of legal entity that you should use to operate your business. This kind of professional advice will be extremely helpful in assisting you to conduct your investment affairs in a business-like manner. Be prepared to tell them:

- Your current financial condition
- Your experience
- Your special talents
- What you hope to accomplish financially
- Any circumstances that might affect your plans

Fictitious Firm Names
Many individuals who go into business ventures have valid reasons for not wanting to use their own names in their individual or partnership enterprises. The laws respect these wishes and permit proprietorships and partnerships to operate under fictitious firm names. The respective names must first be

registered with the proper authorities and must not mislead the public. Registration usually requires that a certificate or affidavit of the fictitious firm name be filed with the county clerk of the county in which the business will be located. A small filing fee is also required. Often, a notice is placed in the local newspaper giving the names of the individual or individuals doing business under the fictitious firm name. This filing is intended to provide the public with legal notice and a source of information as to the real names and addresses of the principals of the business.

The use of fictitious corporate names is usually controlled by the Secretary of State of the state in which the corporation is organized. Sometimes, the state in which business will be transacted also institutes certain controls. To avoid the duplication of corporate names, names are checked by the Secretary of State of the originating state to avoid the duplication of corporate names before the corporate charter is issued to you.

The actual filing of a fictitious firm name or doing business as (dba) certificate does not require the services of an attorney. However, failure to file a fictitious firm name, or failing to renew the application when required by local laws, may result in two penalties. First, the violator is subject to a fine for failure to file. In many jurisdictions, if an individual using the unfiled fictitious firm name is sued as a defendant in a civil action, he is usually defenseless. Second, the individual who has not filed may be precluded from offering a defense to the law suit. He or she could become liable for a money judgment without the benefit of a trial.

Sole Proprietorships

Compared to a corporation, a sole proprietor does not incur the cost of incorporating. Nor does a sole proprietorship require the time-consuming and potentially expensive corporate board meetings and complex record-keeping. Also, a sole proprietor usually does not have to pay a state franchise tax. The overall bookkeeping for a sole proprietor is far less expensive than that of a corporation.

In recent years, tax rates for sole proprietors have been higher than those for corporations. But, after the corporations are taxed on their earnings, the shareholders, in what is referred to as double taxation, are also taxed on their share of the same earnings. This occurs when they receive dividends.

The sole proprietor currently pays a self-employment tax of

13.95 percent for earnings up to $37,800. Sole proprietors are usually not subject to unemployment taxes.

The benefits of operating as a sole proprietor when compared to other legal operating entities include:

- Start-up costs are lower.
- Business decisions are made without consultation.
- Profits need not be shared.
- Integrity and honesty of business associates is rarely an issue.
- Bookkeeping expenses can be minimized.
- Payroll and self-employment taxes may be avoided because a proprietor is not an employee.
- Funds can be withdrawn or transferred at will.
- The business can be sold without involving others.
- A Keogh plan may be used if considered advantageous.
- A friend or spouse may help in the business without authorization from an associate.
- Hours of operation, days off, and vacations are arranged to suit the whims of the sole proprietor.

There are also many disadvantages to operating as a sole proprietorship. These include:

- Personal legal liability for debts or accidents is unlimited.
- A large net profit may be subject to high taxes (place the individual into too high of a tax bracket).
- No one else has a vested interest in the business, either to supervise, watch the business, or to offer advice when required.
- Individuals are deprived of benefits offered by the various types of group insurance and IRA plans that are available to members of the other legal entities. This includes the loss of tax benefits available to businesses using these plans.

Trusts

Basically, a trust is a device whereby property is transferred by its owner, the trustor, to another entity called the trustee or transferee. The trustee holds the property in trust for the benefit of a beneficiary. This is the type of trust that a court might set up to protect a minor.

There are variations. One variation is referred to as a two-party trust, wherein the trustor makes himself the trustee for the benefit of another person. In a second variation, the trustee makes himself the beneficiary. This type of trust is used by public officials when their holdings might be construed as being a conflict of interest if they, and not the trustee, hold title to and manage holdings while in public office. The tax consequences of these trusts vary.

Joint-Tenancies

Some investors own their investments as joint-tenants. This type of ownership provides that if one of them dies, the survivor, be it a spouse or any other person or group, automatically receives title to the joint-tenancy property. A joint-tenancy agreement may provide that while the joint tenants are alive, each may receive unequal shares of the profits. This provision may be necessary because the law considers them to be equal owners, even if their contribution was unequal. With respect to profits and losses for tax purposes, their individual taxes are based on their proportionate share of ownership. Regardless of the size of their investment or the terms of their agreement about splitting profits, if there are two joint-tenants, each is allocated 50 percent of the profits and losses. If there are three joint-tenants, each is allocated one-third of the profits or deductions.

General Partnerships

There are two basic types of partnerships: general and limited. Legally, all general partners are jointly and severally liable for all of the debts and obligations incurred by the partnership. Each general partner has the authority to obligate the partnership to a legally binding contract without the consent of the other partner or partners.

The words *jointly and severally liable* have a special legal connotation that should be understood by all general partners. To illustrate, suppose there are two general partners named Smith and Jones. Assume that Smith has personal assets of $500,000, while Jones has personal assets of $25,000. When Smith and Jones combined their talents to form the Smith & Jones partnership, each contributed $10,000. For some reason, Mr. Johnson secures a judgment of $100,000 against the partnership. This happens at a time when the partnership has no funds. Under the legal theory of joint and several liability, Mr. Johnson has a variety of collection alternatives. These include the right to collect the entire $100,000 from Mr. Smith, or $25,000 or less from Mr. Jones and $75,000 or more from Mr. Smith, who would have recourse against Mr. Jones if and when Jones acquires additional money.

Advantages and Disadvantages of General Partnerships

When individual entrepreneurs consider entering a partnership, the benefits and disadvantages that must be weighed are:

- The amount of their respective investment will be reduced by half.
- If there are losses, a solvent partner will pay his or her share.
- If the partner is insolvent, the legal theory of joint and several liability applies to the partnership; the solvent partner will be responsible for all debts of the partnership.
- If the partnership is profitable, the profits are shared. Each partner will derive the benefit of the other partner's advice and services subject to the terms of the partnership agreement.
- One legal judgment against a general partner, even if personal in nature, can be charged to the debtor's portion of the business assets. This can be disruptive to both the capital structure of the partnership and its operation.

Criteria for Selecting a Business Partner

Five of the best criteria for determining if you should go it alone or accept a partner are:

1. Do you need the partner's capital, or can you get along without it?
2. Does the prospective partner have special skills without which the business cannot survive?
3. Are people with those skills employable at a price that you can afford?
4. If you do not need the capital, can you employ a conscientious skilled worker with the same talents possessed by the prospective partner?
5. Should you relinquish one half of the profits and sole control of the business?

The answers to these questions depend upon whether you want

someone to invest money and to share in the responsibilities and the work, provide advice, and share in the losses.

The Partnership Agreement

Every partnership should have a partnership agreement that is duly recorded. Like the proprietorship, the partnership is recorded in the County Clerk's office of the county in which the business is being transacted. The partnership agreement should be prepared by a commercial attorney. It should spell out:

- The amount of capital to be advanced by each partner
- The percentage of ownership of each partner
- How the profits and losses are to be divided
- The duties of each partner
- The liabilities of each partner
- The compensation of each partner
- The rights of each partner
- How the partnership may be terminated

The partnership ends upon the death of one of the general partners. However, the termination section of the partnership agreement is important, because it provides for the proper and orderly disposal of all partnership interests in the event that one or both partners want to end the arrangement.

Above all, the agreement should contain a detailed *buy-out* clause, in the event that the partners wish to end their partnership arrangement. A buy out clause in a partnership agreement usually specifies the terms and conditions that apply if a member of the firm decides to resign or retire from the partnership. This clause usually becomes extremely important when a business becomes successful. This is especially true in situations where the enterprise is comprised of more than two partners. It is necessary if a majority of the partners decide to eliminate one of the partners for business or personal conduct reasons.

The need for a buy out clause is also demonstrated by the following three examples.

1. A majority of the partners decide to add an additional partner. The candidate may have views that are similar to those of the majority, but not to those of the minority partner.

2. A majority of the partners vote to expand the business, buy a new business, or borrow money for remodeling. A dissenting minority partner believes that these are not advantageous to the business.
3. An equal partner wishes to sell his partnership interest to someone unknown or disliked by the minority partner.

A properly drawn buy-out clause in the original partnership agreement permits the dissenting partner to offer to purchase the interests by the other partners at the same price that he would accept if they desired to purchase his interest in the partnership. It includes a method of determining a fair price and possibly the name of a disinterested party to determine the price and arrange the details.

Limited Partnerships

Investors who want the benefits of a business venture without the joint and several liability have a few options. They may:

- Form a corporation
- Obtain a partner who is willing to be the general partner of a limited partnership and sign up as a limited partner
- Find an established limited partnership or syndication and sign on as a limited partner.

A disadvantage to a limited partnership is that limited partners are not active in the business. They are "limited" in their contributions.

After the partnership is formed, the general partner or partners make all business decisions. They are usually authorized to borrow money for partnership purposes. However, like the general partnership previously described, each general partner in the limited partnership becomes jointly and severally liable for any and all debts or obligations incurred by the partnership.

Examples of Limited Partnerships

The liability of limited partners is restricted (or limited) to the amount of money or assets that they agreed to contribute to the partnership. Once they make their full contribution, their liability is limited to that potential loss. If they have not paid the full amount of their scheduled contribution, then they are only liable for the unpaid balance. Look at the following story.

Mr. Smith, being a promoter, answered an ad to become a distributor for the manufacturer of a fantastic new gadget. When Smith saw the product, he was so impressed that he wanted to become the exclusive distributor for the state of Texas. The manufacturer agreed, provided that Smith supplied him with an initial order for $30,000 worth of gadgets and the agreement to buy another $30,000 of the same or improved gadgets every six months thereafter. Mr. Smith said that he expected to have two partners and that he would immediately begin making the necessary arrangements.

Having only $10,000 of his own to invest, he approached two friends, Mr. Jones and Mr. Johnson. Smith trusted them, and both wanted extra income. They agreed that the gadget had merit. They also had the capital to invest. Neither had any time to help in the proposed business, but both thought that it would be a successful venture.

Accordingly, Mr. Jones and Mr. Johnson agreed to invest $15,000 as limited partners. They went to an attorney and drew up and signed a limited partnership agreement. It provided that Mr. Smith be the general partner and required that his contribution be $10,000 to the partnership. In addition, the agreement provided that both Jones and Johnson be limited partners; their contributions were $15,000 each. As a result, the firm was capitalized at $40,000.

After the agreement was signed, it was duly recorded in the County Clerk's office. Mr. Smith said that he would deposit his $10,000 in a bank account under the partnership name. He promised to take care of everything from that point on. Then, he asked Jones and Johnson for their respective contributions. They promised to deliver their checks to him by the next morning. The next day, as promised Mr. Jones delivered a check for $15,000, but Mr. Johnson only delivered $12,000. He explained that he had miscalculated the amount of money he had available. However, he promised to make up the $3,000 balance in a short period of time.

Mr. Smith opened an office, ordered the merchandise, paid for it, and sold it to various retail outlets. Within a month, another $30,000 gadget order was placed with the manufacturer. These were shipped immediately, but this time he was given 30-day payment terms.

It turned out that Mr. Smith was a good promoter. He did a lot of entertaining and spent a lot of money promoting. However, never having owned his own business, he did not know anything about checking the credit of his retail customer. He simply took their orders and delivered the merchandise. Due to bad accounts, high promotional expenses, and some other factors, the firm quickly experienced a cash squeeze. Smith was unable to pay the manufacturer, who in turn refused to ship further orders.

In the interim, Mr. Johnson had trouble raising the extra $3,000 he owed. When he finally got the money, he sensed trouble. He decided to hold back his payment. When the manufacturer requested payment on the $30,000 due him, Mr. Smith found that by collecting from some of the slow paying outlets and then adding what the firm had in the bank, he would only be able to send the manufacturer $20,000. He closed the office. A few weeks later he sent the manufacturer the $20,000, leaving a balance due of $10,000.

The manufacturer immediately sued the partnership to recover the $10,000 plus legal expenses. The manufacturer won the case and a judgment against the partnership for $10,000 plus his costs. However, when he tried to collect, he found that Mr. Smith had no money, Mr. Jones had money, but he was only liable up to the amount he had promised to contribute to the partnership, which he had fulfilled. That left Mr. Johnson, who now possessed much more money than the amount owed to the manufacturer.

However, as a limited partner, Johnson was nearly in the same position as Mr. Jones, except that he had not paid the $3,000 that he had promised to contribute to the partnership. As a result, he was only liable for the $3,000 and not the $10,000. Based on the limited partnership, only one person was liable for the $7,000 balance. This was the general partner Mr. Smith. If Mr. Johnson failed to pay the $3,000, Mr. Smith would have been responsible for the entire $10,000 plus legal costs.

The purpose of this story is to point out a distinction. If all three people had been general partners, all three would have been responsible for the entire $10,000 balance plus legal costs. The manufacturer could have collected the full amount from any partner having the ability to pay.

The Limited Partnership Agreement

A formal limited partnership agreement, like a general partnership agreement, should always be prepared by an attorney and filed according to the Limited Partnership laws of the state in which the partnership will operate. The agreement should specifically identify:

- The general partner or partners
- The limited partners
- The amount of money or assets to be contributed by each
- When contributions are to be made
- The rights and obligations of the respective signatories
- The compensation of the limited and all general partners

Due to expected amendments to the Tax Reform Act of 1986 and the unexpected interpretations that flow from the various laws, if you contemplate becoming a limited partner to benefit from limited liability, then in addition to having your attorney draw up or check the partnership agreement, you should also consult with your tax adviser. Ask him about the "at-risk rules." In particular, consult your tax advisor if your partnership is involved in real estate, leasing equipment, farming, motion pictures, oil, gas, or geothermal operations.

Basically, the at-risk rules limit a taxpayer's loss for tax purposes to the amount of funds that he has at risk or could lose in the venture. Real estate and closely held leasing equipment ventures are not subject to the at-risk rules. Consequently, and except for these businesses, limited partners cannot deduct more losses for tax purposes than the amount of their investment.

An advantage that a limited partner enjoys over a general partner is that the limited partner is not required to pay a self-employment tax. The general partner, on the other hand, is liable for self-employment taxes even if he already contributes to Social Security.

As previously mentioned, limited partners are at a serious disadvantage because they cannot be active or have an effective voice in the business. This is true even if they know that something is wrong. Further, if they happen to exercise any judgment or control in the operation of the partnership, and this activity is proven by a creditor, their limited liability status vanishes—they become *jointly and severally* liable. The creditor can successfully claim that they are general. They are no longer a limited partners and should be held jointly and severally liable for all partnership obligations.

A recent California law (Revised Limited Partnership Act) permits corporations that are limited partners in a real estate joint venture to have an active voice in the business of the partnership. Limited partners can use a veto without completely eliminating their limited liability status.

One final observation. As with sole proprietorships, neither the partnership nor its members derive the same group-medical and tax benefits that accrue to a corporation and its employees.

Corporations

For those entrepreneurs who have outgrown sole proprietorships and partnerships, a corporation can offer many benefits with very few disadvantages. And, for those who might desire special federal tax considerations while retaining the limited liability features of a corporation, the U.S. Government recognizes *Subchapter S Corporations*. (These corporations are discussed later. For now, be aware that Subchapter S Corporations are not recognized by the taxing authorities of all states.)

One might well ask, "How and why did the use of corporations become so popular?" The corporate structure, by granting individuals the right to incorporate as shareholders, enables them to limit their financial liability to the greater amount between the amount of stock they own in the corporation or the amount that they subscribe to purchase plus any amount that they might loan to the corporation.

In this way, a combination of investors, business people, and managers can combine their funds and talents to become equity shareholders in a general corporate enterprise. They need not fear losing their rights to become actively involved in the corporate business. Thus, they may express their opinions about the ongoing management of the corporate business. This is something they would be prevented from doing as a limited partner without fear of losing their limited liability status.

Most creditors who deal with corporations and limited partnerships are aware of these liability limitations. However, if a corporation is formed with insufficient funds to operate the business or secure credit, it is probable that neither it nor its shareholders will be granted freedom from liability. This is because the law intends for corporations to develop commerce and protect investors. But if it appears that the corporation was formed with an insufficient amount of capital to properly conduct its business, the law will presume fraudulent intent. It will not countenance the perpetration of a fraud on creditors who depend on a corporation that is recognized by a state government.

Stock corporations are recognized legal entities that have been a boon to the overall development of most industrialized countries. Also, they have stimulated the concomitant growth of national, international, and multinational businesses and charitable, non-profit enterprises.

In addition to limiting the financial liabilities of the entrepreneurs who formed or actively participated in these corporations, the original purpose of corporations was to promote the general welfare of the country. They fulfilled that requirement by providing a viable vehicle for raising corporate capital. The result has been the rapid development of commerce, industry, inventions, and international trade.

Years ago, taxes were not a major factor for corporate investors. However, since federal income taxes first became effective in 1913, legislators and corporate lobbyists have tried to get special tax exemptions for corporations. Throughout the years the tax and insurance benefits granted to corporations have varied with the politics and the amount of pressure exerted by tax lobbyists.

One major difference between the other legal entities and a corporation is that it has no sole proprietors or partners. This is true even when a corporation is owned and controlled by one person who is not a director or officer.

Forming a Corporation

A corporation is formed in the following way. Subject to the laws of the state, three or more people, called organizers or directors, sign Articles of Incorporation. The articles include the business purpose of the corporation. The articles are forwarded to the office of the Secretary of State or the Division of Corporations in the governing state. After receiving the appropriate fees and approving the Articles of Incorporation, the state issues a charter to the organizers. The charter authorizes them to conduct business in that state. The corporation may also conduct business in other states by registering as a foreign corporation.

Some states have lower fees than others. The low-fee states

Selecting the Correct Legal Operating Entity 133

attempt to attract corporations to their states to obtain added revenues. According to the *Wall Street Journal*, "Nearly 60 percent of the the companies listed on the New York Stock Exchange are incorporated in Delaware." Delaware offers same day incorporation filings, low fees, and limits the liability of directors. Depending upon where you live, incorporating at home could be much more expensive than incorporating in a state such as Delaware.

Yet, if you incorporate in another state and intend to operate at home, you will probably be subject to local franchise fees and taxes. You should also be sensitive to the fact that taxes and director liabilities vary from state to state. This is particularly true if you intend to operate in multiple states. It is a good idea to have an experienced corporation lawyer and your tax accountant advise you about the best state in which to incorporate.

The corporation is owned by its shareholders. They vote, usually annually, for a board of directors. The board appoints officers that run the day-to-day business operations. The board is controlled by the board of directors. Shareholders have the right to express their opinions about company operations and management by voting their stock shares. They can vote for directors whose thinking parallels their own.

The basic corporate officers are the president, vice-president, treasurer and secretary. The directors of large corporations usually elect a chief executive officer (CEO) who selects the operating officers.

What are the Disadvantages of a Corporation?

There are disadvantages of operating as a corporation. These include:

- The cost of incorporating
- The cost of maintaining special corporate records
- Double taxation of the same profits. (Corporations pay taxes on profits; then shareholders pay personal income taxes on dividends.)
- The requirement for annual franchise fees
- Accounting costs
- Corporate taxes may be too high when compared to the value of corporate income and limited shareholder liability.

Because of constantly changing corporate and personal tax structures, constant advice from a tax accountant is crucial. Operating a corporation without one is tantamount to operating an ocean liner in rough seas without a helmsman.

Shareholders receive earnings and profits from the corporation in the form of dividends. Dividends are taxable, even though the corporation has already been taxed for the income from which dividends are taken. Corporations may also pay dividends in the form of stocks, stock rights, and other property or services.

When a corporation returns capital to its shareholders, it is not taxable if the capital was not derived from earnings and profits. Furthermore, the shareholders cannot have received a return of capital that exceeds their cost basis in the corporation. If the return exceeds their cost basis, it is considered a capital gain—not ordinary income.

Subchapter S Corporations

There are situations when it is advisable for shareholders of a corporation to elect to organize as a partnership called a Subchapter S Corporation. Subchapter S Corporations are governed by Internal Revenue Service codes. Becoming a Subchapter S Corporation requires the unanimous consent of all shareholders. In addition, all of the requirements of the Internal Revenue Service must be met. For example, there are special qualifications governing real estate investments.

By becoming a Subchapter S Corporation, shareholders can avoid double taxation. They eliminate the corporate tax and limit their own tax liability to corporate earning levels. The tax on corporate earnings is limited to the pro-rata income allocable to each of the shareholders based on their proportion of ownership. In effect, the income of Subchapter S Corporations is not taxed. On the last day of the corporation's tax year, its profits and losses are distributed to its shareholders. In turn, each shareholder applies his or her individual tax rate to profit or loss of the corporation.

There are several situations in which a tax consultant might recommend the election of a Subchapter S Corporation. First, the shareholders desire the limited liability offered by a corporation. Then, there are situations when:

- Stockholders are in a lower tax bracket than the corporation.
- Stockholders are in a position to use the corporation's start-up or other long-term losses as tax shelters for their personal incomes.

Some of the disadvantages of a Subchapter S Corporation are:

- The need to understand the complexities of the IRS codes governing Subchapter S Corporations.
- The susceptibility to IRS reclassification if large capital gains are realized. The IRS can claim taxes from both the Subchapter S Corporation and its shareholders.

Concluding Comments

The information in this chapter provides an overview of organizational entities, some common benefits, and some common liabilities. Like the other information in this book, the information is not intended to replace the advice of your attorney or accountant. Because information is rarely timeless, it is important to check on recent events and the current environment. For example, if you believe that you should use the Subchapter S Corporation to prevent double taxation, check with your accountant. Have your accountant evaluate the effect on the corporation and its shareholders. Perhaps there are other, more profitable alternatives. A limited partnership could be a better choice. Once you get the figures and are convinced of the advantages, follow through.

Section 3:
What You Should Know About Finances

Chapter 14: What is Economics and Who Uses It?

What is Economics and Who Uses It?

Prior to the Industrial Revolution, it was not necessary for the average person to have any knowledge of economics. But now anyone who does not understand basic economics is disadvantaged. Today, even the smallest investor or business person must acquire, understand, and regularly use some knowledge of basic economic principles.

Importance of Economics

A knowledge of economics has become so important, it has even invaded the judicial system. According to reports in the *Wall Street Journal*, Federal Judge Richard A. Posner, best known for authoring the leading text *Economic Analysis of The Law*, tutored himself in economics to better understand modern law.

Hundreds of federal judges have received university training in economics in a new movement referred to as Law and Economics. This background encourages rulings that are based upon efficient competitive behavior as opposed to a strict interpretation of antitrust laws.

Fortunately, public education systems have also begun to recognize the importance of economics in our lives. Some educators are stimulating students to learn about economics by referring to it as a "knowledge of money."

Economics Defined

Here is a simple but comprehensive definition of economics. Economics involves the production and distribution of all goods and services and the effects of that production and distribution on everything connected with the health, wealth, and welfare of people and their respective countries.

Unfortunately, most attempts by known types of governments to effectuate a practical, long-range economic system that benefits both the majority of its people and the best interests of the country usually fall far short of the goals. That is because even the most honorable political leaders as well as the most creditable economists cannot agree on which economic principles will produce the desired or most beneficial results. Some believe that the government should regulate nearly every phase of life, finance, and business. Others advocate varying degrees of deregulation.

Unfortunately, experience indicates that even when people seem to find what they believe to be the most practical and efficient system, there are still problems. There are always groups who suffer financial or social hardships, while others enjoy life and prosperity. Hopefully, an understanding of economics will help you to enjoy life and prosper, regardless of what economic systems affect you.

Economic Contradictions

As a beginner, you should become aware of the large number of different and contradictory economic beliefs that motivate the lawmakers. It is these contradictions that both baffle and discourage most new investors from trying to understand the basic principles of economics. This section is intended to simplify these principles.

Some of the major problems a practical economist must try to reconcile at the same time are inflation and its affect on the value of the dollar. With respect to inflation, which is either an ever present threat or benefit to you, the economists differ again. One group of economists says that inflation can be avoided by taxing people at higher rates. This is intended to take away their money and curtail their spending. Higher taxes dampen their demand for goods and services which causes prices to drop. Hence, this approach combats and controls inflation. Critics of this theory claim that these government advocates are merely saying to the consumer-taxpayer, "If you spend too much of your money, it is inflationary. However, if we collect it in the form of higher taxes and then spend the money (instead of allowing you to spend it), the result is not inflationary."

Yet, if the government would use the tax-money to reduce budget deficits by saving the money instead of spending it, the idea might have merit. But alas, bureaucrats tend to spend all available funds, and even more.

As an investor, it behooves you to become familiar with the conflicting economic philosophies. This includes the various regular surveys that both government and private organizations conduct.

By examining the surveys, you get an indication of the thinking of the various influential economic analysts and politicians. You can anticipate what they are going to recommend to the government and which economic philosophy the administration will likely implement. Then you can better determine how these things might affect your current or future investments.

For example, Alan Greenspan, who was appointed Chairman of the Federal Reserve Board in the latter part of 1987, believes in controlling credit according to the money supply, foreign exchange rates, and other growth and inflation indicators. The National Association of Purchasing Managers conducts a monthly survey of more than 250 industrial purchasing managers. When their reading is above 50 percent, then the economy is expected to expand. For October 1987, all of their indicators were positive. Unfortunately, that was the month the stock market suffered a devastating loss.

The United States Department of Commerce's index of leading indicators reflects stronger or slower growth. It showed a decline of 0.1 percent in September 1987. Some of the indicators that are used by the Commerce department include:

- Overall business inventories
- The ratio of inventories to sales
- Business sales
- The production of durable and nondurable goods (durable goods have a three-year life cycle).

The government also prepares an index of 22 commodities of which 13 are industrial commodities and 9 are foodstuffs. Dow Jones has an index of spot commodity prices and of commodity futures.

The Encyclopedia of Economics by Douglas Greenwald is one of the easiest sources to use in securing the names of leading economists and their specialties. It contains the names of more than 160 distinguished contributors.

You may not want to become an amateur economic forecaster. You may prefer to try to interpret the economic forecasts of others or review forecasts in the financial news services. In any event, you should stay abreast of the underlying philosophies of these forecasts. In so doing, you will probably become familiar with and begin to understand the important philosophical differences between Keynesians, supply-siders, and monetarists. These three economic philosophies contain the most important economic theories of our times.

Keynesians

Keynesians are people who follow the theories of John Maynard Keynes, a distinguished British economist. He advocated monetary and fiscal policies early in this century that stimulated employment. He wrote many books and was considered the most influential economist of the 20th century. The word Keynesian came from his 1936 book, *The General Theory of Employment Interest and Money*.

Keynesians believe that if full employment levels cannot be provided by the private sector of the economy, then the answer lies in increased expenditures by the public sector. Further, because they deplored economic stagnation, they also suggested that large expenditures by the government—even if it meant deficit financing—would increase consumer demand for goods and services. They believed that the banks should make the necessary loans to support a full-employment economy. In the second Roosevelt administration, (1937-41) Federal Reserve Chairman Marriner Eccles, following Keynesian theory, recommended deficit spending to balance the federal budget.

In later years, the Keynesian theory had to be modified to meet changing circumstance. But even in its hey-day, it had many opponents. Among these were the monetarists and the supply-siders.

Monetarists

Monetarists criticize the Keynesian fiscal policies because they do not want unnecessary government interference. Monetarists believe that over a period of time, the economic level of output is determined by the forces of supply and demand. Milton Friedman, one of the best known economists and monetarists of the 20th century, helped make monetarism famous when he and Anna J. Schwartz wrote *A Monetary History of the United States, 1867-1960*, which was published in 1963.

The authors proposed that the high rate of inflation in the United States would not have occurred if the Federal Reserve Board had used a tighter money policy. Since then, Friedman has held many government posts and has been associated with many Universities.

From 1941 to 1943 he was the principal economist with the U.S. Treasury Department. In 1981, during the first year of the Reagan administration, he was appointed to the President's Economic Advisory Board.

Friedman believes that in order to achieve a reasonable degree of stability in economic activity and the price levels, the government should control money growth at a steady rate similar to the way a commodity is controlled. Neo-Keynesians prefer to restrict wages and prices but sometimes suggest tax increases or reduced government spending.

Monetarists believe that an excessive money supply or growth rate indicates an inflationary trend. That is why they endorse governmental regulation of both the money supply and the economic growth rate.

Supply-Side Economics

Supply-side Economics is believed to have started with Adam Smith in the 1700s. It was revived in the 1970s because its theories seemed to offer a way to combat inflation. Supply-siders oppose high interest rates on the grounds that they hinder economic growth. Supply-siders believe that providing incentives to produce merchandise is more important than providing incentives to consume merchandise. They believe that reductions in taxes are an incentive to increased production.

In 1979, Congressman Jack Kemp of New York, backed by a group of other Republicans, unsuccessfully tried to get a 30 percent tax cut for the 1978 tax year. They argued that the tax cuts would stimulate economic activity to the extent that the lost tax income would be replaced by increased revenue. In 1981 a similar type of tax reduction was tried by President Reagan but without catering to the supply-siders. He tried to get tremendous reductions in U.S. government spending in order to secure a balanced budget. The supply-siders would have been happy with the tax cut.

Supply-siders are not afraid of huge deficits. They are divided about government spending. Sometimes they endorse a flat tax or sales tax using the theory that such a tax collects revenues from many taxpayers who are able to avoid paying income taxes. Their belief is that those once uncollectible taxes would vastly increase tax revenues and materially reduce any budget deficit.

Even though monetarist policies—such as those espoused by

Milton Friedman—do help to curb inflation, there have been times when interest rates and unemployment have soared under such policies. On the other hand, Keynesian theories, which advocated manipulation of the economy by the government through tax and spending policies, could not deter the sky-rocketing inflation of the 1960s and 1970s.

Minor Economic Theories

Following are some additional economic theories that you might encounter. However, these have not had the same degree of approval as the major three just covered.

Libertarians desire a minimum amount of government interference. They are aware of the importance and implications attached to money-supply growth but abhor governmental regulations.

Micro-economists are usually only concerned with how the economy is affecting individuals and households.

Macro-economists are concerned with the broad economic picture, such as the relationship between the country's income and its investments.

Rational-expectationists endorse monetarist views about money supply but believe that people, by their anticipatory actions, will negate any governmental attempts to regulate the money supply too finely.

The importance of these theories is that you should be cognizant of the fact that different administrations and politicians attempt to run the government according to the economic principles in which they have faith. This is often without regard to whether or not they are effective under prevailing economic circumstances.

Important Economic Indicators

To be a knowledgeable investor, you should always be aware of the following economic indicators.

- Money supply
- Interest rates
- The present and anticipated Federal Reserve Board's policy about both

The basic money supply has a direct impact on interest rates. Although it has not always received a high priority, at the present time it seems that most economists agree that the money supply has a tremendous impact on the economy. They do not agree, however, on how, when, and by whom the money supply should be regulated. It should also be noted that the disagreements between the economists also extend to the executive, administrative, and legislative arms of the government. Furthermore, most governments in the world disagree with each other's economic policies.

Many people do not understand the role that our commercial banks play in the creation of money. Neither do they understand the role played by the central bank in controlling the money supply. Commercial banks may create money and expand the money supply by issuing loans and investing in large projects. They are backed with reserves by the Federal Reserve's central bank which charges them interest.

Foreign Exchange

The rate of interest that the central bank charges is calculated and designed to accomplish a dual purpose—to make a profit and to control the economy. If the economy heats up, they increase the interest rates in an attempt to curb borrowing. If the economy is sluggish, they lower the interest rates to encourage borrowing.

Equally important are:

- The strength of the dollar in foreign-exchange markets
- The balance of trade figures
- Whether or not the U.S. is a creditor nation or a debtor nation
- The amount of the Gross National Product (GNP)

These figures and statistics usually appear in the daily press, and particularly in financial papers such as the *Wall Street Journal*.

The strength of the U.S. dollar in foreign exchange is a very important consideration. Our rate of exchange with foreign countries varies with each country in ratio to the strength of the respective currencies. Basically, the more debt that a country incurs, the weaker its currency becomes. Those countries that export more finished goods than they import usually have a stronger currency than the importing countries. Therefore, when that country or its citizens want to buy merchandise from or travel to another country, they must pay more of its currency than they would if their currency was stronger than that of the export country.

The foreign exchange rates between Canada and the United States offer an interesting example of how rates of exchange can affect neighboring countries, businesses, and visitors. In 1976, people paid $1.03 U.S. dollars for a Canadian dollar. This benefited Canadians who bought from or visited the United States. Thereafter, the Canadian dollar began to decrease in value. During 1987 the United States dollar was worth approximately $1.31 Canadian dollars. This means that if in 1976 a U.S. resident invested in a Canadian enterprise that agreed to pay a fixed amount of 1,000 Canadian dollars annually, that 1,000 Canadian dollars was only worth 750 U.S. dollars in 1987.

Balance of International Trade

The difference between a country's imports and exports is called its *balance of international trade*. In its ordinary and narrow context, that definition does not include income from investments abroad. Other than to make comparisons, the balance of trade figures are not important to you unless the country with a trade deficit is required to use international reserves or borrow funds from outside of that country to pay for the balance of trade deficit. That type of borrowing, if extensive, may affect the future exchange rate of the borrowing country's currency because its currency will be weaker.

Gross National Product and Gross Domestic Product

The Gross National Product (GNP) is the total monetary value, at market prices, of all final goods produced in a country during one year. To this, the income accruing to domestic residents arising from investments abroad is added. Finally, income earned by foreigners is subtracted. Financial transactions are not included in Gross Domestic Product (GDP) figures.

The GNP and GDP figures enable governments and you to compare and analyze current economic conditions with those of prior years. And, if there were any changes in monetary and fiscal policy during the year, you could see their effect on the totals.

Having a valid economic opinion about current conditions is important to every investor's peace of mind if not his or her success as an investor. You should base investment decisions upon either your own economic views or the views of selected, respected economists with whom you agree. Is the government administering the right or wrong economic medicine for the current business climate? Will it benefit or hurt the majority of the people and the welfare of the country? With an economic basis for your investment decisions, you will have answers to these questions. The answers give you more confidence in your investment decisions. If you are right, the result of your investments will be higher investment yields.

Chapter 15: How to Interpret the Investment Climate

How to Interpret the Investment Climate

After investors agree upon or select an investment with which they believe they will be comfortable, one of the questions they most frequently ask their adviser or broker is, "Is this the right time to invest?" This question is one of the most difficult to answer and, frequently, only subsequent events can provide the answer.

Timing the Economic Climate

Selecting the most advantageous time to make and successfully dispose of your investment is as important as the quality of the investment itself. It may be even more important than the amount of the dividends or profits the investment will have made for you. Timing is also as important as all the knowledge and skill you may have acquired about the merits or details of your investment.

Unfortunately, even if one selects the most meritorious investment, the answer to correctly timing the profitable disposal of it depends upon two very important considerations:

1. Accurately determining the current economic climate
2. Forecasting and interpreting the future economic climate

Accordingly, you should try to acquaint yourself with the various types of economic indicators and indexes that are available, such as those mentioned in Chapter 14. The information you glean from the indicators, together with some knowledge you may have about economic history and business cycles, can prove to be invaluable to you.

You should also compare the different interpretations the economists give to the signals with your own observations. Sometimes these interpretations may give you an idea of the problems that your investment will experience currently or face in the future. The problems could result from new legislation or restrictions with which you may not be familiar.

The point is, you cannot bury yourself in the details of your business or investment without being conscious of the economic climate that surrounds them and which will affect their future productivity and value. The least you can do is to read the trade papers or magazines that cover your investment or business. If a kindred trade exists in your area, join it and find out what is transpiring and what its members think the future seems to promise.

Interpreting the Indicators

Investors must become aware that some knowledge of economic history and current indicators can help their intelligent and timely selection or sale of a business or investment. Although you may possess an innate dislike of economics and be inclined to believe that it is an arcane subject best reserved for students or professors, every investment made by you will be directly or indirectly affected by some aspect of economics. These may include indicators that refer to financing, interest rates, unemployment, auto sales, housing starts, money in circulation, taxes, budget problems, or import/export trade balances.

Each businessman and investor must ask himself or his accountant how each of these aspects of economics will affect his venture. For example, if you are in a capital-oriented business, the trends in financing may indicate smaller or larger net profits. If interest rates are going to climb, will you be able to afford them? An increase in housing starts would be encouraging to building supply manufacturers and retailers; banks would be encouraged because of their increased financing role in both construction and loans to furniture manufacturers and retailers, and so forth. To the lay person, it will indicate that many people are optimistic about the future.

If a person has a labor-oriented investment, it follows that a future scarcity of labor may disproportionately affect costs, sales, and percentage of profit per sale. The volume of new auto sales generally reflects the optimism or negativism of the majority of the people. A high volume of automobile sales would indicate that a good portion of the auto buyers' monthly payments will be going towards paying off their cars.

In short, each of the above aspects can be interpreted to aid the thinking processes of the investor or business person in their short-term deliberations about when they should get in or out of a venture. There is no guarantee that your interpretations or mine will be correct, but using figures or indicators to determine the investment climate is the intelligent approach to investing.

Fortunately, hundreds of economic indicators are easily available to help you determine the best time to buy or sell or attempt to forecast future trends of business, economics, and politics. Be aware that although the economic indicators mentioned above are used by the leading economists, the correct use of these indicators is more of an art than an exact science.

One of the prime reasons why the leading economists disagree with each other so frequently stems from their inability to reach the same conclusions from the same facts. Nevertheless, because of the many variables that are involved in leading indicator forecasting, I would suggest you let the economists do the interpreting for you. If you look for them, you will find their conclusions reported in the business sections of your newspapers and in the financial trade papers of the industry. Get an idea of which indicators are key from this book. Then learn more about them by letting the recognized economists interpret them for you.

Each month the Bureau of Economic Analysis of the U.S. Department of Commerce publishes 300 economic indicators in its Business Conditions Digest. Sixty-five of them are called *leading indicators* because the events through which they were formed occurred before the general economy was affected by them. The balance of the indicators are called *coinciding* or *lagging indicators*. As you might guess, coinciding indicators reflect what happened when the economic processes caused the event to occur when the economy was affected. The lagging indicators refer to those events that occurred after the economy was affected. For example, in the construction industry, plans to build a large complex would be a leading indicator. The layoff rate could not be a leading indicator because it would probably occur after the complex is completed. It would be either a coincident or lagging indicator.

Twelve Leading Economic Indicators

The average layman will probably have an interest in a set of indicators published by the Bureau of Economic Analysis referred to as a *leading indicator composite*. It lists 12 different leading indicators that are supposed to give you an idea of what the economy will be like in the months ahead. These include money supply, liquid assets, housing permits, average work week, stock market, plant/equipment orders, layoff rate, inventories, vendor performance, new consumer orders, sensitive prices, and business formations.

At the same time, you should be aware of the public's sensitivity to what they hear about the economy and their resulting confidence or lack of it concerning the future. This sensitivity has a tremendous impact on the course of the economy. This is because confidence determines whether people buy tangible or intangible goods and services or save or invest their money.

Sensitive Economic Factors

Pronouncements by the Federal Reserve Board are referred to by economists as the most sensitive economic factors for determining future economic activity. They issue statistics about:

1. The tightening or loosening of credit terms or money
2. Actual and projected interest rates
3. The Gross National Product (GNP)
4. The export/import balance of trade
5. The budget deficit or surplus
6. Inflation
7. The strength of the dollar in foreign trade
8. Unemployment and employment figures (these are not the same and comparisons can be misleading).

Both indicators and sensitive factors are so interrelated that frequently it is difficult to distinguish which is the cause and which is the effect. As the events that created them begin to mesh, they continue to create new results. It may very well be that the difficulty of forecasting and interpreting evolving economic changes causes professional analysts with the same economic philosophies to disagree so frequently with each other, even when they start with the same set of basic facts or economic indicators.

Some economists believe that the actions of the consumer are the best indicator of both the state of the economy and the investment climate, and indicate which corrective measures should be enacted.

While learning the importance of the sensitive indicators, new investors should not overlook the importance of two other signals with which they should be concerned:

1. Current and anticipated interest rates
2. Confidence of foreign investors in our economy.

If foreign capital is withheld because of our domestic excesses, then the economic climate usually will not be too favorable for most ventures.

The following information is intended to help you interpret some of the indicators and also to help you time your purchase or sale of investments based on your interpretation of the investment climate.

When the general economy (*investment climate*) is slow or stagnating, one of the government's options is to stimulate the economy through a fiscal policy in which the government sets out to spend huge sums of money. It is difficult to pursue this type of loose financial policy when a country is already heavily debt-ridden. Thus, the only viable remedies left to stimulate the flagging economy are to either cut the short-term interest rates or increase the amount of money in circulation.

You should be aware that when the type of money placed in circulation is of the paper currency type not backed by hard assets, the value of that currency soon diminishes, resulting in monetary deflation. That increases prices without any increase in the demand for goods and services. Ordinarily, in the absence of inflation or deflation, prices are increased or decreased by supply and demand.

An increase in domestic prices tends to curb exports, which decreases employment figures; whereas a loose money policy discourages foreign investments.

The modalities that are recommended in this chapter for evaluating the investment climate are not the only ones that can be used. But they are the ones that are used and referred to by most economists.

Chapter 16: Who Regulates the Money Supply?

Who Regulates the Money Supply?

This chapter describes the money supply and its controls. Every investor who wants to earn money should be aware of how the money supply is created and controlled.

In the United States, all of the domestic currency, coins, and credit for which you work or which you spend, save, invest, or give away, are part of the United States monetary system. The control of this money and credit is divided between the Treasury Department and the Federal Reserve System, both of which possess vast powers.

The Treasury Department

For example, the Treasury Department can decide that the United States should intervene in foreign exchange markets in order to prevent the dollar from rising too high. Its decision would then be implemented by the Federal Reserve System.

The Secretary of the Treasurer is an appointed cabinet member and usually represents the Administration's viewpoint. The main function of the Treasury Department is to raise and control cash. One of the methods used by the Treasury to raise cash is to sell its Treasury bills or bonds through a bidding process in the open market. The bills, which are sold and traded in the money market, are similar to the bonds but usually are repayable within a year.

Treasury bills are non-interest-bearing discount securities that are issued to finance the national debt. They are sold at a discounted price that reflects the going short-term interest rates. Although short-term bills are discounted at low interest rates, they are purchased by those who seek liquidity.

Treasury bonds are of longer duration and are sold and traded in the capital market. The *Capital market* refers to private or public places, including organized markets and exchanges where financial instruments denoting debt or equity are traded. Because they are not as liquid as the shorter-term instruments, they must yield a much higher rate (about 9 percent) of interest than the short-term bills.

When interest rates were more stable, Treasury bills and bonds did not fluctuate in value as much as they do now. Currently, because of the excessive fluctuation in the daily prices of previously issued Treasury notes and bonds, many investors are more likely to trade them than invest in them. These investors prefer trading in them to secure quick capital gains profits rather than buying treasuries for their fixed revenue for a long period of time during which higher rates might seriously depreciate and cause them to be discounted at a lower price than the one at which they were originally issued.

The Federal Reserve System

The Treasury may increase the nation's money supply by selling its bonds to the Federal Reserve System. The payment by the Fed will be in the form of credits to the Treasury deposited at the Fed upon which the Treasury can write checks. When the checks are issued, the banks that cash them send them to the Fed, who credit the banks' reserves. The increased reserves, as explained below, enable the bank to loan more money, which has the affect of increasing the money supply. When the Treasury bonds or bills are sold to the public, the Treasury Department spends the money, no reserves are built up, and the nation's money supply has not been increased.

The Federal Reserve Board is empowered to regulate the banking system, the amount of money in circulation, the amount of credit used, and the range of interest rates that prevail.

Specifically, the Fed has five major functions:

1. To send examiners to member banks to ascertain that they are heeding Federal Reserve regulations
2. To supervise the printing of currency at the mint
3. To regulate the money supply
4. To establish reserve requirements for member bands
5. To act as a clearing house for the funds in the system

The Federal Reserve System is controlled by 12 directors, one from each of the 12 regional banks that are spread across the United States. These regional banks are located in Boston, New York, Philadelphia, Cleveland, Richmond, Atlanta, Chicago, St. Louis, Minneapolis,

Kansas City, Dallas, and San Francisco. The decisions of the twelve directors are subject to review and determination by a seven-member Board of Governors of the Federal Reserve System. Each of the seven members is appointed by the President of the United States for a 14-year term and must be confirmed by the Senate.

This central bank of the Fed, as it is frequently called, has a policy-making group called the Federal Open Market Committee (FMOC) which consists of the seven members of the Board of Governors and the presidents of six Federal Reserve Banks. The FMOC usually meets in private sessions, and its decisions are seldom announced. It is the group that determines the amount of money growth it would like to achieve. But it is not always successful. If the growth rate rises or drops too quickly, the Committee alters its strategy and either tightens or loosens the credit conditions under which its banks can operate. Also, upon request, the head of the board expresses his views to Congress, whose reaction tends to influence the economy.

Money Supply

Naturally, because the Federal Reserve Banks control all other banks under their jurisdiction, their regulations greatly affect the general economy. One of their regulations that seems to affect the economic monetarists, the public, and business the most is how they regulate the money supply. Economic monetarists, such as Milton Friedman (his theory holds that central banks, such as the Fed, can stabilize interest and exchange rates by control of the money supply growth), believe that the money supply is more important to the economy than deficits, and make the average person more conscious of it. Now, newcomers to economics constantly ask, "How can the Fed affect the money supply?"

In order to understand the answer, we must learn first what the money supply comprises. Although many people were taught the broad definition that the money supply consists of the total of the amount of deposits in checking and savings accounts plus the currency that is in circulation, newer concepts have replaced that definition.

The money supply (referring to the amount of money, funds, and credit available for use) is constantly monitored and measured by the Fed in its Washington offices. It prepares, issues, and uses specific monetary measuring indexes, which are referred to as M-1, M-2, M-3, and L (explained next). When the FOMC meets, usually monthly, it reviews these indicators (mostly M-1 and M-2) to see if they are consistent with the committee's current goals. These goals normally include the expansion or contraction of the money supply. From their conclusions, they issue directives to their Open Account Manager in New York, who then tries to comply with their wishes.

Monetary Indexes

M-1 In addition to being an important indicator, M-1 is a broad, basic measure of the money supply that is readily available for spending. It includes:

1. Demand deposits
2. Money in circulation
3. Non-bank travelers' checks
4. Credit union accounts
5. Checkable deposits at banks and thrift institutions.

M-2 This measure includes M-1 plus:

1. Money-market accounts
2. Most personal savings accounts
3. Money-market mutual fund shares
4. Overnight Eurodollars
5. Time deposits under $100,000
6. The overnight repurchase agreements entered into by commercial banks.

The Department of Commerce, which issues an index of Twelve Leading Indicators, uses an inflation-adjusted M-2 index as its single money-supply indicator.

M-3 This measure includes all of the M-2 indicators plus institutional money-market accounts (non-bank savings institutions) and large certificates of deposit (over $100,000).

L This measure includes M-3 and all other liquid assets.

The M-1 figures are released weekly while the M-2 and M-3 figures are released monthly. The figures are maintained under the careful scrutiny of the Fed because they determine the changes, if any, that have occurred in the nation's money supply and help the Fed determine its future course of action. Although the overall goals of the Fed include high employment, price stability, and a stable dollar, its immediate goals are to regulate the monetary indicators M-1 and M-2. When they evaluate M-1 and M-2 figures, they compare the percentage growth or decline within the last month or two. For example, the following passage according to *The Money Market: Myth, Reality and Practice* by Marcia Stigum, summarizes the meeting of the FMOC on October 18, 1977. "The committee agreed that the growth of M-1, M-2, and M-3 within ranges of 4% to 6½%, 5½% to 9%, and 8% to 10½%, respectively, from the third quarter of 1977 to the third quarter of 1978 appears to be consistent with those objectives."

Thus, the average investor should remain familiar with the goals of the FMOC and changes in M-1 and M-2 indicators and make comparisons between them and the GNP. Different economists have additional views as to what should be compared. Some suggest computing the ratio of M-1 to the adjusted monetary base to determine if the amount of money supplied is growing at a different rate than the amount of money demanded.

According to the Board of Governors of the Federal Reserve System, a comparison of respective M-1, M-2, M-3, and L statistics would look as follows. The numbers are in billions of dollars.

MONEY STOCK AND LIQUID ASSETS
YEAR

ITEM	1970	1975	1980	1985	1986	1987
M1	217	291	415	627	638	
M-2	628	1,023	1,631	2,566	2,591	
M-3	678	1,172	1,989	3,200	3,260	
L		816	1,368	2,325	3,838	3,891

History of M-1 and Black Monday

The following is a chronological history of M-1 to the June preceding the Black Monday of 1987:

In the week ending Dec. 22, 1986, M-1 jumped $8.7 billion to a record $731 billion for the quarter. In the week ending January 19, 1987, it fell $2.6 billion. In late January, it rose $500 million. For March, the money supply rose to $739.8 billion. At that time, the *Los Angeles Times* reported that "James C. Miller III (OMB Director) warns of danger of recession if the Federal Reserve tightens the money supply." It rose $1 billion for the week ending April 6th. For the week ending May 11, 1987, it rose $1.6 billion and on June 12, the FRB reported a drop in the money supply. On July 3, 1987, the money supply had jumped $.9 billion but the stock market was reported as being unaffected.

If you are wondering whether Black Monday could have been predicted by the money supply figures provided by the government, you will be interested in a brief discussion by Daniel L. Thornton that appeared on the front page of the October 1987 issue of *Monetary Trends*. This publication was issued by the Federal Reserve Bank of St. Louis with the caveat "The views expressed herein do not necessarily reflect the official position of the Federal Reserve System."

"By almost any yard stick, monetary growth has been very slow since January: the rate of M-1 growth during the first eight months of the year was only 2.7%. This compares with an 18.3% growth rate during the prior eight months and a 15.7% growth rate for the same eight-month period in 1986. A similar, though less pronounced, slowing occurred in the broader monetary aggregates, M-2 and M-3. Recent growth is slow even when a much longer-term perspective is taken. The growth rates of M-1, M-2, and M-3 since January (1987) are about one-fourth, one-third, and one-half of their respective growth rates over the prior four years.

Alternatively, M-1A (M-1 less interest-bearing checking account balances), which some argue is a better measure than M-1 when it comes to measuring the impact of monetary influences on the economy, declined at a rate of nearly 1% during the past eight months. This compares with an 11% growth rate for the previous eight months and a 7.1% rate over the previous four years."

Monetary policy refers to the efforts of the Fed to control the economic activity and status of such items as employment, production, and prices through their power to restrict or enlarge the money supply. The *monetary base*, a popular term among those who measure the effects of the money supply, is determined from the decisions of the Fed as to what the monetary policy will be.

For an example of how you can interpret these aggregate figures denoted by M-1 and M-2, note that M-1 includes money held in savings accounts. Many banks provide incentives to keep certain levels of money on deposit with them. Yet, if interest rates rise sufficiently to cause a considerable amount of money to be transferred from M-1 commercial accounts into M-2 savings accounts, or vice versa, then percentages in the M-1 and M-2 figures would change and be a signal that some of the commercial banks might get into trouble if the volume of dollars or accounts they lose become too high.

Controling the Availability of Money

Two of the major tools that the Fed employs to control the availability of money to banks are the *Loan-Loss Reserve Ratio* and the *Discount Rate*. The loan-loss ratio refers to the amount of reserves that the bank must maintain to protect the demands of their depositors in the event the bank must make up losses incurred from unpaid loans. By ordering the banking system to increase its loan-loss ratios to the amount of their assets, the Fed decreases the amount of money available for loans. This automatically increases interest rates and curbs borrowing.

The discount rate, the major tool used by the Fed, is the rate the Fed charges member banks for loans. By raising or lowering the discount rate, the Fed controls the amount of money that the banks will borrow. This, in turn, affects the money supply's looseness or tightness. In September of 1987, before October's Black Monday, the discount rate to banks was 5½ percent. Before the crash, it had been raised to 6 percent to tighten the money supply, but after the crash the government announced a loose, liquid money policy and kept the rate at 6 percent. A few weeks after the crash, it remained at 6 percent when President Reagan suddenly announced that he was not trying to lower the value of the dollar.

Actually, when it comes to establishing a loose or tight dollar, some economists do not consider the interest rate as important as the third method used by the Fed to control the money supply; namely, the *open market* activities of the government. In its open market operations, the Fed buys or sells government securities from or to the banks, which adds or subtracts money to or from the banking system.

On November 11, 1987, an article by Alan Murray and Walter S. Mossberg in the *Wall Street Journal* summed up a discussion on monetary policy with this conclusion: "At the moment, the central bank (the Fed) seems to be walking a narrow line, using 'open market' operations to keep rates down, but holding the discount rate stable in an attempt to keep the exchange markets stable.''

Usually, banks only borrow from the Fed when their customers' deposits outbalance their required reserves. The reserves should be in the form of currency in their vaults, although some of the large banks deposit a portion of their reserves with their local Federal Reserve bank. The banks may try other loan sources first, but when they need emergency funds for reserves, they go to the discount window of their appropriate Federal Reserve Bank. The discount window gets its name because the banks procure money at discount rates by putting up government securities or other acceptable collateral. In turn, these requests for loans give the Federal Reserve System a clue as to the current market rates for loans that are available to the borrowing bank.

A Fed Dilemma

A typical example of a Fed dilemma occurs when one of its targets becomes the control of run-away inflation, and it decides that the solution for preventing rapid money growth is an increase of interest rates. However, if the strength of the United States dollar in foreign trade rises so high that the United States imports much more than it exports, we find that the higher interest rates that are usually used to restrict credit and money also create a large increase in foreign investments in this country. In turn, this increases the value of the U.S. dollar and further restricts U.S. exports.

In this vein, it is interesting to note that in 1985, when the U.S. intervened to reduce the strength of the dollar, the dollar at first strengthened, even though U.S. interest rates were lower than in other countries. At the time, it seemed that faith in the U.S. dollar was possibly as important as the Fed's control of the money.

It should be noted, however, that as the U.S. persisted in its efforts to reduce the value of the dollar and secured the cooperation of other countries, the value of the dollar did drop. But then, faith in the U.S. economy led many of the investors in foreign countries to invest in U.S. stocks, bonds, and factories. After the stock market crash of 1987, both West Germany and Japan urged the United States to reduce the value of its dollar by drastically reducing its trade deficit, thereby making the dollar weaker through lower interest rates. The thought was that lower interest rates would deter foreigners from investing with the U.S., and that our lower interest rates and weaker dollar would help us reduce our trade deficits. A weaker dollar would slow imports by increasing their price in the United States while reducing the price that foreigners would pay for goods exported from the United States.

A Review

In summary, let's review a few points made in this chapter. The Fed controls the money supply of the U.S. using a variety of means, including the following:

1. Ordering banks to increase or diminish their reserves
2. Raising or lowering the discount rate when banks borrow to maintain their reserves
3. Using open market operations such as buying or selling government securities

They measure their effects against M-1, M-2, M-3, and L. These indicators help them to predict future trends and bring some sanity to an otherwise insane area.

By now you should have a fair idea of the important roles played by the Treasury Department and the Federal Reserve Board in their regulation of the money supply and what prompts them to act. Thus, in the future, should either of them announce a change of thought concerning their future money policies, you should be able to correlate those policies and their anticipated results with your own future financial activities. The bottom line is that interest rates will usually fall with a loose money supply and rise with a tight money supply.

A word about Black Monday. Some economists blamed the crash on the fact that the reported U.S. trade deficit prior to the crash produced expectations of a lower-valued dollar and higher interest rates at a time that people had expected higher interest rates and a stronger dollar. Shortly after the crash, 35 economists surveyed by the *Wall Street Journal* expected less inflation and lower interest rates.

Other people blamed the crash on the attempts of the Federal Reserve Board to defend the value of the dollar by increasing interest rates. As people tried to shield their money by purchasing bonds, it was reported that interest rates dropped 1.75 percent from a high of 10.5 percent to 8.75 percent. As time goes on, additional theories for the crash will emerge. Strangely, all of them may contain some grain of truth.

Chapter 17: Forecasting Inflation, Deflation, Recession, and Depression

Forecasting Inflation, Deflation, Recession, and Depression

Whenever anything dramatic occurs in the economy, economic analysts begin to forecast different opinions as to what may happen in the future. As a serious investor, you should be able to formulate your own opinion as to which forecasts are correct and even formulate your own economic forecasts. This is the purpose of this chapter.

The reason that economic analysts disagree with each other in their attempts to accurately forecast the future of the economy is that they do not always agree on how the economy developed to its current level. Neither do they agree on the weight to be given to the different factors they used in arriving at their conclusions. For example, some economists will use a trade deficit to forecast a possible recession. Others may view these same deficit figures, but will not give as much weight to the deficit total.

These economists break down the specific figures to show that there has been a steady increase in the dollar volume of exports over the past few months, despite the imports outbalancing the exports. They might also observe that the exports were mostly labor related which, in that case, can be interpreted to mean additional take-home pay for U.S. workers, an increase in consumer consumption figures, and extra taxes for the government.

Definitions

The easiest way for you to forecast the future of the economy is to first learn the definitions of the major economic conditions that can affect your life. These conditions are inflation, deflation, recession, and depression. The simple definitions that follow should temporarily suffice.

Inflation refers to a general rise in prices.
Deflation refers to reducing the availability of money in a country.
Recession refers to a decline of economic activity in a country.
Depression refers to a period of high unemployment and low economic activity.

Statistics

It is very important that you begin to make a distinction between the quoted statistics that people use to make their theoretical point that one of these conditions defined above actually exists. Beware that facts or statistics are interpreted in more than one way. For example, if the stock market rises by 15 percent one day and the next day you hear a TV news report that "today the stock market dropped a record 10 percent," that report cannot be interpreted without a complete record of stock market events. Also, if you hear or read that "inflation increased or decreased X percentage points," compare these statistics to the difference between the actual overall prices that prevailed six months ago with the current prevailing prices for the same items.

Just because statistics have been issued does not make them accurate. If they are important to you, then you should ascertain where the survey took place, how many items were considered, the source of the figures, and the relationship of each of these to the whole picture. The figures may indicate that the inflation rate has been going down steadily. Of course this may only mean a temporary leveling off of prices—not that prices will continue to drop.

Throughout the history of the United States, a series of inflationary periods have greatly increased the overall price level of most goods and services. These periods often were interrupted by slight recessions, depressions, and interludes of reduced inflation rates. When considering the different economic stages, one should bear in mind that each condition eventually gets its turn and does not stay at any one particular level. Moreover, different groups of people benefit in each of the defined economic conditions. For example, during a depression, low-priced cars may outsell luxury cars, whereas during the phase of prosperity that leads to inflation, luxury cars may outsell economy cars. This, of course, benefits the respective dealers.

Conflicting Beliefs and Forecasts

For long-term forecasting, give consideration to the inflationary history of the United States instead of the effects of short-lived economic stages. Next, familiarize yourself with the major economic theories that are employed by our leading politicians. They are Supply-side economics, Keynesian economics, Monetarist economics and the Laissez-Faire theories of Adam Smith. These were discussed in Chapter 14. They are summarized again for you in the following four paragraphs.

Supply-siders believe that reducing taxes and the size of the government will stimulate productive investment by corporations and wealthy individuals and thereby assure economic expansion. They are opposed to high interest rates because they slow economic growth. They claim that President Reagan used the principle when he cut taxes to achieve an economic recovery.

Keynesians believe in government intervention. They believe that an insufficient demand produces unemployment, that too much demand causes inflation, and that the remedy is to have the government adjust expenditures and taxation. Further, they advocate that to avoid a depression, governments should loosen money and increase spending so that consumer spending, employment, and investment can be stimulated.

Monetarists, such as Milton Friedman, believe that the future of the country is dependent on the money supply. Monetarists recommend growth to be taken at a slow, steady pace. (In October 1987, Friedman was appointed as Economic adviser to the President.)

The Laissez-Faire theory, which dates back to Adam Smith's book *The Wealth of Nations* in 1776, is that government intervention in business and economic affairs should be kept to a minimum. However, that was before large corporations began to exert influence on the economy of the nation. But people still endorse the theory whenever government intervention becomes excessive.

Next, you must familiarize yourself with the Gross National Product, the actions of the Federal Reserve Board, and those leading indicators (M-1, M-2, M-3, and L) that usually provide a clue to the future economy. Then derive your answer by determining what action you think the government or industry will most likely take to change current conditions. The balance of this chapter is designed to help you make this kind of analysis.

Inflation

The major harbingers of inflation are a general and continuing rise in prices of available goods, usually caused by an increase in the volume of money and credit and a shortage of goods. Under inflation, the purchasing power of the prevailing currency decreases. Sometimes the inflation rate in a year can amount to 100 percent. Even when it is less, the resulting loss of purchasing power increases the need for additional money, stimulating credit requirements. This in turn creates a demand for additional money, thereby creating higher interest rates. The higher interest rates increase the cost of living, and the cycle continues until people stop buying or borrowing and begin to liquidate their assets. This is why some economists believe that higher interest rates will eventually cause deflation or a recession rather than inflation. Ordinarily, expectations of deflation (lower prices) contribute to lower interest rates.

The public usually ignores the storm warnings that always precede the rapid onset of double-digit inflation and its takeover of the economy. Most governments and corporations, it would seem, encourage and do not fear low, single-digit inflation under the theory that it stimulates growth. Actually, many economists continue to endorse a moderate amount of inflation because they believe that inflation creates jobs for the new crop of workers spawned by population increases that result from new births or new immigrants.

Somehow, the public becomes accustomed to single-digit inflation and ignores the signals of approaching double-digit inflation. Double-digit inflation might be tolerable if everybody in the population had their assets or spendable earnings increased at the same rate that double-digit inflation increases and affects prices. Unfortunately, two major factors prevent this from happening. First, much of the population does not have the kinds of assets—such as various forms of real estate and/or heavy inventories—that increase in value with the transition from tolerable low-inflation rates to intolerable double-digit inflation rates. Secondly, much of the population—particularly the large body of today's retired people—are on fixed incomes. Aside from those who receive minor cost-of-living adjustments, their earnings do not enable them to cope with the debilitating effects of double-digit inflation.

Price increases for postal services, phones, transportation, and insurance, plus cost-of-living adjustments, are always inflationary, regardless of whether they occur during a period of depression or inflation. Higher rates for financing utilities and necessary services increase the cost of doing business for every family or business enterprise.

Perhaps the greatest inflation in our history was caused by the oil shortage of the 70s. It resulted in heavy increase in prices that adversely affected nearly everyone's spendable income except that of the oil companies.

If you anticipate unusual inflation and need to protect yourself from its dire consequences—such as unaffordable prices for your necessities—it is recommended that you use credit to buy tangibles now and pay for them in the future. This is because the dollars or credit you use now have more purchasing power than they will in the future when their value decreases. I also recommend that you purchase investments, such as real estate, with low-interest trust deeds or mortgages. By doing this, you will be paying back in the future with money that will have decreased in value and have less purchasing power than it has now. Moreover, inflation will most likely cause your property to increase in value. Some people recommend the purchase of gold as a hedge against inflation, but this requires specialized knowledge.

Stay away from long-term bonds, because inflation or fear of it will reduce their value, even if they are guaranteed by the government. The government only guarantees payment of the face amount of the bond if held to maturity. It does not guarantee the purchasing power of the face amount of the bond at the time it is sold or redeemed. On the other hand, the value of tangibles that you purchase, whether leveraged or owned outright, may increase in value and more than just compensate for the loss in value of your inflated currency. Thus, during inflationary periods, most investment advisers will usually recommend capital growth-oriented investments rather than income investments, and vice versa during non-inflationary periods. Capital growth investments refer to long term investments of money to expand your money, usually by investing in industries that produce other goods or income and include buildings, machinery, and equipment.

A major decline in the strength of the dollar can usually produce inflationary tendencies. A minor decline in the strength of the dollar, on the other hand, can help multinational companies recover export business that they may have lost to foreign competition due to the dollar's prior strength. (This occurs when, due to the strength of the dollar being greater than that of the foreign currency, the dollar buys more and the people of a country such as the United States import an excess of foreign goods.) When the strength of the dollar declines, U.S. citizens pay more for foreign goods. The resulting decline of foreign competition permits domestic companies to increase their prices, all of which is inflationary.

At times, you may become confused by the contradictory opinions of economic analysts. They frequently mistake short-term economic signals for long-term signals and vice versa. When this happens, it's time for you to compare the actual facts that you have ascertained yourself. From these facts, secure your own answer by combining these facts with the following economics explanations.

Major Causes of Inflation

The major causes of inflation are usually referred to as cost-push, demand-pull, or monetary-debasement.

- *Cost-push* refers to a principle in which taxes are decreased so that people can spend more money. This then spurs employment and creates additional taxpayers to pay more taxes. Cost-push inflation refers to the cycle of price increases that start when the demand for goods exceeds the supply. This causes the price of most products to rise.
- Under the *demand-pull* theory, the government increases taxes to reduce spendable income. This lowers the deficit (if the money taken in is not squandered elsewhere), which eventually is supposed to require less taxation. Demand-pull inflation is similar to cost-push inflation.
- *Monetary-debasement* refers to "fiat" money, the name given to money that is not backed by adequate reserves. Fiat money cheapens the value of the dollar and assures higher prices. Conditions for this situation are always concomitant with the issuance by any government of more money than there are goods and services available.

On the other hand, whenever inflation is caused by too many dollars chasing too few goods and services, someone always suggests taxing the excess money away from the consumers. This, theoretically, is supposed to cut down the excessive demand while helping the government's financial position.

It is unfortunate that so many politicians and governments believe their spending of surtaxed dollars is less inflationary than when consumers are allowed to spend them. Consequently the government and politicians usually do end up spending them instead of concentrating their efforts on reducing the deficit or the national debt.

Whenever the majority of major corporations develop strong, after-tax profits, look for the possibility of explosive inflation. This is because higher corporate profits usually yield higher dividends, which increases the values and prices of their respective stocks. This can also lead to increased corporate and personal spending, which automatically stimulates capital outlay and employment, the frequent forerunners of inflation.

Deflation

Deflation refers to a decline in prices and profits without any change in the cost of production. Consumers may receive a short-term price benefit, but if they own a share of the companies whose profits are reduced, their reduced income may counteract the long-term benefits that they receive from short-term, lower prices.

Deflating the United States dollar refers to creating a lower demand for it in world monetary markets. On the other hand, it should be noted that lower foreign oil prices help the American consumer but weaken the domestic banks (and their stockholders) that have made questionably large loans to foreign oil producers based on the high, pre-1980 value of their oil reserves. Lower foreign oil prices also increase the value of U.S. dollars while reducing the costs of transportation, manufacturing, and energy costs—all of which tend to curb inflation.

When the economy of a nation is affected by deflation, assets, such as real estate, gold, silver, and corporations, decrease in value. This reduces the asset value and borrowing power of their respective owners and curtails the demand for loans, keeping interest rates low. Deflation, like inflation, seems to feed upon itself until there is a backlash from the public. Usually, when the public anticipates deflation, they start saving money to take advantage in the future of anticipated increases in the purchasing power of that money. However, when deflation actually occurs, there is a reduced demand for goods. This curtails employment and production and frequently the prices of goods that increased with inflation do not come down.

If you anticipate deflation, you can look forward to a period in which the prices of goods and services decline, unemployment increases, and production drops. This condition will continue until such time that an unfilled demand for goods and services encourages production and employment.

Recession

When the Gross National Product of the U.S. *declines* for two consecutive quarters, it indicates the start of a recession. Basically, the GNP reflects the total of government and consumer purchases plus the total of private, foreign, and domestic investments in this country, along with the total value of exports for a year or less.

According to a February 25, 1985, Associated Press Report, "Fifty-two percent of the National Association of Business Economists expected the next recession to begin in 1986, with only 17 percent of those surveyed predicting that the current growth will last until 1987 or beyond." Interestingly, in the prior recession of 1981-82, some economists said that the deficit was stimulating us out of a slump. Be aware that recessions and unemployment can co-exist with high interest rates. After the crash of 1987, economists began to discuss possibilities of a recession if the money supply was kept too tight.

There are two opposing theories about how to recover from a recession. Supply-side economists endorse across-the-board income tax reductions to stimulate production, employment, and earnings. They believe that the tax reduction will increase the total tax receipts of the government, even at a lower tax rate. In other words, lower taxes would increase output and income, which in turn would increase the amount of taxes collected. This would then result in a decreased deficit. This is the plan that was espoused by President Reagan and his economic advisers in 1981 and which has resulted in the largest budget deficit in history.

This is not to say that the 1981 tax plan was the sole reason for the large deficit.

The opposing view was implemented by the Trudeau government in Canada from 1982 through 1984 to combat the recession at that time. The plan was based on restoring healthy corporate balance sheets. The concept was that if corporations are helped to increase their profits, the results will be a heavy increase in business investments which should stimulate jobs and production. That theory only works if labor receives the benefit of full and well-paid employment through which it can purchase the increased supply of goods. Higher prices come about because the loans that are required to increase factory production produce higher interest rates and thereby result in higher prices. In actual practice, when higher priced goods could not be purchased, as was the case in Canada, unemployment figures rose. The plan was considered a failure, and the recession continued.

On the other hand, while increased housing starts in Canada and the U.S. can benefit construction workers, manufacturers, and suppliers of building materials, these same housing starts tend to increase the demand for credit from first the builders and then the purchasers of the housing. This increased demand for credit usually boosts the interest rates, which, if excessively increased, can lead to inflation followed by recession.

Whenever investors and business people in the U.S. marketplace begin to believe that economic growth is heating up excessively, they carefully watch the actions of the Federal Reserve Board. They look for indications of the Fed's inclination to combat inflation by tightening up the money supply.

During a recession, the Gross National Product provides a similar observation. When two consecutive declines in the GNP quarterly reports indicate a recession, any anticipated increase in the GNP increases the value of the dollar in Europe. Meanwhile, in the U.S., investors fear that any major increase in the GNP growth rate will automatically stimulate the demand for credit, causing interest rates to rise. Their belief is that such a rise will invite an inflationary atmosphere and send a clear signal to the Fed that the money supply should be restricted.

Loans to oil-producing countries along with excessively large loans to third-world countries (that may never be repaid) can cripple the U.S. banking system, impair international credit, and produce inflation. In addition, because wholesale oil prices are now close to being two-thirds to three-quarters less than what they were in the late 70s and early 80s, banks that loaned huge sums of money to American oil producers—based on the old, high-cost way of producing oil and the old, high value of oil placed on their underground reserves—no longer have sufficient collateral to cover the loans. As a result, many of the banks that made these loans face insolvency. Those that are still solvent have temporarily discontinued loaning money for any kind of new oil production ventures. In the past, when banks collapsed, a general recession or depression occurred.

Depression

An economic depression is a stage in the economy in which manufacturing, housing, business, banking, and investment activities are at very low ebbs. These factors produce unemployment and a low M-1 (a Federal Reserve Board leading indicator for available cash and credit).

Not counting a possible 1988 slump after 1987's Black Monday, the U.S. has experienced 11 slumps since 1939. The *Wall Street Journal* reported that the most recent one lasted 15 months—from July 1981 to November 1982. During this time, the drop in industrial output was 12.3 percent and the peak jobless rate was 10.7 percent.

By contrast, the big depression that started in August of 1929 lasted until March of 1933. During this period the national industrial output dropped by 53.4 percent and the peak jobless rate reached 24.9 percent. Some eminent economists today warn that shrinking the money supply back in those years helped produce and prolong the 1929 depression. Others believe that in the future, a too severe shrinkage of the money supply by the Fed, because of a fear of or reaction to an overheated economy and inflation, could create a future depression.

During a depression, there is usually an attempt to reduce unemployment by stimulating production. Governments attempt to accomplish this by loosening the money supply so that interest rates can be lowered to induce manufacturers to borrow and employ people. Experience indicates, however, that during a depression, even low interest rates are not an inducement to stimulate borrowing by credit-worthy people. They are not confident in their ability to pay back the interest and principal.

Recent Lessons

Forecasting inflation, deflation, recessions, and depressions is not easy. Accordingly, economists look to the past for useful clues. For example, what lessons can be learned from the economics of the recent past? In 1987, we experienced the Black Monday market crash and subsequent declines that severely reduced the assets and financial strength of many individuals and large corporations. During the same period, the markets of other major countries also tumbled. Yet, no one knows whether the short-term or future consequences for any of these countries or the U.S. will culminate in a recession, inflation, depression, or deflation. If we can learn from history, we should be cognizant of the observations of the leading economists who, depending upon their personal philosophies, background, and the school of economics to which they subscribe, cited at least one of the following reasons for causing the crash.

An Excessive Domestic Budget Deficit Many economists said that the value of the dollar was too high. Some blamed too extensive a defense program and tax reductions for the rich, while others blamed excessive social welfare programs. Still others said that taxes were too low and should be raised. Some said that "government spending cuts and tax increases would be unwise as the economy faces possible recession." On November 5, 1987, shortly after the market crash, a *Los Angeles Times* poll found that although 69 percent of those polled agreed that the federal deficit was a serious problem, 64 percent did not want their taxes raised to reduce the deficit.

Trade Deficits were caused by an overpriced dollar. This made U.S. prices for domestic merchandise so expensive to foreigners they could not purchase enough domestic products to balance the imbalance of trade caused by excessive imports.

Excessively High Interest Rates were used to attract foreign capital to support the large U.S. budget deficit. The government created those high interest rates through a tight money policy. When money is scarce, people who have it increase their interest rates. Also, the Fed (see Chapter 16) can increase or decrease interest rates at will. Since the crash, the government has decided to initiate a loose money supply policy and interest rates have been declining. By loosening the money supply, it is calculated that the resulting loss in the value of the dollar in foreign exchange markets will cut down the U.S. ability to import. This boosts exports which, of course, reduces the trade deficit. Economists warn, however, that reducing the value of the dollar could produce inflation as it did in the 1970s, while creating attractive bargains for foreign shoppers looking for income producing real estate or corporations. Also, fear of inflation causes lenders to place their investments in short-term securities rather than in long-term bonds. This alternative does not provide the capital required for substantial growth.

An Overpriced Stock Market with dividends averaging about 3 percent on stocks was too much below the 9 percent interest paid during one period on safe government bonds and the 12 percent that was being paid on some corporate bonds. Consequently, investors sold an unusually high amount of stocks so that the proceeds could be reinvested in high-yielding bonds. This results in an oversupply of stocks and the consequent severe drop in their prices.

Faulty Government Accounting and Budgeting Some economists have said that the currently used "cash-basis budget and accounting system" of the U.S. government must be replaced by Generally Accepted Accounting Principles (GAAP). GAAP is an accrual-basis and budget accounting system used by many major corporations to assure correct financial reporting. As an example of GAAP's impact, if Congress passes a bill that requires an expenditure of $1 million per year for ten years, that expenditure would appear on the budget books as a $10 million obligation. On the cash-basis system presently used, the budget deficit would only show the $1 million paid in that particular year and the $9 million would not be reflected in the budget for the current year. Thus, from the accounting example just cited, one can see that the annual budget does not reflect all of the debt. It is not a true reflection of the financial condition of the budget, especially when it is compared to the Gross National Product on a percentage basis. The meaning of this is: large accounting firms that could use a replica of the GAAP system for determining the condition of U.S. finances, could advise important clients who can influence the market of their assessment of the real budget deficit. This could be done before the average person, who depends upon a cash-basis system, is aware of what is happening in financial markets.

Lack of International Cooperation Between Japan, West Germany, and the United States. There has been a failure of these to recognize their interdependence. There have also been attempts by the U.S. to enact restrictive trade bills.

Too Much Margin, according to some economists, produced too much speculation by people who did not have enough financial backing to make their margin calls when stocks first began to drop.

Actually, all of these reasons, whether they are true or false, have deterred foreign capital from investing in U.S. stocks. Interestingly enough, right after the 1987 Black Monday crash, the Fed immediately loosened the money supply and lowered interest rates. Undoubtedly, more reasons for the crash will be forthcoming as will prophesies of future depression and inflation. For example, within two weeks after the Black Monday crash, an Associated Press article said "The dollar was off again today in New York, near postwar lows, raising the prospect of instability that could frighten away foreign investors, push up *inflation* (italics are mine) in the United States and hurt economic growth overseas."

One other signal that you must watch is who gets appointed to the important financial posts. For example, the appointment of Alan Greenspan to replace Paul Volcker as Chairman of the Federal Reserve System in late 1987, was a notice to the world that the Administration would favor looser money and a lower dollar.

Regardless of whether you believe the reasons noted above, other investors will believe some or all of them and will react with fear. Thus, in the future, whether or not you play the market, watch for the economic signals described above that portend inflation, deflation, recession, and depression. Review their potential effects on the markets (both foreign and domestic), the general population, corporate, and individual investors in your investment bracket. If you can interpret the economic warning signals, you can protect your holdings before it is too late by switching to more timely investments.

Crashes do not come suddenly and they are not easy to forecast. The fact is they are usually preceded by warnings. But most people don't see them or don't want to believe them even though they should know that market crashes also affect nonmarket investors. A review of the papers a few weeks before the Black Monday debacle indicates the dive was preceded by many unusual drops and aberrations in the market. Alert, wise investors should have been able to use and interpret those drops, along with the public statements from politicians about interest and the money supply.

After you have made your investment decision and implemented it, you should be able to justify the actions you take. Your actions should be based on intelligently minimizing your risks.

Chapter 18: How the Federal Budget Affects You

How the Federal Budget Affects You

The annual budget for the United States is prepared prior to the preceding fiscal year by the Office of Management and Budget (OMB). During the budget's formation, many branches of the government—including the separate Budget Offices of the House and Senate—submit their intellectual inputs. In addition, all the departments of the government submit requests for operating funds.

Investors are Affected by the Budget

Many investors pay little attention to either the formation of the federal budget, its deficit, or its surplus. Perhaps they are indifferent. Or, they may believe that the federal budget is being taken care of properly by elected officials under close scrutiny. Basically—but all too mistakenly—they do not see how the budget can affect them.

First, if there is a deficit, they will pay for it unless they can persuade those in power to tax another economic group. Regardless of what happens, most investors will be affected by the consequences. Taxing any group of people extracts money out of the economy. A reduction in spending, besides affecting the money supply, can also increase unemployment and decrease social service benefits, such as welfare and unemployment compensation. Each of these actions decreases the bank savings of the taxed group and ultimately affects all investors.

On the other hand, a large surplus creates a good feeling among those who care about the budget. However, many economists will start complaining that the surplus indicates that either the government has overtaxed its citizens or is purposefully depriving the consumers of the pleasure of spending their own money.

Surplus or Deficit

Like the average citizen, the investor is caught between these two philosophies. Regardless of who is right, the investor indeed is affected by the budget and the arguments about it. They are certainly affected by the important economic decisions and laws that the deficit or surplus provokes legislators to enact. Before analyzing how the budget is formed, let's review a thought-provoking question.

Will this new budget create a surplus or a manageable deficit?

- An excessive budget deficit will cause inflation. The extra money that the government extracts from the taxpayer to offset deficit spending prevents the taxpayer from saving a part of it. Thus, the government will spend what the taxpayer would have saved. The extra spending creates additional spending which, in turn, produces inflation.
- The key to a good economy lies in a well designed employment program.
- Disciples of the Keynesian school of economics say, "Budget deficits are permissible even if they create a national debt, as long as they stimulate wealth, growth, and employment." (Supply-siders disagree.)
- We should use taxes to try to control costs, curb inflation, and prevent unemployment.

Meanwhile, during all this discussion, the Gramm-Rudman-Hollings bill was enacted. This bill requires that $23 billion be cut from the fiscal year budget running from October 1, 1987, through September 30, 1988.

The Budget Deficit

If the average investor is interested in the federal budget, he will probably focus on whether the budget will produce a deficit or a surplus. He has been led to believe that if the anticipated revenues exceed the anticipated budget, then there will be a surplus. But if the revenues do not equal the expenses, there will be a deficit.

Not a Fiscal Policy

It should be understood that a federal budget deficit or surplus is not a country's fiscal policy. There is more to it than that. Budget deficits get added to the national debt, which must be financed and on which we pay interest. It is the amount of the national debt that we are willing to carry that represents our fiscal policy. Other countries look at this when determining our fiscal worthiness and how much of our indebtedness they should carry. If there is a budget surplus, which seldom occurs anymore, Washington may apply it to the national debt or spend it. If there is a budget deficit, the amount of the deficit is added to the existing national debt. In 1983, the national debt was reported at $1.337 trillion. The interest on that sum can amount to over $22 billion a month at current rates. As we observed in Chapter 17 about different accounting systems, the accrual-basis budgeting system reflects a true budget better than does a cash-basis accounting system. However, the OMB currently uses a cash-basis accounting system to construct the federal budget.

Not a Trade Deficit

Another big problem is that too many people confuse a budget deficit with a trade deficit. They are not the same. A trade deficit refers to the balance of international trade and is explained in Chapter 19.

The anticipation of a large fiscal surplus would make many people very happy. To others it would mean that the government overtaxed them and in the process unnecessarily tightened the money supply. The anticipation of a large federal deficit usually provokes many domestic and international problems, with which the U.S. Senate, House, and President must cope.

Large deficits usually give rise to innumerable, vociferous, diametrically opposed viewpoints from all segments of the economy. Many of the viewpoints come from politicians, financial planners, and economic analysts who are trying to determine the size of the budget and how to pay for it. Some economists and legislators allege that it is morally wrong and unbusinesslike for a government to continually spend more money than it collects. Others condone a large deficit under the theory that it helps to control the economy and to maintain lower unemployment levels. Still others shrug off large deficits because of their strong belief that the vast assets of the country are more important than its deficits. For those who claim that we should not burden our children with our debts, there are counter-attackers who say that there is nothing wrong with having our children paying for an improved world when they become taxpayers.

A simple comparison between a family and the government might throw some light on budget deficit principles. In today's sophisticated society, a family's normal living requirements, aside from adequate housing, usually include a car for transportation, electronic equipment to keep up with what is going on in the world, education to get ahead, and quick cash to pay for unexpected medical bills and emergencies. Very few families could earn enough money to be on a cash-basis accounting system. Accordingly, to satisfy their normal wants, they must secure credit. Thus, for any year that they obligated themselves to pay out more money than their net income after taxes, they incurred a deficit. When they start to pay interest on that deficit, they, like the government, are involved in deficit financing. Sometimes they may pay interest on their interest. Thus, the family, while recognizing the need for deficit financing, must be careful to pay their obligations on time before creating additional deficit financing and long-term debt for non-essentials. If they require deficit financing for education that could help them increase their earnings, or if the deficit financing is required to nurse them back to health from an illness, the deficit financing can be condoned. If, however, they get into deficit financing for debts that they could have avoided, they have no excuse.

The government is in the same situation as the family, but with a few important exceptions. Because the government must be concerned with the welfare of its people, it is obligated to get into deficit financing whenever the welfare of its citizens demands it. This is especially true when you consider that the government has the power to borrow funds, create funds, and raise funds through its power to tax. It can compel willing or unwilling taxpayers to contribute to the general welfare. However, when the government gets into deficit financing that requires paying interest on interest, then its budget planning may be getting out of hand.

The government may also be taxing those people whose deficit financing was unplanned and who cannot pay taxes. Under these conditions, the government must borrow money through bond issues and pay high interest rates. This tightens the money supply, increases the national debt, and impairs our business and export-import relationship with other countries with whom (like it or not) we are interdependent. If the taxes are used properly, they may reduce or eliminate the government's having to pay interest on its accumulated amounts of interest. While some deficits can be economically sound—particularly when emergencies cause them—in normal times the federal budget should be controlled to avoid an excessive deficit.

Pump Priming

The use of a budget deficit as part of the monetary policy of a country is referred to as pump priming. It is part of the Keynesian economic philosophy developed in the early part of this century. This type of budget is of extreme importance to all investors because it indicates that an attempt is being made to stimulate the economy.

Pump priming has been used rather extensively in the U.S. since 1930. Many economists believe that deficit financing is acceptable if it increases economic activity, stimulates employment, and increases purchasing power. These economists claim that a budget deficit may be good for the economy. They believe that when the government spends more money than it has collected in taxes, the resulting beneficial expansion of the economy can be worth carrying a deficit. This is because: 1) the government's excessive spending would give a boost to the economy by putting more money into circulation, and 2) a budget shortage could also reflect a low tax rate. This presumably would give the public more money to spend.

When it comes to domestic and foreign investors, most of them are wary of deficits that could induce explosive, double-digit inflation. Yet, in the face of a large deficit, foreign investors will invest in the U.S. if the rate of inflation happens to be less, or the interest rates are higher, than those of their own or other countries.

Effects of GNP

Experienced budget analysts, however, prefer to use the Gross National Product (GNP) as their guideline. (GNP is the nation's total output of goods and services adjusted for inflationary factors.) They think in the following terms: What percentage of the GNP will the annual budget be? What percentage of the GNP will the deficit be?

For an example of this principle in action, consider that in 1985 the Congressional Budget Office estimated a budget deficit for fiscal 1985/86 of $214 billion. At that time, President Reagan estimated that the budget deficit would be $222 billion. Learning of these two estimates, the *Wall Street Journal* estimated that "either could be equal to about 5½% of the fiscal year's gross national product" and would require that the U.S. "pull in funds from foreign sources by an amount equal to about 12% to 15% of the requirements."

The situation just cited could produce high interest rates abroad and in the United States. This could affect import/export trade balances and contribute to unemployment in the United States. Prior to the issuance of the preceding budget figures, the announced fiscal policy of the U.S. had been to reduce the deficit to 4 percent of the GNP by the beginning of the October 1, 1986, fiscal year.

Some economists fear that a huge deficit can restrict growth and produce a period of deflation with its severe consequences. In 1984 the *Canadian Globe-Mail* reported that "some economists believe that a sudden loss of confidence in the ability of the United States to handle its deficit could trigger economic disorder."

Some stock market analysts predict that rising stock market prices will accompany any reduction in deficits and inflation. Many economic and financial analysts do not fear a large deficit, itself. They are more concerned about the huge interest payments that will be incurred to finance an increasing deficit. Some analysts use the size of a deficit to help them forecast long-term interest rates. Interest rates, however, depend upon many international considerations, such as the size of other countries' deficits and the basic economic wealth of the U.S.

After Black Monday, the *Wall Street Journal* printed an editorial by one of its contributors, Professor Irving Kristol. While making an interesting point that the budget deficit had nothing to do with the dollar, he asked, "How can the budget deficit explain the collapse of all major stock markets—British, Japanese, French, German, even Hong Kong?" He then blamed "the sharp rise in interest rates—especially in Germany and Japan—as a signal of impending inflation," and added that "inflation fears, not recession, was the problem."

Deficit-Reduction Theories

There are four major theories that concern themselves with how to reduce the deficit:

1. Increase taxes (cut tax shelter loopholes, increase corporate taxes, curb the tax evaders with a consumption tax).
2. Reduce government spending.
3. Increase taxes and reduce government spending.
4. Increase the GNP so that increased taxes without an income tax increase will produce the surplus revenue that can reduce or eliminate the budget deficit.

These theories are important to you because the implementation of any one of them will affect your business earnings or investments. But bear in mind that the subject of federal or state budgets is not an exact science. There are many variables that can affect the many calculations and compromises that are used to create the budget. Trying to interpret them is more of a philosophical art than a science. So, listen to the budget debates. Adopt a philosophy from the material present in this book. Use your own experience and enjoy the world of amateur budget forecasters. If you can, apply your conclusions to your own investment program.

Chapter 19: The Import/Export Balance of Trade Quandary

The Import/Export Balance of Trade Quandary

How can international trade, the strength of the dollar, and import tariffs affect your investments? How can you watch for economic signals to help you plan your investments? This chapter provides information and clarifies terminology to help answer these questions and others. It also tells you how events of the past influenced the investments in certain industries and commodities. Your understanding of how international trade, currencies, and import/export legislation can increase your chance for success as an investor.

The Trade Deficit

Prior to October 19, 1987, most investors were not aware of how they could be affected by trade deficits. Suddenly, after Black Monday had come and gone, both trade deficits and budget deficits were in the forefront of the news. Both were cited as the major reasons for the precipitous drop in the market. Even then, many investors still wondered how or why a trade deficit could influence their investments. They could understand how a budget deficit has to be made up with surplus. To them, a trade deficit meant that the dollar volume of imported goods exceeded the dollar volume of exported goods. Why should this concern them? And why did many investors lose their nerve and sell their stocks en masse? Why did they move to bonds when the trade deficit figures continued to show no improvement?

Economic Signal

Investors used the trade deficit forecast as an important economic signal. They did not concern themselves with the enormity of the $15.68 billion trade deficit for August 1987 as much as with the continuing deficit trend. Few realized that the comparative trade figures had not been adjusted for inflation. To the investors, the signals were loud and clear. If the U.S. continued to import excessively more than it exported, a larger trade deficit would be incurred. The U.S. would be unable to improve its trade deficit. This signified the creation of an economic cycle that, to the U.S., would mean:

1. Less raw materials being produced
2. Less employment
3. Less manufacturing of finished goods
4. A slackened consumer demand from those involved in the export cycle
5. An outflow of money or credit.

Therefore, instead of the export of U.S. goods or services to foreign countries to balance the heavy debts caused by the trade deficit, the news was all bad.

When the trade deficit is balanced, the discouraging conditions listed above are corrected. Then the burgeoning economic activity that follows provides investors with confidence. They are encouraged to use their time, money, and credit to invest. Those investors who can predict the positive and negative reactions of the mob to trade deficits or surpluses are able to plan successful investment programs.

Still, many investors worried about additional repercussions prompted by fear in response to news about the trade deficit. They were also concerned with the restrictive U.S. legislation that was being leveled against foreign countries that were not buying U.S. goods. Specifically, some investors were disturbed about the hotly debated Gephart amendment. This authorizes the President to retaliate against countries that use market barriers to prevent the U.S. from reducing its huge trade surplus with them. While this amendment may sound good, it is a form of trade protectionism that presents many problems. These are discussed later in this chapter.

The Balance of Trade

To most, the "balance of trade" is the figure derived by subtracting the amount of goods or services exported from the amount imported. But, this is too general. Although methods of analysis have varied through the years, import/export trade balances should be considered from a minimum of five categories:

1. The trade of goods, sometimes correctly referred to as the merchandise balance or incorrectly referred to as the balance of trade
2. The trade of services
3. The balance of goods and services
4. The current accounts measure of international trade
5. The balance of payments on capital accounts.

The figures from any one of these categories may be useful. However, you cannot understand the total balance of trade picture until all of its components are combined.

The Trade of Goods The *trade of goods* deficit or surplus for a specific country refers to whether more or fewer goods were exported or imported. The difference between the amount of goods imported and exported creates the deficit or surplus.

For example, assume that the value of each country's currency is about equal. Also assume that the total amount of money spent by one country for soft goods, such as clothing, and for hard goods, such as machinery, exceeds the amount spent by the other country. In this situation, the country that receives the most amount of currency for the items defined in the specific category—in this instance, the trade of goods category—is considered to have a trade surplus. The other country has a trade of goods deficit. A variation to this example follows.

During the middle 1980s, the United States continued to experience an overall trade deficit at the same time it experienced an overall trade of services surplus. This is why it is frequently important that trade and service figures are assembled and stated separately.

One problem with trade deficits is that they indicate that more money left a country than came in. This situation can cause a money shortage to develop. When this occurs at a time when the money is already in short supply, many people find it necessary to begin using more credit.

When the demand for credit becomes excessive and is added to the funds that have left the country to pay for imports, banks and other credit institutions can charge high interest rates. This concerns investors who seek high interest payments on the money they lend.

The Trade of Services There is more to foreign exchange than the trade of goods. We must also consider the *trade of services* mentioned in a prior example. Assuming that we are referring to the U.S., the trade of services includes, but is not limited to, the total amount of money that each country's trade participants receive from the other's trade participants. These funds include such categories as:

- Interest and dividends
- Interest for investment holdings
- Payments made for transportation, travel, food, and lodging
- Any form of financial or medical advice

The Balance of Goods and Services The total services, when added to the trade of goods classification, comprises the *balance of goods and services* component. For a few years prior to 1985 the U.S. experienced a "services surplus." This surplus helped to counter the trade deficit.

The Current Accounts Measure The fourth measure of comparison is the *current accounts measure* of international trade, or *balance of current accounts*. This category is the excess of imports over exports of goods and services plus or minus the difference due in the payment of services, such as interest and dividends.

The current accounts measure of international trade is the most important of the five classifications. It is determined by combining the "trade of goods" total with the "trade of services" total. The result indicates whether the overall financial position makes a country a debtor or creditor nation. Does the U.S. and its people owe more or less to other countries than foreign countries and their investors owe the U.S.? This is the determining factor. Whenever the debt to foreign countries exceeds what they owe, the U.S. will be compelled to pay out more interest and dividends than it receives.

The Balance of Payments on Capital Accounts The fifth measure of comparison, the *balance of payments on capital accounts*, may seem similar to the "current accounts" measure. But it is different. "Capital accounts" include purchases by a foreign buyer of an enterprise in which the buyer must purchase the money of the seller's country in the foreign exchange markets. If too many of these sales transactions are conducted, they tend to increase the foreign trade deficit.

If U.S. citizens purchase too many foreign enterprises, some economists become concerned that the U.S. trade deficit may become unmanageable. Unfortunately, when the dollar is strong, it is unlikely that the U.S. can improve the trade deficit. This is because a strong U.S. dollar is less attractive to foreign buyers than a weak U.S. dollar. (When the U.S. dollar is weak, U.S. citizens have to pay foreign buyers more dollars to equal their equivalent currency. With more dollars, foreigners can buy more exports from the U.S. than when the dollar is strong.)

Thus, a strong U.S. dollar means the use of fewer raw materials, less employment, reduced manufacturing, less consumption, and less tax income for the U.S. After Black Monday, the Reagan administration's goal was to loosen the money supply to weaken the dollar. This was designed to increase exports.

How strong or weak is the dollar? Consider the following two questions. Are interest rates normal, high, or low? How many dollars—on a comparative yearly basis to past levels—are now required for domestic or imported merchandise or services?

Protectionist Bills and Tariffs

Excluding third world (developing) countries, some countries whose future outlooks are bleak because of weak currencies offer good business and investment opportunities to those who possess stronger U.S. dollars. A country's ability to remain financially solvent while continuing to manufacture products or mine minerals that are required in world trade is vital. In addition, a country with weaker money attracts foreign capital to purchase attractively priced merchandise and services.

With respect to the inherent problems in the Gephart amendment referred to above, the foremost problems are these:

1. Protectionist bills usually carry pork-barrel clauses. These benefit special interests or industries such as sugar and steel in the United States. This can be costly to the U.S. taxpayer. For example, if the Gephart amendment passes, the U.S. will pay millions of dollars to certain U.S. sugar companies. Payments will be made in the form of refunds on tariffs that these companies paid in past years for imported sugar that they refined and re-exported. (Interestingly enough, these refund expenditures were approved in a bill that was allegedly attempting to protect U.S. trade while the country was talking about reducing budget deficits.)

2. Protectionist bills may attempt to restrict imports, (such as Australian lamb) from countries with whom the U.S. already has an export surplus. Then, too, we must consider that some foreign nations carry so much debt that they cannot afford to buy U.S. exports. They may have to depend on their exports to the U.S.
3. The retribution that can be launched by foreign powers is not healthy for the U.S. economy. Such powers abroad could, for example, restrict hard-to-get raw materials that are required for manufacturing.

Opponents of protectionism want U.S. industry to modernize its equipment, use better materials, and have better quality control. This is exactly what the Japanese did when they learned what Americans want. If these steps are taken, Americans will buy more well-made, well-priced, guaranteed American products without the need for protectionism and its numerous hazards.

Tariffs

As an investor you must consider whether your investment will be affected by protectionism in the form of tariffs. *Tariffs* are a form of taxation (custom fees and import/export duties) that can be imposed by a country on both imports and exports. Generally, tariffs are confined to imports. Their basic purpose may be to further an economic policy, restrict trade, or to raise revenue. Although items may be taxed individually, the ad valorum method of assessing duties (i.e., taxing a certain percentage on the value of each item) is the one used by most nations. The ad valorum method is preferred because the percentage need not be constantly changed to keep pace with inflation or deflation.

The theory behind protectionism is to restrict imports through tariffs, such as import duties and quotas. The purpose is to protect both labor and manufacturers in the U.S. from imports that are priced below the domestic cost for the same item. Usually, prices are lower because of overall lower labor, raw material, and manufacturing costs in the exporting country. You can be affected as an investor—even if you are not directly involved with the impact of the tariff—if you are involved with a product that is principally exported. When a foreign country feels that the tariffs on its exports are unfair, it may place punitive tariffs on merchandise that it imports from the U.S. This has a direct affect on U.S. interests.

Protectionism as an economic tool may be used in a number of ways. It may be used to combat the dumping of low-priced goods; to protect new, essential, or experimental industries; to protect agricultural products; and to reduce the balance of payments deficit.

It has been estimated that because of protectionism, inefficient U.S. management costs the average American consumer about $250 a year. Industries protected by excessive import duties or quotas (limitations on imported merchandise) are usually inefficient. Neither the employer nor the employees have an incentive to compete with or be as efficient as an unprotected foreign manufacturer.

Fortunately, a weakened domestic economy and a weak dollar usually produce a decline in imports and an increase in exports. A *weak dollar* generally means that in foreign markets, such as Japan, England, France, and Germany, the value of the dollar is weaker than their standard currency equivalent. Thus, the purchasing power of the foreign currency is expanded. Consequently, foreign buyers are able to buy more goods and services from the U.S.

A strong U.S. dollar buys more foreign goods. It buys less from an exporting country when the exchange rate of both countries is stable. A strong dollar, however, makes the U.S. an importing nation rather than an exporting nation. As an investor, you are concerned with the value of the dollar in foreign exchange. Fortunately, the daily press lists the foreign exchange rates because of their importance.

The Quandary

The word "quandary" appears in the title of this chapter. It is used because many experts express opinions for which they do not have the answers. Every country would like to balance its export/import trade without creating heavy budget deficits, tragic Black Mondays, recessions, or economic depressions. Everyone theorizes, but neither public officials nor acknowledged economic experts seem to know how to avoid the events that produce trade and budget deficits, depressions, prosperity, or even a surplus.

This subject is of vital importance to you as an investor. The value of your assets and potential investment is significantly impacted by the size of your country's import/export trade deficit or its surplus. It is especially important if you are involved in, or contemplating, a business or investment that is linked to the U.S. or another country's economy. For good or bad, you are affected by the trade imbalances of both countries.

You should understand the applicable nomenclature used in the press and the relevance of the figures that are used. Unfortunately, too many conscientious but uninformed citizens relate trade deficits too narrowly. They only consider the amount of petroleum products that are imported from the Middle East or cars and electronic equipment imported from Japan and Germany. They must also count the U.S. exports aircraft, aircraft parts, trucks, passenger cars, tractors and tractor parts, office equipment, and farm goods.

With respect to deficits caused by petroleum imports, a decrease in the price of petroleum can reduce the deficit dramatically. However, petroleum imports comprise only a small portion of the economic picture. More is required to comprehend the balance of trade quandary.

The Trade Cycle The cyclical wheel continues to turn and different scenarios are revealed. With minor exceptions, the workers and their employers in a country with expensive currency become inefficient. Their workmanship gets sloppy, quality diminishes, and costs rise. In the absence of strong quality controls, these factors, plus others, cause the country's money to again become lower in value. Other factors that affect such changes include labor problems and competition from other countries for that same business.

In 1985, after the U.S. had experienced many years of trade surpluses, it began to experience heavy trade deficits. It is likely that these deficits may continue into the 1990s. Even if a reversal of the current trade deficit occurs prior to the end of 1989, a considerable amount of time will be required to assemble, coordinate, and interpret the data before it is announced.

After 1984 the weakness of the U.S. dollar was at first disregarded. This was the first time in several years that the U.S. had experienced an unfavorable balance of international trade. The desire of major countries to benefit from the strong U.S. economy and reserves has resulted in heavy foreign purchases of U.S. Treasury securities, corporate bonds, real estate, and manufacturing facilities. This type of surplus is only as good as the faith of "monied" foreign investors in the overall strength of the economy.

Whenever foreign owners lose faith in their U.S. investments and decide to dump them quickly, the U.S. encounters a serious problem. Wholesale selling depreciates the value of investments, dropping price levels below their intrinsic value. Consequently, investors should monitor international balance of trade signals that could affect their personal holdings.

Third World Debt Another factor that clouds the export/import balance of trade is the huge debt owed by third world (developing) countries to the U.S. and its banks. If these debts remain unpaid, it will be difficult to estimate the enormous amount of financial damage to the banking system and the U.S. The U.S. disguises the problem and helps debtor nations and the unpaid banks by not calling the debts delinquent or attempting to settle for partial payments. This benefits U.S. banks. Despite the huge delinquencies, the debtor countries continue to post favorable debt balances; interest is often collected while the principal on loans remains unpaid.

There is a paradox to this scenario. To help third world countries survive their debt crisis, many economists suggest that these debtor nations become exporters. However, this would make creditors out of the third world nations that import from the U.S.—the long term losers might be U.S. industries and the labor force.

U.S. farmers are part of another group that suffers from the excessive unpaid debts of foreign nations. It is difficult for farmers to borrow money from financially troubled domestic banks that are waiting for payments from third world countries.

Foreign Investment When the dollar becomes weak against foreign currencies, a cycle begins. Capital from foreign countries is often used to purchase U.S. real estate, bonds, securities, and businesses. The U.S. gets the opportunity to increase exports during this period. This provides employment, increases production, and eventually strengthens the value of the dollar. When the dollar becomes too strong, the export business declines and the U.S. becomes an importing nation. When the U.S. imports too much, the government loosens the money supply. This again weakens the dollar and the cycle continues. Although it is scary to learn that U.S. buildings and factories are being bought and controlled by foreign interests, only future business cycles can determine whether or not the foreigners made wise investments.

There is a major problem with permitting foreigners to own U.S. interests at will. What if, for reasons that benefit their countries, they decide to shut down all their U.S. factories at the same time? Chaos would result for every person or industry connected with these foreign companies.

Competing in the World Market A strong U.S. dollar curbs U.S. exports and induces domestic manufacturers to spend more money on research and development. The goals of U.S. manufacturers should be to develop new technology, improve their products, and trim production costs. These goals can be accomplished by obtaining the latest technology and manufacturing equipment available. The fulfillment of these goals assures manufacturers that they can be more competitive with both domestic and foreign manufacturers. Further, their competitiveness and profits also improve when exorbitant executive salaries, unjust labor benefits, and the excessive costs of domestic marketing programs are reduced.

Historically, there has been a heavy domestic demand for foreign cars and electronics. Many economists believe that the U.S. could achieve a more favorable trade balance without a favorable monetary exchange rate. They believe that the trade balance could be altered if U.S. management and labor joined forces to design, engineer, and manufacture better quality merchandise. Also needed is better follow-up service and less built-in obsolescence than is now offered by foreign exporters.

Therefore, if you are asked to invest in a business that involves cars, electronics, or associated items, learn if any possible changes in the trade laws would affect your investment. Good information sources include your congressman or a domestic trade organation affiliated with the product you want to investigate. (The names and addresses of such organizations can be obtained from your local library.)

Canadian Lumber and U.S. Wheat

Lawmakers who must decide whether or not to restrict imports through protective laws or tariffs are usually confronted with difficult decisions. Two examples are cited. In one, the U.S. government tried to impose a duty on Canadian lumber. In the second, it attempted to sell subsidized wheat to the Soviet Union.

The Canadian Lumber Tariff Until recently, the United States imported about one-third of all the soft lumber used in the housing industry from Canada. Naturally, this did not sit well with U.S. lumber interests, who then sought legislative protection. Requests for protection from imports are usually based on actual or potential unemployment and low profits or losses. Frequently, however, when tariff protection is being sought, the complete facts are not disclosed.

During the tariff discussions concerning Canadian lumber, many assumed that the major reason for the large volume of lumber imports to the U.S. was Canada's inexpensive dollar. It was being exchanged at the time for about 70 U.S. cents. Lumber users could take advantage of the 30 percent savings. Those assumptions, however, were not completely correct. There were two other important factors that were not considered.

The first factor was that the Canadian lumber was kiln-dried—an expensive process that requires special drying ovens. To dry wood properly, it takes time, is costly, and requires additional capital. Kiln-dried wood is preferred by conscientious builders or furniture makers. The drying process reduces shrinking and warping. In the U.S., domestic kiln-dried wood is not in great supply because of the attached expense. In some instances, the orders must be for at least 100,000 board feet, thus taking it out of reach for many users.

The second factor, probably forgotten, is that in the late 1970s the rate of exchange between the U.S. and the Canadian dollar was $1.03 U.S. to $1.00 Canadian. Even at that exchange rate, a tremendous amount of Canadian lumber was being bought by U.S. lumber yards.

After the value of the U.S. dollar increased in value to approximately $1.30 Canadian, the U.S. demand for kiln-dried lumber continued to increase. For the U.S., this meant both benefits and disadvantages. The benefits were that buildings and houses could be priced lower, making them more affordable. Also, the buildings were not likely to shrink or warp. On the other hand, the major disadvantages for the U.S. were that unemployment increased for its lumbermen, and lumber yards could not make as much profit from the lower-priced, imported wood. Many believed that U.S. protective legislation would increase employment while increasing the cost of housing. Some feared that these increased costs would stimulate inflation.

Following is a chronological report of the preceding events. In March 1986, the U.S. International Trade Commission claimed that the importation of shingles, shakes, and wood from Canada were a detriment to domestic production. They suggested that the U.S. place heavy duties on such products to protect U.S. lumber interests.

Although Canada is a friendly neighbor, it did not take kindly to this idea. Meanwhile, President Reagan was trying to create a free trade pact with Canada. Lumbermen and farmers on the U.S. side of the border were opposed to the pact.

In May 1986, the U.S. claimed that red cedar shakes and shingles had been subsidized by the Canadian government. In response, the U.S. granted temporary protection to domestic producers of these products in the form of a 35 percent tariff phased out over 5 years. This did not sit well with the Canadians. By November rumors had emerged that their government would impose stumpage fees paid by Canadian producers to their Provincial governments for standing lumber. Finally, by the end of December, it was expected that Canada would agree to impose a 15 percent export fee on the soft lumber that its producers exported to the United States.

An interesting sidelight to these events is that in September 1987, 11 of the western states in the U.S. experienced the greatest amount of damage from forest fires that had ever been recorded. Here was a signal (for anyone contemplating an investment in any project requiring lumber) that a shortage of lumber might increase the prices of both the raw materials and the finished products. Potential investors should know how their investment will be affected by either the imposition or lifting of a subsidy or tariff for a product that might be connected with their investment.

The Wheat Subsidy In August 1986, at a time that the U.S. farm economy was in deep trouble, President Reagan again moved away from his free trade policy. Even though the Soviet Union had reneged on a previous agreement to purchase U.S. wheat in 1985, President Reagan pledged to subsidize 4 million metric tons of U.S. government-owned grain sales to the Soviet Union at $91 a metric ton. This was $13 less per metric ton than the $104 a metric ton that the U.S. had paid for it through its "export enhancement program." Under this program the government had bought surplus commercial farm goods for export with the understanding that it had to be sold at a certain date. The price is usually derived through a bidding procedure. President Reagan's plan was viewed as an attempt to cut the expected $160 to $170 million trade deficit for 1986. In addition, it would show Congress and the electorate in an election year that he could have a tough trade policy towards foreign trading partners.

As might be expected, grain selling allies were disturbed. If the Reagan plan was approved, Canada, Australia, and Argentina—who had been large grain exporters to the Soviet Union—were expected to lose millions of dollars in grain sales. The National Corn Growers objected because they felt that if the Soviets bought the wheat, they would not buy their corn. (This is another reason why the word "quandary" appears in the title of this chapter.) Prior to this time, President Reagan had rejected the idea of subsidizing communist countries with U.S. tax dollars. Also, on the same date, the United States was considering the imposition of restrictions on the importation of certain textiles.

Although it was estimated that the Reagan plan would cost the U.S. $52 million in government-owned farm goods, many legislators supported it and requested additional export promotion. An editorial by Vin Weber in the *Wall Street Journal* proposed that the sale should not be viewed as a subsidy but "as a businesslike attempt to gain a foothold in the world agricultural market."

President Reagan's actions were a double signal to investors. It was an alert to those who were interested in textiles. Restrictions would increase the value of domestic textiles. It was also a signal to anyone connected with wheat-related products. The subsidy to support the distribution of more wheat might create a future shortage that could favorably influence the profitability of their investment.

Unfortunately, in November 1986 the Soviets again reneged on their deal. Some traders thought the Soviets reneged because of currency problems. A short while later, the Soviets announced that they would be harvesting 200 million metric tons themselves, which would be the largest crop since 1978. (Incidentally, skeptics disbelieved this announcement, believing it to be an attempt to depress world wheat prices.)

These examples are only a small sample to show the relationship between investing and the problems and opportunities connected with the export/import trade quandary. If you still doubt that major economists are in a quandary, consider this: In the early part of this century, the U.S. was tied to a gold standard. In an attempt to relieve economic pressure, the U.S. abandoned the gold standard. Then in late 1987, just a few weeks before the Black Monday of October 17, the Secretary of the U.S. Treasury made a startling recommendation. He suggested to the ministers of the World Bank and International Monetary Fund that they should consider relating the value of the dollar to commodities instead of to the value of other currencies. Are you aware that gold is considered a major commodity?

Black Monday will be remembered as the day The Dow Jones Industrial Average plunged an average of 22.6 percent and reflected a drop of 508.2 points. It was the biggest drop in the market's history. The markets in other countries also dropped. No one knows why, but a lack of confidence was apparent. On Black Monday, however, while the commodities market also dropped, one of its components—the precious metals group—rose. Gold rose $10.10 an ounce to reach $481.70 an ounce. The precipitous drop in the market combined with the increase in the price of gold affected the dollar volume of future international trade. It also affected the future living standards for untold millions of people throughout the world.

Look for Signals

As an investor or business person, you must continually watch the economy, the international balance of trade, foriegn exchange rates, and the stock market. Look for signals that help you get into or out of the right investments at the right time. When economic conditions are in a state of flux, import/export businesses are in danger. When signs of new or revised international trade tariffs surface, determine their affect on the related industries or commodities. Above all, use these signals as a basis for your investment plans.

Chapter 20: Interest Rates and the Value of the Dollar

Interest Rates and the Value of the Dollar

As an investor, it is imperative that you have some concept of the importance of interest rates and the value of the dollar. In varying degrees these factors affect nearly every investment you make.

How Interest Rates Affect You

First, interest rates are important to you, particularly as an investor, because they indicate the cost of using the money or credit used to operate a business venture.

Second, interest rates affect the value of your dollar. When interest rates are high, your dollar is usually stronger. It will buy more in international markets than when it is weak. When interest rates are high, manufacturers are able to import lower-priced raw materials. This helps them produce lower-priced finished items in the competitive field in which you may have a financial interest.

Third, interest rates are important to you whenever you become interested in investments that are interest-sensitive. By interest-sensitive, I mean that profits and values derived by a company or governmental branch are closely connected to prevailing interest rates. The most interest-sensitive organizations are federal, state, and municipal governments and their agencies and financial institutions. Public and private utilities include the type that provide transportation, gas, electric, water, and telephone services. The prices of public utility stocks frequently fluctuate according to the amount of interest they are required to pay for the cash or credit they borrow, even though the consumer eventually foots the bill. Professional business analysts, when determining the efficiency and value of a company, determine the number of times a company has earned the amount it pays for interest.

Interest rates, of course, are seldom stable. They fluctuate according to the demand for money, the money supply, and government regulations. But your understanding of them, and what makes them fluctuate and affect the value of your investment, should help you evaluate when to refinance, expand, or sell your venture. The balance of this chapter is designed to acquaint you with information that helps you formulate decisions based on the interest rates and the value of the dollar.

Who Controls Interest Rates?

In 1984, President Reagan was quoted as saying, "Fear of the future causes high interest rates." The matter of interest rates is deeper than fear alone. International interest rates are controlled by the central banks of the major countries. Domestic interest rates are controlled by Federal Open Market Committee (FOMC) of the Federal Reserve System (see Chapter 16).

Though it has the power to regulate the money supply, the FOMC controls short-term interest rates according to its opinions (usually kept secret). It determines whether a tight money supply and high interest will better serve the economy than loose money and low interest rates. The impact of short-term interest rates on long-term rates was discussed in a recent article in *Monetary Trends* a monthly publication issued by the Federal Reserve Bank of St. Louis. On September 4, 1987, after discussing the rise in the discount rate from 5.5 percent to 6 percent (where it had been since August 1986), when it was lowered back to 5.5 percent, the article made this statement. "Other interest rates responded immediately to the increase: the prime rate moved upward to 8.75 percent from 8.25 percent; the three-month Treasury bill rate for the week ending September 11 jumped 18 basis points from the previous week's level of 6.21 percent; and the long-term Treasury securities' rate increased 29 basis points in the same period."

(Basis points refer to the yields paid on securities such as bonds and notes. The smallest basis point is translated into 0.01 percent of yield. Thus, the 18 basis points referred to above meant that the new yield on three-month Treasury bills was 6.39 percent. Basis points are distinguished from rates of increase.)

Affect of Interest Rates on Spending

Experience indicates that high interest rates usually slow down economic growth. The high rates reduce the amount of dollars people spend on vacations and business travel, all of which contribute to unemployment. When interest rates are high, manufacturers tend to avoid capital improvements that could spur employment. Also, in a period when interest rates are high—which usually occurs whenever the economy is enjoying moderate growth—people begin to save their money. They want to profit by investing at the higher rates of interest that prevail during an expanding economy. When interest rates become exceptionally high and inflation seems to be increasing out of control, many savers and investors become concerned that the value of their savings will diminish. Thus they may use their savings for either pleasure or the acquisition of tangible goods (i.e., gold, art, real estate, etc.) which they hope will not lose value.

Affect of Interest Rates on Debtor Nations

An increase in interest rates can also play havoc with the economy of debtor nations whose large international debts are tied to prevailing interest rates. Conversely, lower interest rates lower debt burdens and help to improve the economy. If the debtor nations are producers of gold or oil, an increase in interest rates may compel them to sell off their precious commodities at lower prices to meet their payments. For example, in June of 1986 Mexico, a heavy debtor nation, considered the exchange of its oil to creditor nations.

When debtor countries are required to sell their assets to pay debts, the consequences may be a decline in the value of their assets at a time when they are trying to improve their credit. Also, when foreign debtors are compelled to pay high interest rates, it is unlikely that they will help the U.S. increase its volume of exports to them.

Theoretically, if foreign countries decide to compete for world investments by increasing the interest rates they pay, the U.S., whenever it is in need of foreign investments, might be compelled to increase its interest rates. This would increase the volume of foreign investment in the U.S. and could eventually create an inflationary atmosphere and trigger a downturn in the U.S. economy. If you desire to be an informed investor, you must follow these trends.

Affect on Dollar Value

Whenever the U.S. GNP is strong at the same time that U.S.

interest rates are at a high level, the U.S. dollar should have a strong value in the international marketplace.

Influence of Federal Reserve

The Federal Reserve Board has the power to set forces in motion that will increase or lower the value of the dollar. One good example of the Federal Reserve Board acting to lower the value of the U.S. dollar occurred in late January of 1985. The Federal Reserve Board feared the value of the dollar might to be too high for the good of the economy. At that time, the Federal Reserve Board and the U.S. Treasury consulted with each other about the value of the U.S. dollar being too high abroad. The Treasury agreed to join other industrialized nations in a combined effort to help stabilize foreign exchange markets.

Consequently, the Federal Reserve Board, the implementing arm of the Treasury, began a program designed to lower the value of the dollar by lowering interest rates. This created a situation wherein the U.S. dollar would not be as desirable as the equivalent currency of countries whose interest rates, or yields on securities, exceeded those of the U.S. That created a weaker U.S. dollar which reduced its importing power. Meanwhile, the weaker U.S. dollar induced foreign countries to buy U.S. exports, thereby strengthening our economy. At first, the program was unsuccessful, but by the following month, it appeared that the program would work. Shortly thereafter, however, the dollar regained its strength, even though the interest rates in many foreign countries were higher than those in the U.S.

How Foreign Investors React

But the continued strength of the dollar was viewed as proof that foreign investors were impressed by both the strength of the U.S. economy and the security of their investments in the U.S. The Federal Reserve Board persisted in its efforts to lower the value of the dollar by increasing the money supply and reducing the value of the dollar by reducing interest rates. Shortly thereafter, the value of the U.S. dollar dropped. Subsequently, U.S. exports began to increase.

Different countries use the same financial techniques. During the aforementioned period, the Japanese became concerned about losing their export market to the U.S. The Japanese yen had increased in value, which could reduce their volume of exports.

Consequently, in mid-1986 the Japanese were worried about the increased value of the yen. They attempted to raise and support the strength and value of the yen by buying dollars. However, toward the end of 1986, to increase its volume of exports, Japan decided to lower its interest rates.

When countries become fearful of the declining value of the U.S. dollar and want to retrieve the capital their citizens have invested in the U.S., they:

- Try to improve their own economy by providing tax incentives to encourage investors and entrepreneurs to invest at home.
- Try to either prevent additional money from leaving their countries or tax investment funds that are invested abroad.
- Try to urge the U.S. to reduce its interest rates to discourage continued foreign investment in the U.S. while making their own interest rates more favorable. (Foreign nations could also claim that too much foreign money in the U.S., attracted by high interest rates combined with an excessively large trade deficit, could make the U.S. too much of a debtor-nation and cause it to collapse. The latter event could occur when and if the amount of foreign holdings in the U.S. greatly exceeded the U.S.' investments abroad.)

Corporations and Equity Financing

If corporations that require additional capital use equity financing (issue corporate stock) instead of selling bonds, the pressure for higher interest rates is reduced. Equity financing or equity capital refers to funds that are used to secure an ownership interest in a corporation by purchasing its stocks. There are many types of corporate stocks, such as common, preferred, capital, etc., and each offers a different type of ownership. Most equity financing is secured by a corporation through the sale of its common stock, which gives its owners a claim on the corporation's earnings and assets as well as the right to vote for the directors of the corporation.

Common stocks, however, do not pay interest and cannot pay dividends unless the corporation earns a profit. Dividends, sometimes referred to as earnings per share, also refer to the amount of profits that the board of directors votes to distribute, usually quarterly, to the different classes of shareholders, according to the number of shares they own. Bonds, on the other hand, while also used to secure financing, are not considered as equity financing because a bondholder does not acquire a share of the corporation. Bondholders do not receive a share of the profits and are limited to receiving their stipulated interest (the set fee that they receive for loaning their money). What is important is that even the smallest bondholders receive their scheduled interest payments before the largest shareholder becomes entitled to receive any cash dividends. In effect, bondholders loan money to the corporation whereas stockholders buy a share of it and profit from an increase in the corporation's asset value and profits.

When a growing U.S. economy keeps interest rates high, the prices of stocks may be affected. Often various regulations are implemented to control interest rates that must be charged for margin accounts maintained for you by the various stock brokerage firms. The prices of securities may also be affected by the federal regulations that specify the amount of the margin account that may be financed on credit. By having a margin account, an investor is able to have his brokerage firm finance a certain percentage of the securities he purchases. The investor is required to maintain a sufficient margin balance in his account in the form of securities or cash.

When interest rates become too high, people who depend on margin accounts to purchase stocks are discouraged from making additional purchases. This tends to depress prices by increasing the available supply. Conversely, lower interest rates stimulate margin account activity for two reasons. First, the lower carrying charges cut the maintenance costs for the buyers and enable them to hold on to their investments longer at a lower cost. Second, they can make a quick profit from a smaller increase in the margined stock due to the buyers' lower interest costs.

Bonds and Other Securities

Usually, if the investing public believe that the Federal Reserve Board will not raise interest rates, bonds can rally. The opposite is also true. If you own a bond that pays interest, for example, at the rate of 10 percent, and the interest rate rises to 11 percent, your current bond will not be worth as much as a new bond. On the other hand, if you possess a 10 percent bond and the interest rate drops to 9 percent, then the value of your bond will be worth more than the face value of the new bond.

Some economists feel that if inflation and commodity prices remain low, interest rates will also remain low. Other economists, however, insist that servicing a huge budget deficit will require heavy Treasury financing, which will produce higher interest rates. Always expect that a large demand for money will increase interest rates. Without government intervention to weaken the money supply and reduce interest rates, paying off a large budget deficit will also increase interest rates.

Whenever securities, such as bonds, pay higher interest rates than banks, and their rates of interest for the same amount of investment yield more than stock dividends, many investors will draw their money out of both banks and stocks to take advantage of the higher financial rewards offered by such securities. (A security refers to any written instrument that indicates an obligation by a debtor to a creditor. It may be in the form of bonds, stocks, warrants, options, or subscription agreements. Each of the last three items are rights to buy. All instruments called Treasuries issued by the U.S. are securities, whether they are called Treasury bills, Treasury bonds, or Treasury notes. Although they are issued differently, their major difference is in the size of their dollar denominations and their periods of maturity.)

Recently, a strong demand for 30-year U.S. Treasury notes drew a mixed response from financial analysts. (Treasury notes range from $1,000 to $1 million or more and may mature in from one to ten years.) To some analysts, the heavy buying demand meant that investors believed that long-term interest rates would provide a lower yield than the current yield. Under these circumstances the bonds that were being issued would be a good investment. Others suggested that lower interest rates in the future would increase the value of stocks and make them a better investment. Why? When corporations can borrow money at low interest rates, they can show larger profits while increasing in value. In my opinion, a mixed portfolio is best.

So far, I have presented you with accurate information about the importance of interest rates and the value of the dollar. The following examples are offered so that you will have other opinions on this very important subject that could affect your investment program.

According to the February 24, 1985 issue of *Los Angeles Times*: "Even if the higher interest rates did not bring foreign capital to the U.S., the higher profits of U.S. industry over foreign profits would have been an inducement."

During 1984-85, the U.S. dollar was strong with high interest rates. Because of that strength, Japan began to invest heavily in the U.S. by amassing a trade surplus that amounted to a reported $50 billion by 1986. Despite the large U.S. trade deficit, which usually weakens financial strength, the presumed strength of the U.S. dollar was also being supported by American investors who shunned foreign investing in favor of investing in the United States.

In the early part of 1985, the U.S. dollar was still very strong. Foreign investors were convinced that U.S. investments were the best available, even though many economists contended that the dollar was overvalued. This, in effect, could cause the U.S. to lose jobs to foreign manufacturers. According to these investors, the only solution was to reduce the deficit. Meanwhile, other economists disagreed.

On February 26, 1985, Associated Press business analyst John Cuniff quoted Edward L. Huggins, an economist and Heritage Foundation Fellow, as follows: "Conceding that while the strong dollar has hurt the U.S. economy and exports, low cost goods imported to the U.S. help to keep inflation down; that if measured by a certain International Monetary Fund Benchmark, the dollar in 1984 merely equaled its 1970 strength" and that "as strength in the value of the dollar in foreign exchange has increased, unemployment in the U.S. decreased." Cuniff also questioned the causal link between deficits and interest rates by asking for an explanation of the "depressed values of the currencies in France with a 12 percent prime rate and of Italy with a rate of 18 percent."

Some analysts believe that if foreign investors withdraw their money from the U.S. while the interest rates of their respective countries become so high they cannot be ignored by all investors, then their respective currencies will become stronger, resulting in a weakening of the U.S. economy.

In mid-1986, interest rates were low and inflation was under control. After the U.S. dollar lost its foreign exchange strength due to the combined actions of the Federal Reserve Board and cooperating countries, the U.S. economy became flat and uncertain. At that time, there were some indications that some foreign investors might withdraw investment funds from the U.S. to secure higher interest rates elsewhere. However, some countries, such as Japan, were investing additional funds in American plants.

Inflation and Economic Cycles

There are two additional points that investors should bear in mind, without forgetting the importance of interest rates and the value of the dollar.

First, some economists believe that too strong an economy will produce inflation. Therefore, they prefer a weakened U.S. economy. On the other hand, many economists believe in and work for a strong economy in which they see more investment opportunities. My reaction to these beliefs is that the United States is not the only country in the world that controls the economy. And, although we must adjust the economy for our benefit, we must also consider the economy and plans of our allies and trading partners when formulating programs.

The second point, which has been tested and verified by time, is that all economic conditions are cyclical and are sure to change. Although there are true and tested investments, constant improvements provide new opportunities for those with foresight. Moreover, if you want to invest and avoid losses, you must watch changes in interest rates and the value of the dollar. This way, you can sell your investment at the right time, preserve your assets, and try another type of investment.

Chapter 21: Income Shelters and Tax Traps

Income Shelters and Tax Traps

A tax shelter is an investment that uses certain types of legal bookkeeping expenses. A tax shelter enables one or more participants to either defer paying or permanently save a specific percentage of money on their respective income taxes. The most common bookkeeping practices are the recording of depreciation, depletion allowances, and interest payments. These are covered in this chapter. Although capital gains are not a pure tax shelter, they are also discussed because they receive preferential tax treatment. It should be understood, however, that without an investment and without certain types of permitted expenses, you cannot benefit from either a tax shelter or preferential treatment. While the Internal Revenue Service collects the taxes according to its own interpretation of the tax laws, an aggrieved taxpayer can appeal in a tax court.

Although tax shelter investments once offered many ways to avoid taxes, their current use, as approved by Congress, has eliminated most. Actually, Congress now only permits their use in qualified circumstances in which the investment risks are considerably greater than ordinary investments. However, without the benefit of at least some minimal relief, the industries being sheltered could suffer from a lack of investment capital. In most cases, the shelter that is provided is not total shelter but only refers to the amount of money that can be depreciated for items such as buildings or equipment and for the depletion that is allowed in oil and gas drilling and production.

The term "tax trap" refers to such risky investments that might be advertised as tax shelters but which are really a trap for the unwary. Congress has not, nor will the IRS, approve them as tax shelters. To avoid those traps, before you invest in what you think is a tax shelter, refer to The Tax Reform Act of 1986 and its applicable regulations, interpretations, and their possible amendments with your accountant— especially regarding tax shelters. Subject to changes, the major industries that are sheltered currently include real estate and oil and gas exploration.

The benefits of legal tax shelters are that they permit the beneficiaries to use deferred or saved tax dollars for other purposes. Such dollars may be used to either further the best interests of a business or to make other investments with the hope of earning additional money and enjoying a better lifestyle.

Many tax shelters were designed not so much to earn current net profits but to shelter personal income earned from other sources. The Tax Reform Act of 1986, however, restricted the use of most tax shelters that do not have a sound, economic basis.

Abuses

Invariably, many of these legal shelters have lead to abuses that favor certain private interests and deprive our country of millions of revenue dollars. Consequently, such blatant misuse of these shelters has lead to an inevitable outcry to equalize taxes in favor of the oppressed taxpayers. This is when lobbyists attempt to promote special-interest tax legislation that will benefit those industries that pay their salaries. It will be interesting to watch what new amendments will be made to the Tax Reform Act of 1986.

Unfortunately, our political system permits too many elected legislators to become dependent on the largess of lobbyists and those they represent to cover most of their election expenses. As a result, even if legislation is passed to give the honest taxpayer a fair shake, the chances are high that the lobbyists will eventually succeed in enacting changes that will favor their clients.

But even under a system that could provide fair taxes for all, many taxpayers will still seek to save tax dollars. Knowing this, both promoters of tax evasion schemes as well as honest and dishonest taxpayers will always conjure up new or forgotten tax shelters. Some of them will be legal; the others will eventually be declared illegal.

It is lawful to use every honest tax advantage that is available to you under the law. Thus, the problem becomes one of determining what is honest and what is lawful. In that purview, the first step that a conscientious tax adviser takes is to discover and omit, if possible, whatever approach will trigger an audit by the taxing authorities.

Tax Audits

Of the many factors that trigger IRS audits, certain tax shelters are high on the list. In the forefront are tax shelter activities with high write-offs relative to the amount of money invested. It has been reported that the Internal Revenue Service collects an average of $19,000 in back taxes for each "potentially abusive" tax shelter return that it audits; and that the IRS is in the process of collecting $2.5 billion in revenues from fines, negligence penalties, and civil fraud penalties, plus taxes owed with interest.

Because of the risk involved in tax shelter ventures, they are only recommended for people who can afford the risk and who are in large tax brackets. Ownership in an oil well may sound promising to people who are not in a high tax bracket. However, the risks of losing their entire investment are too high to warrant taking a chance. Their losses may well exceed their normal taxes. Unfortunately, in many instances where the deductions could have been used profitably, the tax shelters were disallowed by the IRS.

In the past, the competition to partake in some of the tax shelters caused their prices to rise. They rose so high that many of them became unprofitable and unaffordable for the average investor. Hopefully, that situation will be rectified in the future by the new tax laws.

Thousands of ingenious tax avoidance schemes have been created and still flourish. These schemes involve real estate, cattle breeding, stamps, master recordings, gemstones, oil exploration, movies, and nearly anything that can make money, including self-ordained ministers who set up churches to hide their income.

Since 1984, the IRS has begun to squeeze promoters of tax shelters. Currently, these promoters are required to register tax shelters before offering them to the public and to maintain a list of investors for inspection by the IRS.

Legal Tax Shelters

There are three major types of legal tax shelters which are described below. It is in pursuit of these shelters that many honest taxpayers encounter unlawful schemes and run afoul of the IRS.

- One type is actually more than just a shelter. It enables an investor to earn and retain a certain proportion of tax-free income that cannot be touched by the IRS. These are usually in the form of capital gains, depletion, interest payments, and certain business losses. Any of these shelters can be eliminated at any time by a new tax law. Further, state laws may not coincide with federal laws.
- A second type enables an investor to shelter (temporarily avoid paying taxes on) the amount of money depreciated on business-related equipment. This includes such items as drilling equipment

in a petroleum venture or the unpaid profit of an installment sale by only paying income taxes on that portion of the installments that have been received that tax year.
- The third type of shelter is a combination of the first two. These shelters enable a taxpayer to permanently save tax dollars and are usually the result of exemptions or preferences granted by the law.

Capital Gains

One such preference, relating to capital gains, started being phased out at the end of 1986 by the Tax Reform Act of 1986. Until then, this exemption provided that if investors profited from long-term capital gains (investments held for six months or more), their net tax liability could not exceed 20 percent of the amount of the capital gain. Thus, if an investor held stocks, real estate, or other investments that were sold for a profit after the legally prescribed holding period of six months, the maximum net tax rate that could be applied was 20 percent. If the profit was earned in a shorter period, it was referred to as a short-term capital gain, and a maximum tax of 50 percent applied. Over the years many taxpayers have considered the tax benefits of capital gains to be the equivalent of a tax shelter.

For 1987, the maximum tax rate scheduled for long-term capital gains was 28 percent, and 38.5 percent for short-term capital gains. In 1988, both long and short-term capital gains were treated alike using the maximum rate of 28 percent.

Interest

Until the end of 1986, interest that was paid was a deductible tax item and a good form of tax shelter. It was used for all types of investments and purposes, including real estate, buying stocks on margin, and consumer loans. The Tax Reform Act of 1986 caused the elimination of interest as a deduction to be phased out over a period of five years (from 65 percent in 1987, 40 percent in 1988, 20 percent in 1989, 10 percent in 1990 and to zero thereafter).

This means that most investments will have to be bought for their merits rather than for their tax deductibility. Investors will have to make higher down payments and finance smaller amounts of the purchase price. Congress began to eliminate interest as a tax-deductible item because too many taxpayers were using their interest payments in an unrestricted manner, mostly to live well and to increase their investment earnings while reducing their taxes.

Homeowners are still permitted to deduct interest in a limited fashion on the mortgages of first and second homes. For homes purchased after August 1986, the interest deduction is limited to loans that do not exceed the original purchase price of the homes plus improvements. By way of comparison, in some countries interest that is paid by an investor is deductible as an operating expense to reduce the amount of income that will be subject to tax. This also has had the effect of lowering the investors' tax bracket (the tax rate that applies to the net profit).

Beginning in 1987, if you owned securities on margin you were only permitted to deduct margin interest up to the total amount of your entire investment income. This included any capital gains profits plus any interest and dividends received by you. Margin is the amount of money and/or the value of the securities an investor places with a broker to open a margin account. If the investor's deposit with the broker is insufficient to pay for the stocks purchased, the broker, subject to the limits set by the various regulatory bodies, loans the customer the balance of the money that is required, at above average interest rates. The securities are held as security for the loan. Under the tax rules that prevailed prior to the Tax Act of 1986, the customer could deduct the entire interest amount paid from whatever profits were made, regardless of the source.

Depreciation

Depreciation is considered to be one of the major tax shelters. It reduces taxable income by amortizing the life of buildings and equipment even though the buildings and equipment may be increasing in value due to inflation. Ordinarily, depreciation refers to bookkeeping charges against earnings for the purpose of writing off the cost less the salvage value of a business asset over its estimated useful life. Depreciation does not involve a cash outlay but contributes to an individual's or company's bookkeeping reserves.

For example, if you purchase a piece of business equipment that has a ten-year life span, you may deduct a set percentage of its cost each year. At the end of ten years, when it is not expected to have any value, you will have been compensated for your business loss. But, if the item is sold for more money than the amount for which it has been depreciated, a tax must be paid on the difference between the sales price and the total amount that has been depreciated.

There are many types of depreciation. When selling depreciated items, the tax rates can vary according to the length of time that the items are owned and the method of depreciation that you use. The method of depreciation should be determined by your accountant.

With respect to tax deductions for depreciation, the overall annual depreciation deductions for businesses have been lowered. The depreciation life of real estate has been extended from 19 years to 27½ years for residential property, and to 31½ years for commercial property. Factories, machinery, and equipment also take longer to depreciate. Incidentally, land is not a depreciable asset.

Securities

Many governments, in an attempt to subsidize or encourage the growth of certain industries, grant special tax exemptions on all or partial earnings. Frequently, these privileges are extended to purchasers of bonds or securities that the government sponsors.

Although the future tax fate of municipal bonds in the U.S. appears to be uncertain, municipal bonds have enjoyed tax-free income status and have been considered an excellent tax shelter. However, if they are sold for a profit, they become taxable as short or long-term capital gains. But any attempt to borrow money to finance the purchase of municipal bonds and then deduct the interest paid to buy or carry such a loan is not allowed by the IRS.

A municipal bond is one that is issued by a state or a political subdivision, such as a county, city, town, or village, and includes bonds issued by state agencies and authorities. Interest paid on municipal bonds has been exempt from federal income taxes, but the federal government is attempting to change this. When the federal government attempts to restrict this deduction, there is the likelihood of a legal battle that could involve the right of one sovereign power, such as the U.S., from interfering in the taxing ability of other sovereign powers, such as the respective states.

It may be of interest that in recent years tax-exempt municipal bonds have yielded about 30 percent less than U.S. Treasury bonds, which are subject to federal income tax. If the tax exemption of municipal bonds is reduced, more people may begin to purchase Treasury notes.

Installment Sales

Another method of sheltering income, although always subject to tax revisions and interpretations, is the installment sale. Through this device the profit from a sale is deferred from either one year to the next year or for a number of years, depending on the dates of payment for the sale. This has the effect of reducing the amount of earnings that are subject to tax in the year of the sale. It also could reduce the applicable tax rate on the reduced income.

However, the Tax Reform Act of 1986 says that after December 31, 1986, the gains on publicly traded securities shall be reported as of the trade date and not the settlement date. (The trade date is the date that the order to buy or sell is executed. The settlement date is usually five working days after the trade date, at which time the brokerage firm and its client balance their accounts with each other.)

Short Term Losses

Prior to the new law, short-term gains could offset short-term losses. In the absence of short-term gains, short-term losses could offset long-term capital gains and net short-term losses could be offset against ordinary income up to $3,000. However, since it took $2 of losses for every $1 that was offset, a short-term loss of $6,000, for example, would secure a $3,000 deduction. Carry-over losses could be carried forward during your lifetime until they were exhausted. However, such losses had to retain their original character and be treated as either long- or short-term capital losses, or short- and long-term capital gains.

A capital gain is the profit made from any asset that you have held for the period of time prescribed by the applicable law. This is currently six months and always subject to change. Capital gains are important as tax shelters whenever their applicable tax rate has been less than the tax rate charged for ordinary income.

Under the Tax Reform Act of 1986, beginning in 1987, both short-term and long-term capital losses were treated alike and could be used to offset up to $3,000 of ordinary income. The most that you could be taxed for capital gains was 28 percent, but in 1988 capital gains were being taxed as ordinary income. In 1987, short-term gains were taxed at a maximum rate of 38.5 percent but in 1988, both long- and short-term capital gains are treated alike. The maximum rate for most investors is now 28 percent for both long- and short-term capital gains.

One problem that concerns business people and corporations is how to get the IRS to accept the cost of running an essential part of the business as a normal business expense and not as a capital expense. The difference is that the normal business expense can be deducted from taxes during the year in which the expense occurs. Capital expense must be recorded and depreciated as an expense over a period of years. A capital expense can only be recovered according to the applicable depreciation rules of the IRS for both personal and real property.

No one knows when Congress or new interpretations of existing laws and regulations by the IRS will change the present tax structures. Yet, any changes to the tax laws can dramatically alter the worthiness of your investments. Therefore, unless you can thoroughly understand tax matters and interpretations, consult your tax accountant about investments that are based on the benefits of various tax shelters.

Tax Shelters or Tax Traps

As discussed above, shaky tax shelters may prove to be tax traps. One example involves promoters who may offer to sell investment units in projects that include such things as films or leasing equipment. The promoter promises that the investor can secure large write-offs (a form of tax shelter) against earned income by making a relatively small cash deposit and signing a promissory note for the balance. In some instances, the investor also agrees to sign future promissory notes.

Frequently, promoters persuade investors to sign such notes with the following explanations:

- The notes are just a formality to show the IRS that the investors are sincere and not just looking for a tax shelter.
- Payment will be made from the profits or the promised payments on the notes will be forgiven.

Next, the promoters assign these same executed promissory notes (IOUs) to their respective banks. The banks accept them in good faith as security for the loans that the promoters require to finance their operations.

(Sometimes, during the period that the promoters are soliciting funds from the public, the venture may already be in managerial or technical trouble. It may be without sufficient working capital and have no hope of being bailed out with additional funds.)

Of course, if the project fails, the bank will ask the investors to make good on their respective promissory notes. On the other hand, if the investment is successful, the contemplated amount of money that was expected to be sheltered may greatly exceed the relatively low cash investment. This is when the IRS may deem the cash-investment ratio (when compared to the amount of the requested tax shelter) to be too small and disallow the investment.

Before permitting a taxpayer to use a tax shelter, the Internal Revenue Service must be satisfied that the main motive of the alleged tax shelter investment was to earn money. This is the underlying reason that Congress permitted tax shelters. Knowing the types of promoters who use these tax traps, combined with the relatively small amount of cash advanced by the taxpayer, the IRS is inclined to believe that the promotion was designed as a tax avoidance scheme and not to legitimately earn money. Hence, it was indeed a sad day for those trusting investors when they learned they had lost much more than the cash they had invested without getting the benefit of the promised tax shelter.

Some real estate syndicators have claimed that their investors could deduct from their taxes approximately $1.25 to $4 for every $1 invested. This may be within the parameters allowed by the IRS but should also be thoroughly investigated before investing.

Unusual Tax Breaks

If you have ever been caught in a tax shelter trap, don't feel too bad about it because governments also trap themselves, even when trying to help the economy. For example, consider two cases that occurred in Canada.

In the first case (in a program that ended in October 1984), the Canadian government made the mistake of attempting to grant tax credits to investors in a scientific research tax-credit program without providing an effective holding period. As a result, until the law was rescinded, investors and companies bought billions of dollars of securities that had tax credits attached. They obtained the tax breaks even though some of the investors "flipped" (sold) their investments the same day they bought them. It has since been estimated that the Canadian government's failure to anticipate the quick turnovers cost it close to $2.9 billion in uncollectible tax revenues. The costs of both the administration of the program and the investigation of complaints are not included in this figure.

The program, originally designed to promote $5.6 billion in research activity, left the research companies $2.9 billion short. One subsidiary of a major oil company made over $25 million in tax savings with its "flip use" of the credits. Under the program, 74 percent of the transactions used the "quick flip" according to a Canadian watchdog committee report.

The second case, based on a June 1986 report in the *Globe and Mail* (a Toronto-based newspaper), demonstrates how dishonest promoters took advantage of legitimate tax shelters. These would have permitted them to make money honestly. According to the newspaper report, millions of dollars disappeared under the following circumstances.

Under the provisions of a government plan, for every $100 an investor paid to a research company he would receive a $50 tax credit from the company, along with a commitment to immediately repay the investors a cash amount of $55. This amount combined with the $50 credit gave the investor an almost instant risk-free $5 profit! At this juncture, the company would have an unearned $45 and a commitment to do $100 in research. Aside from the advantage taken of this plan via the "quick-flip" use of the tax credits involved, it is alleged that many other companies found it more profitable to use the money for non-research purposes. Revenue Canada (the Canadian Taxing Authority) estimated that as much as $2.5 billion was invested in the research projects, much of which was bogus, during the 18 months the program existed.

Some tax shelter promoters ask investors to advance them the same amount of money that their respective taxes totaled for the past three years. In return, they promise the investors a full refund of the taxes. Also, if they suffer losses, they can deduct portions of their investment losses from current income. This will reduce their current taxable income and reduce or eliminate taxes for the next few years. Unfortunately, in addition to the investment not turning out to be successful, the IRS does not allow the deductions.

When income tax rates are high, there is a reluctance on the part of the captains of industry to spend money on capital improvements. The government, in an attempt to stimulate both the economy and employment, may offer special incentives to companies that spend moneys on capital expenditures. Such government incentives frequently induce some business people to purchase machinery and equipment to help shelter some of their income. When tax rates are decreased, these same people shun capital improvements and forego tax-sheltering depreciation.

A Few Suggestions

Here are some tax savings suggestions:

- **Income Deferment** If at any time you expect next year's tax rates to be lower than this year's rates, try to legally defer as much of this year's anticipated income as possible.

- **Municipal Bonds** In view of anticipated reductions in tax rates, if you are interested in the tax exemptions offered by municipal bonds, you should make a determination as to which ones may be vulnerable to tax changes. If the reduction in taxes makes untaxed bonds as desirable as they once were, then consider acquiring them.

Since August 15, 1986, some municipal bonds that were once tax exempt have lost their federal exemption. As a rule of thumb, municipals that lose their tax-exempt status are those whose funds will be used for nonessential purposes.

- **Parental Support** Ordinarily, if you contribute to the support of your parents by helping to pay off their real estate taxes and/or mortgage payments, such payments cannot be deducted by you. However, if you first secure an ownership interest in their property and then help to pay their taxes and mortgage payments, you will be able to shelter the deductible portion of your payments.
- **Certificates of Deposit** Some tax advisers recommend a six-month Certificate of Deposit that credits interest to you monthly. If you mature the CD after the tax year, you do not have to pay any taxes on the interest that was credited to you, but not received. Premature withdrawals, however, incur substantial penalties.
- **Real Estate Deductions** As previously discussed in this chapter, any homeowner may deduct real estate taxes and mortgage or trust deed interest payments up to two homes. If either spouse is 55 years of age or older, they do not have to pay taxes on the first $125,000 of the capital gain obtained through the sale of their home, provided that the home was their principal residence for each of the last three out of five years.
- **Individual Retirement Accounts** Some of the most popular tax shelters for employers and employees under the age of 50 have been Individual Retirement Accounts (IRAs). IRAs permit a specified limited amount of savings to be placed into these money-earning funds, which are exempt from current taxation and are only taxable on withdrawal. Under the Tax Reform Act of 1986, IRAs will not be as attractive as they originally were since a number of restrictions govern their acquisition under the new tax laws.

Contributions to IRAs may be made up to the age of 70 plus six months. They enable taxpayers to shelter from current taxes the authorized maximum annual amount of moneys placed into their respective accounts. They permit taxpayers to accumulate in their IRA fund an unlimited amount of interest, dividends, or profits, all without taxation until the money is withdrawn, at which time the amount withdrawn is subject to the regular tax rate.

Prior to 1987, contributions were limited to $2,000 per year per wage earner, ($4,000 per working married couple) and $250 for a nonworking spouse. Since 1987, tax deductible contributions to IRAs have been limited to people who are not covered by an employer-sponsored retirement plan.

Funds accumulated in IRA accounts can be self-directed or placed into various types of investments, such as stocks and bonds, real estate, mineral deposits, such as oil or gas, certificates of deposit, annuities, mutual funds, and certain types of limited partnerships. Those who do not wish to self-direct their investments usually use mutual funds.

In 1986, it was reported that the IRS ruled that the interest charged on a loan that was created to borrow funds with which to start an IRA fund was tax-deductible, thus providing a tax deduction while generating tax-free income. This ruling, however, could be affected by the changes or amendments made to the Tax Reform Act in the future.

Penalities are imposed if the money is withdrawn before the contributor reaches the age of 59½, but this rule is waived if the contributor dies or becomes disabled. The penalty for early withdrawals amounts to 10 percent, plus the payment of income taxes on the amount withdrawn. It should be noted that there is an interesting exception to the penalty clause for early withdrawal. The contributor is permitted to "roll over" (borrow) his or her funds for any reason, provided they are returned within 60 days.

Although reputable planners suggest that most wage earners should have IRAs, they are not recommended for everyone, particularly if the penalty for early withdrawal is increased.

Prospective contributors who may need the money soon for a reason such as a child's college education, should avoid the hardships they could encounter with an early withdrawal. Such hardships could include the possibility of being required to pay the combination of the early withdrawal penalty plus the payment of taxes on the withdrawn (previously untaxed) funds, all at one time. They might be better off if, instead of contributing to their IRA, they pay taxes on the money that they are using for their IRA contribution and use the net balance to try to make capital gains (profits) in other investments.

Also, if you expect any of your investments to generate capital gains or losses, it is suggested that you keep them out of an IRA. That way you take advantage of any special tax treatment that is accorded to long-term gains, and you can use a percentage of losses to offset certain types of income, as previously explained in this chapter.

Other tax exempt income, such as the interest from tax-exempt municipal bonds, should not be placed into an IRA. The reason for this is that their tax-exempt status is lost (wasted) in the IRA, and when the funds, including tax-exempt earnings, are withdrawn, they are taxed as ordinary income.

When there is a wide age difference between a couple, the bulk of their IRA funds should be placed in the younger person's account so that it can generate tax free income for a longer period of time. If, however, there is an intent to use the funds in the near future, try to place the bulk of the contributions into the older person's account. It can be withdrawn at an earlier time without penalty.

A Final Word

All the current regulations and interpretations are subject to change. Therefore, it is suggested that you secure competent, up-to-date advice before you act on any information outlined in this chapter.

＃ Section 4: X-Raying a Business

Chapter 22: How to Understand Financial Statements

How to Understand Financial Statements

Suppose some of your friends approached you because they knew that you were looking for an investment. "A few years ago," they begin, "we formed a small company. We're doing pretty well, but we need some additional capital. Rather than borrow, we would prefer to sell an equal interest to someone we know. Would you like to join us as an equal partner?"

Before you could make a non-emotional, intelligent decision, what specific, salient questions would you, as a prudent investor, be compelled to ask? And what financial know-how would you need to have to understand fully the answers that you receive?

If you knew the correct questions to ask, you might be able to find some of the answers in the company's financial statements. Unfortunately, most people do not know what questions to ask, what they mean, or how to interpret the answers they elicit.

To remedy such a deficiency, this chapter describes the correct questions to ask (56 to be specific) and outlines what the answers to these questions should be. This will help you determine the worthiness of nearly any type of investment opportunity to which you may be exposed. Also included are clear, understandable interpretations of all the answers with relevant definitions of accounting jargon and ambiguous financial terms that you will encounter in most financial statements.

Without some knowledge of how to evaluate the financial structure of an investment, the average investor should abstain from investing. I might point out to you that untold numbers of sophisticated investors, despite professional guidance, have lost large amounts of money through propositions similar to the one cited at the beginning of this chapter. They had not learned the importance of protecting themselves with additional safeguards.

Before experienced investors consider the merits of any proposition—especially if it involves sharing an investment with others—their first thought is: "If I get into this deal and don't like it, how much will it cost me in time, money, and aggravation to get out of it?" Aside from securing legal advice on this point, their next question is usually: "Will all parties sign a 'Buy and Sell' agreement?" If the answer to this question is negative, their answer to the proposition is generally also negative without any further consideration of its merits.

Protective Clauses

"Buy and Sell" agreements serve two major functions. First, they protect new investors from having the interests of the preceding investors sold to people who, for any of many reasons, might be objectionable to you without providing you with the first opportunity to purchase the interest that is for sale. If an offer to purchase the project is made to the original investors, a properly drawn "buyout agreement" gives new investors the first preference to purchase the offered interest at the same bona-fide price offered by prospective purchasers.

Second, you must be protected in the event that essential partners become disabled or die. For example, could you or your partners buy each others' interest in the venture if one of you died? Also, could inheritance taxes become a problem and cause the business to be sold to pay them? This matter should be discussed with your attorney, your accountant, and a qualified insurance agent.

Next, because your 20 percent interest in the proposition would be a minority interest, you must be concerned about who has the voting power. Frequently, propositions are offered that require an investor to furnish most of the money, but the majority of the voting rights are usually reserved for people who make no cash investment, such as friendly relatives. Avoid such propositions because, in essence, you would be giving control of your money to other people who might not care about it as much as you would. Whenever you advance the bulk of the money, look for propositions that give you at the very least a 51 percent control of the voting rights so that you will have control over how your money is used.

Sophisticated, successful investors will protect their funds by not purchasing a 20 percent interest or 20 percent of the stocks, or for that matter any other percentage of a company. Instead, they will offer to loan the money to the company in exchange for a fair rate of interest. In addition they will often require an agreement that will entitle them to receive as a bonus the future right to purchase either the discussed interest in the company or the stocks that were originally offered for sale.

The protection they receive from this type of agreement is that if the money they loan is squandered or even lost honestly, they will have a general lien against the assets of the company for the value of their loan. If they had accepted the stocks without the loan—and their money was wasted or appropriated by those controlling the majority of the voting rights—they not only would not have a lien against the assets of the company but all of the other general lien holders would have preference over them.

But, temporarily, if you are not yet a sophisticated investor and are being offered an investment by strangers or your closest friends, you can avoid bad deals and conserve your investment funds by absorbing the information in this chapter.

Request Important Financial Documents

You can start pretending to be financially sophisticated by asking for copies of the company's latest Balance Sheets, Profit and Loss Statements, and Statements of Retained Earnings. If there is an objection, you can always say that your attorney will insist that your accountant review the statements before you make a decision.

While this request is normal and business-like, it can scare away unscrupulous people who offer investment propositions with suspicious record-keeping. Whenever financial records are presented to you that you do not understand, it is always wise to refer them to your accountant for professional interpretation. The proper financial documents, properly interpreted, can reveal the true status of a business or even uncover attempts to doctor the records. If your accountant spots a legal problem, make the effort to secure legal advice.

When possible, make a visual inspection of the project. Get the aid of someone who is familiar with similar types of tangible and intangible assets.

There are two major reasons why most people do not understand financial statements: 1) they have an innate aversion to arithmetic or reading numerical data; and 2) they neither understand simple bookkeeping nor the accounting terms (technical jargon for conflicting accounting procedures used by different accounting firms).

No intelligent investor can afford to ignore or gloss over financial records. These records are the prime source of vital data from which highly important statistics and revealing ratios can be gleaned. The ratios, in particular (which are described for you later in this chapter) can provide the best clues as to whether a specific investment will fit your needs.

Since most successful investors and business people know how to use figures, they seldom involve themselves in a business or investment without first performing the required analysis. Usually, they will examine pro forma (theoretical) or specific statements and make comparisons with percentage figures already known by them from their experience. Or, they may refer to similar reliable statements from other sources in the same line of business.

Every business or investment you own, operate, or contemplate purchasing deserves the time required to understand the financial documents. These should always be maintained and kept available for review. While financial documents are always necessary for both financial and tax reasons, they cannot necessarily always be taken at face value. They must be carefully explained and interpreted.

Determine Their Accuracy

The first consideration is to determine the accuracy of the financial documents. In other words, who prepared them? And next, from where and from whom did the presenter of the documents secure the information? Finally, was the supplied information verified? And if so, by whom?

Thus, as you progress, you will begin to look for and encounter *unaudited* reports and *audited* reports. Preparers of unaudited reports may be either a bookkeeper, an accountant, or a Public or Certified Accountant in the U.S. (Chartered Accountant in Canada). While unaudited reports may be correct, they require more investigation and interpretation than audited reports. Unaudited means that the preparer accepted the figures and information without checking their reliability. When the statements contain a verification such as "the auditing steps that were followed to verify the account were in conformity with the generally approved standards of accounting principles" or "the statements have been prepared according to generally accepted accounting principles," you have what is called an audited statement.

Generally—but not always—you can rely on an audited statement to present a fair picture, provided you read the footnotes and properly interpret them along with the accompanying statements. You should know that audited statements have come under severe criticism in recent years. There have been an increasing number of expensive malpractice suits filed against both large and small members of the accounting profession.

The accounting profession has been hit so heavily that in 1985 the *Wall Street Journal* reported that "the American Institute of Certified Public Accountants, the profession's biggest trade group, is launching a campaign to convince Congress to limit accountants' liability exposure." Furthermore, the accounting profession now believes that financial reports issued by public companies are the main responsibility of management and not outside auditors. Some firms have failed almost immediately after having received clean audit opinions.

Accountancy firms that report on public corporations, such as those listed on the stock exchanges, have a choice of making four types of certification statements (opinions):

1. The "clean" opinion states that the records have been examined and fairly represent the company's activities in accordance with generally accepted accounting principles.
2. The "subject to" opinion certifies that the fairly presented results are subject to certain adjustments, such as liabilities that are not yet known.
3. The "except for" opinion is used when some part of the company has not been audited. This type of opinion is not acceptable to many governmental regulators.
4. The "disclaimer" opinion disclaims any opinion about the company's financial condition.

Qualified opinions can hurt the credit rating of the "qualified company," and may cause the company to change accountants. A "clean audit" may be worthless to you until you are able to interpret it properly because there are many legitimate variances in accounting procedures.

Whenever you analyze and compare the statements of two

inventory intensive companies, you must study their inventories. This is particularly true when prices of raw goods and finished products are fluctuating heavily. You must first determine if both companies used the same type of inventory control system. Then find out if they changed their control system during the year (if so, the change would be revealed in the footnotes).

Some companies use the LIFO system of inventory control accounting. LIFO is an acronym for "last in, first out." Other companies use the FIFO system, which is an acronym for, "first in, first out." Under the LIFO system, the inventory is valued at the latest cost, whereas in the FIFO system the inventory is valued from its earliest cost forward (actually, the inventory may be valued at its cost over a period of time). Under the FIFO system, the inventory reflects a higher price because the cost of the goods sold is lower and the gross profit is higher at the end of the accounting period. On the other hand, with the LIFO system, the cost of the goods sold during an inflationary period will be higher because they are tied to the latest purchases. These will reflect less profit. If a LIFO company buys inventory during a highly inflationary period at a low price—and the price of the inventory rises before the material is worked on and sold—the company makes a paper profit even if there is no demand for the finished merchandise.

At the same time, a FIFO company using its last cost (which because of inflation or other reasons might be much higher) will show a smaller profit for that period. This is true even if its other operating costs were equal to the LIFO company and its sales volume at the same price exceeded those of the LIFO company.

Many of the expense items that you must look for depend on the type of company you are analyzing. For example, if you are checking a transportation company, you must check insurance or self-insurance costs for accidents. This is in addition to looking at the length of its franchises, the number of passengers carried, labor, maintenance, and energy costs.

If you are checking a real estate company that owns apartment houses they want to sell you, you would have to check the total amount of rent concessions that have been granted for both the past and the future. Sometimes, you may even have to make someone else check every lease with every tenant or check the apartments to see if they are actually occupied.

Sometimes, some of these items are mentioned in the footnotes, which can also include: changes in the company's method of depreciating fixed assets, stock dividends, and splits that change the value of outstanding stocks; profit-sharing; employment contracts; and retirement plans. If you require information that is not in the reports or in the footnotes, contact the officers of the company or have your attorney or accountant secure the information for you. Usually, a company's annual report, professionally and conscientiously prepared, will contain nearly all of the financial documents that you will require.

The basic three documents are usually referred to as The Balance Sheet, The Profit and Loss Statement, and The Statement of Accumulated Retained Earnings. Sample forms of these important documents are shown on following pages. Unfortunately, the figures in these statements, when read by themselves without comparison to either the company's prior records or those of similar companies in the same industry, are not as useful as they could be. They are, nevertheless, vital documents for decision-making on your part.

Whether evaluating banks, private companies, public entities, specific businesses, or investment ventures, the best way to handle these statements is to use them comparatively. Make written comparisons between the various important items reported for different periods of time. First, compare the most recent quarterly and annual figures with those of the last few quarters and also for the past few years. Then compare them with those of other similarly-sized companies in the same industry. You will find a Blank Investment Analysis Chart provided for your use.

Next, the differences between the various financial statements are described. Then you are shown what they look like in an abbreviated form. Finally, the 56 questions that you should ask, secure answers to, and understand are presented. These should be applied before making an investment, whether it be in business or the stock market.

The Balance Sheet

The first financial statement discussed is the Balance Sheet, sometimes referred to as a Statement of Financial Condition. When it is not complete, it is called a Condensed Balance Sheet. When it refers to a corporation and its subsidiaries, it is called a Consolidated Balance Sheet.

In its condensed form, a Balance Sheet shows (as of a specific date) the nature and amount of the entity's liabilities and capital assets. It reveals:

- The amount of money that an individual, company, or corporation owns
- What it owes
- The ownership interest of the stockholders or owners of the company

The Balance Sheet is so named because the total amount of the assets must balance with (equal) the Total of Liabilities plus the Total of Stockholders' Equity.

The Total of Stockholders' Equity consists of the totals of all of the outstanding common and preferred stock (the total ownership interest, not loans), plus the Accumulated Retained Earnings.

Earnings

Another important financial document is called either the Profit and Loss Statement, the Income Statement, a Statement of Income, or an Earnings Report. The function of these documents is to list the profits and losses of a company over a specified period of time. It lists earned income, expenses, and the resulting profit or loss.

The third major financial document is referred to as either a Statement of Retained Earnings, Statement of Earned Surplus, or an Accumulated Retained Earnings Statement. These statements measure the value of assets accumulated against a period of time over the total of Liabilities and the stockholders' Equity. An Accumulated Retained Earnings Statement reflects the total of all of the annual Net Surpluses since the inception of the company.

If you want to know the amount of money, goods, and properties the company owns and how much money is owed to it, look at the Balance Sheet under *Total Assets*. Assets that will be realized within a year are called *Current Assets*.

The claims of creditors against the Total Assets are called *Total Liabilities*. The liabilities that fall due within a year are called *Current Liabilities*.

SAMPLE BALANCE SHEET

ASSETS

CURRENT ASSETS		
Cash in Banks	$ 50,000	
Accounts Receivable	100,000	
Inventories	50,000	
TOTAL CURRENT ASSETS		$ 200,000
Net Value of Property, Land & Equipment	50,000	
TOTAL ASSETS		$ 250,000

LIABILITIES AND STOCKHOLDERS' EQUITY

CURRENT LIABILITIES		
Accounts Payable	$ 45,000	
Accrued Expenses Payable	25,000	
Federal Income Taxes Payable	25,000	
TOTAL CURRENT LIABILITIES	95,000	
TRUST DEED DUE IN TWO YEARS	5,000	
TOTAL LIABILITIES		$ 100,000
STOCKHOLDERS' EQUITY		
5% Preferred Stock	$ 50,000	
Common Stock (1000 shares)	50,000	
Accumulated Retained Earnings	50,000	
TOTAL STOCKHOLDERS' EQUITY		$ 150,000
TOTAL LIABILITIES & STOCKHOLDERS' EQUITY		$ 250,000

When you want to learn the amount of a company's net profit or loss for the year, you refer to the income statements. Samples are shown below. These statements may also be called a Profit and Loss Statement, because they show all of the profit less costs and expenses.

Sample of Abbreviated and Condensed Income Statement

Net Sales:	$ 500,000
Other Income:	5,000
Gross Income:	$ 505,000
Cost of Sales and Operating Expense:	$ 420,000
Interest on Bonds:	None
Federal Income Tax:	25,000
Total of Gross Expense:	45,000
NET INCOME	$ 60,000

If you want to know how much *Net Income* was retained by the company after paying all of its dividends, you total all of the net surpluses since the inception of the company to derive the *Accumulated Retained Earnings*. These need not be in cash.

Sample of Accumulated Retained Earnings Statement

	Balance (At Beginning of Fiscal Year):	$ 1,000
	Add: (Net Profit for the year):	60,000
	Total	61,000
LESS	(Dividends Paid On: Preferred Stock	2,500
	Common Stock)	5,000
	TOTAL	$ 7,500
NET SURPLUS		53,500
ACCUMULATED RETAINED EARNINGS		
	(balance at end of fiscal year)	$ 54,500

The 56 Question Test

You are provided with detailed information about the importance of each question, how to solve the question and understand the answer. Necessary definitions are also included. Answers to some of the questions, such as those used for researching manufacturing companies, may not be necessary for non-manufacturing businesses.

An Investment Analysis and Comparison Chart is included at the end of this chapter. This chart helps you review financial

How to Understand Financial Statements 255

statements in order to extract, record, and analyze the vital information of any company. It also helps you compare those companies that are in the same industry.

A Quick Preview of the 56 Questions That You Should Ask (Detailed answers and explanations follow question 56.)

In most instances, the following questions are restated for easy understanding or clarification.

1. How much were the net sales? (How much business did the company transact in the last 12 months?)
2. In the reasonably near future (less than a year), how much of the company's cash and assets will be available in cash? In other words, what are its current assets?
3. What is the value of the company's physical assets (such as land) after deducting book depreciation on such assets as buildings and equipment? These are distinguished from other assets such as cash, current assets, and intangibles (patents and goodwill).
4. How much of the company's assets are tied up in inventories? This includes raw materials to be used in the product, partially finished goods (or work) in process, and finished goods.
5. What are the company's intangible assets? (How much of the total assets are comprised of non-physical, intangible assets and rights, such as goodwill, patents, trademarks, copyrights, franchises, etc.?)
6. What is the tangible net worth? (What is the total value of the entire stockholders' investment in the company?)
7. What are the total assets? (If the company were to go out of business as of the date on the balance sheet, how much cash would all of the assets produce?)
8. How much are the total current liabilities? (What is the total amount of money that the corporation will be compelled to pay out in the normal course of its business within one year of the date on the balance sheet?)
9. Aside from the bonds and the total current liabilities, how much money does the company owe its creditors that is not repayable within one year from the date on the balance sheet?

10. What is the amount of accrued federal income tax at the date of the balance sheet or earnings statement?
11. What are the total liabilities? (What is the grand total of all of the money that the company owes to all its creditors excluding stockholders and bondholders?)
12. What is the capitalization of the company from bonds? (How much money has been loaned to the company in the form of funded debt such as bonds?)
13. What is the common stock capitalization of the corporation? (How many shares of common stock are outstanding that will share in the net proceeds after the owners of the bonds and the preferred stock are paid their respective interest and dividends?)
14. What is the amount of the preferred stock capitalization of the corporation? (How many shares of stock have a preferred claim on the company's earnings before payment can be made on the common stock?)
15. What is the net worth of the total of the stockholders' equity? (Assuming that on the date on the balance sheet the corporation was liquidated and every asset was sold for its balance sheet value, what dollar value would the stockholders receive after all liabilities were completely paid?
16. What is the annual amount of total interest payable on the bonds and dividends on preferred stocks? (How much money is required each year to pay both the prescribed dividend rate for the preferred stock and the interest rate on the bonds?)
17. What is the net working capital—net current assets? (If all of the current liabilities are paid off within one year from the date on the balance sheet, how much money would be left?)
18. What is the amount of the accumulated retained earnings— earned surplus? (How much money has the company retained out of its past earnings, including money that may have been used to purchase new machinery or equipment, etc., that has not been paid out in dividends?)
19. After paying taxes, but before paying any dividends, how much profit did the company earn in each of the last three years?
20. What are the pre-tax profits? (Without considering income tax obligations, how much money did the company earn?)

How to Understand Financial Statements 257

21. What is the company's cash flow from operations? (How much additional working capital could the company show if all of the bookkeeping deductions were added to the reported net income?)
22. What is the book value of the common stock? (If the company were to be instantly dissolved as of the date on the balance sheet, how much money would each share of outstanding common stock be worth?)
23. What is the percentage of net income to net worth? (What is the percentage of net profit that has been earned by the company compared to the value of the investment that has been made by the stockholders?)
24. What is the company's current ratio? (What is the proportion of working capital—current assets—to liabilities?)
25. What are the quick assets of the company? (Out of the current assets that can be converted into immediate cash, how many dollars will there be for for each dollar of current liabilities?)
26. What is the company's liquidity ratio? (What is the ratio of the amount of total cash, U.S. Government securities, and marketable securities owned by the company when compared to its total of current liabilities?)
27. What are the company's respective capitalization ratios for bonds, preferred stock, and common stock? (What percentage of the company is owned respectively by the bondholders, preferred stockholders, and common stockholders?)
28. What is the ratio of the total stockholders' equity to debt? (Compared to the stockholders' total equity—net worth—how much are the total liabilities?)
29. What is the ratio of debt? (What is the amount of debt for each share of stock?)
30. What is the ratio of total liabilities to total net worth? (Does the company owe too much money in proportion to what the stockholders own in the company?)
31. What is the ratio of the funded debt to tangible net worth? (Is there too much bond indebtedness for the amount of the company's tangible net worth?)
32. What is the ratio of current debt to inventory? (Is the company's debt too high when compared to the amount of inventory it has on hand?)

33. What is the company's overall coverage? (By how many times did the company's adjusted operating profit—profit before paying interest on bonds but after taxes—exceed the combined total paid for interest on the bonds and the dividends on the preferred stock?)
34. What is the ratio of fixed assets to the tangible net worth? (Does the company have too much of its net worth—as asked in Question 6—invested in fixed assets—as asked in Question 3?)
35. What is the miscellaneous assets to net worth ratio? (What is the quality of the assets that comprise net working capital?)
36. What is the quality of the working capital assets in relation to the net worth ratio? (How much of the current assets consist of the type of inventory and accounts receivable that are not easily collectible?)
37. How much money was paid as a dividend on each share of common stock for each of the past three years?
38. What was the percentage of dividend payout from earnings? (How much of the income was paid out in dividends?)
39. What is the percentage of yield? (What percentage of profit is returned to the stockholder for the amount of money paid for the stock?)
40. What is the earnings ratio per share of common stock? (What percentage of money did each share of common stock earn?)
41. What was the preferred dividend coverage? (How many times were the preferred dividends earned?)
42. What was the percentage of profit on the stockholders' equity? (What was the profit percentage on the total amount of money invested by the stockholders?)
43. What was the ratio of net profits to net working capital? (Is the company making enough profit for the amount of working capital that is available to it?)
44. What is the ratio of net profit to net sales? (What percentage of profit does the company earn for each dollar of sales?)
45. What is the ratio of pre-tax profits to sales? (How efficient is the management?)
46. What is the ratio of sales to fixed assets? (Is the money that has been allocated by management to enlarge the production facilities of the company being spent wisely?)

47. What is the ratio of net sales to inventory? (Is the company buying too much inventory for the amount of sales that it is transacting?)
48. What is the ratio of net sales to net worth or turnover of tangible net worth? (When compared to the amount of money that the company is worth, is the sales volume too high, too low, or adequate?)
49. What is the ratio of net sales to working capital or turnover of net working capital? (Is the company making enough sales for the amount of working capital that it has available?)
50. What is the ratio of inventory to working capital? (Does the company have more money invested in inventory than is warranted by the amount of its working capital?)
51. How much backlog is there? (What is the dollar value of unfilled orders for future delivery?)
52. What is the ratio of stock price to price-earnings? (If I want to buy the stock, how many times what it earned per share—not dividends—will you have to pay for it?)
53. Could the proper evaluation of the financial report have been affected by a change in the company's accounting procedures or the inclusion in the report of non-recurring profits or losses, for an extraordinary income derived from the sale of a plant asset, or some unusual deferment such as tax?
54. Will the earnings be affected by the company's contemplation of (1) a new major product, (2) an acquisition of another company, or (3) the discontinuance of an unsuccessful part of its business?
55. Is it contemplated that any major amount of money derived from additional capitalization or from accumulated retained earnings will be used for capital expenditures?
56. If the company in which you have been invited to invest is not a stock company, will your capital contribution be used to pay indebtedness, such as back salaries or part of the company's excessive obligations, or can you control your investment so that it will be used to enhance future growth?

When you have secured the answers to these questions, you may consider that you have done part of your investment homework. The other part of your financial education consists of understanding the answers to the questions.

As previously recommended, you should compare your answers for the same company for different quarterly periods and years. Then compare them with the balance sheets of similar companies in the same business. With this analysis, you should be able to make intelligent investment decisions.

However, before you can properly evaluate answers, you must become familiar with ratios, how to create them, and how to use them.

Ratios—Their Importance and How to Create and Understand Them

What is a ratio? Literally, a ratio is a comparison between the quantities of two different things. It expresses the number of times that the first number contains the second number. Every answer that states a numerical comparison, such as 4 to 1, is a ratio. It can be expressed as a percentage (400%), as a "times" basis (4 times), or simply as a comparison to the figures that were intended to be compared (4 to 1).

Let's assume that you want to find out the stock-to-bond ratio of a corporation that has issued 4,000 shares of stock and 1,000 bonds. To create the ratio, you divide the amount of the first item that is being compared—in this instance the 4,000 stocks—by the second item, 1,000 bonds. The 4,000 stocks divided by 1,000 bonds gives you a stock-to-bond ratio of 4 to 1, meaning four stocks for each bond.

If you want to express the same answer as a percentage, the figure that precedes the percent sign means it is fraction of 100. Thus four percent equals 4/100, or the decimal equivalent of .04. A four percent ratio of stock to bonds means one share of stock to every 25 bonds. A 400 percent ratio equals four stocks to every bond.

When the word "times" is used in the ratio, such as how many times the annual net profit exceeds the amount paid on preferred dividend payments, the second number in the ratio—the number that is not given—is always 1. Thus, if the times ratio number is 10, the meaning is 10 to 1. From this point on, unless otherwise indicated, the ratios expressed are in percentages.

The Explanations of the 56 Questions and Answers

QUESTION 1.
How much were the net sales? (How much business did the company transact in the last twelve months?)

Definitions: The net sales figures, found in the Profit and Loss statement, disclose the dollar value of the amounts of goods or services sold in one year, less the value of returned goods and allowances for price reductions. Costs or expenses are not included, even though the word "net" might lead you to believe they are.

Railroads and public utilities call it operating revenue. When there are secondary sources of income, these are usually referred to as "other income."

Importance: The primary purpose of any business is to make profits. Net sales or operating revenue give the first clue as to the size and activity of the company. I use sales figures to make comparisons between current annual sales and those of prior years. By comparing those records with records of similar companies in the same industry, and by using the net sales figure as a basis for many of the ratios I create and discuss as we proceed, I am prepared to evaluate the quality of management and make predictions about the company's future profits and value.

Solution: Corporations issue annual, interim quarterly, or semi-annual financial statements. These types of statements are referred to as a Profit and Loss Statement, a statement of Income, or a variation of those terms. Net sales is usually the first figure on such statements.

QUESTION 2.
In the reasonably near future (less than a year), how much of the company's cash and assets will be available in cash? In other words, what are its current assets?

Definition: Current assets are the totals of cash and assets or resources that are expected to be transformed into cash during the normal operating cycle of the business. Current assets are also referred to as working assets.

Importance: Total current assets are a major indicator of the company's cash liquidity and ability to meet its obligations. Because the total current assets figure is invaluable, I use it many times to help you evaluate the company and its management. For example, in Question 17, I use it to determine both the company's working capital (net current assets) and the ever-important current ratio in Question 24.

Solution: Current assets are usually specifically listed on the asset side of the balance sheet. You find the total current assets by adding the following assets: cash, marketable securities at cost or not in excess of market value, accounts and notes receivable for the sale of merchandise in normal trade channels (less provisions for bad debts), and inventories at cost or market, whichever is lower.

QUESTION 3.
What is the value of the company's physical assets—such as land—after deducting book depreciation on assets? Depreciation is taken on items such as buildings and equipment. These are distinguished from other assets such as cash, current assets, and intangibles (patents and goodwill).

Definition: Fixed assets equal the sum of the cost of the value of the land plus the depreciated book value of the buildings, leasehold improvements, fixtures, furniture, machinery, tools, and equipment. They do not include inventory. Depreciation is the amount of decrease in value—due to wear and tear and a decline in prices—that is allowed when computing the value of the property for tax purposes. The actual value is usually greater than the depreciated value. Land is never depreciated; and its cost value remains constant even though its market value may be much lower or higher.

Importance: The fixed assets are an excellent figure for comparison purposes. They do not, however, indicate market value or the replacement cost in the future. This is because the figure is based on actual cost less the accumulated yearly depreciation. It tells us how much money is invested in the type of assets which are used repeatedly in the performance of the entire operation from manufacturing to transportation. A large amount of fixed assets can indicate either deep financial strength or heavy liabilities. Favor the company that can reflect a comparatively good sales job and profits with less fixed assets than its competitors. Industrial companies should not show a constant decline in current assets as compared to fixed assets.

The fixed assets of railroads, transportation companies, and public utilities are usually much greater than those of industrial companies.

QUESTION 4.
How much of the company's assets are tied up in inventories? This includes raw materials to be used in the product, partially finished goods (or work) in process, and finished goods.

Importance: Properly used, inventory figures (found under assets in the balance sheet) may disclose errors or attempted frauds. At the same time they can help you in subsequent questions to evaluate management and future prospects for profits.

Later, to determine the inventory-to-sales turnover, first compare inventory to sales; then compare the ratio of inventory to current assets. The inventory figure can signal danger if it is too heavy or too light for the season, for economic conditions, for general circumstances, or for the amount of sales projected for the year. It can also help gauge the age and salability of the company's materials and goods.

QUESTION 5.
What are the company's intangible assets? (How much of the total assets are comprised of non-physical, intangible assets and rights such as goodwill, patents, trademarks, copyrights, franchises, etc.?)

Importance: An investor can be easily misled by a company that overstates the value of its intangible assets (under assets on the balance sheet). Although goodwill and patents can be valuable, care must be taken that they not be unrealistically overstated in value. You should also use intangible value to determine the tangible net worth of the company by subtracting it from the stockholders' equity.

QUESTION 6.
What is the tangible net worth? (What is the total value of the entire stockholders' investment in the company?)

Definition: Tangible net worth equals the amount of money invested by the stockholders plus accumulated retained earnings. It is also referred to as stockholders' equity or owners' equity or capital.

Technically, intangible assets should be subtracted. Tangible net worth does not mean the present market value of the assets.

Importance: This figure aids in many significant evaluations, such as:

- Does the company require additional capital to increase its sales and profits?
- Does the company borrow too much or have too much worth for the amount of business it transacts?

To evaluate the financial strength of the company, you must compare liabilities to net worth as done for Question 30.

Solution: Total the preference stocks, the common stocks, the surplus, and the undivided profits called stockholders equity. Then subtract the intangible assets as described for Question 5.

Analysis: If the current debts exceed approximately 66 percent of the tangible net worth, or if the total debts exceed approximately 75 percent of the tangible net worth, then the manufacturing company requires careful evaluation.

QUESTION 7.
What are the total assets? (If the company were to go out of business as of the date on the balance sheet, how much cash would all the assets produce?)

Definition: All property of any nature owned by the company to which it either holds title or an equity interest—whether paid for or not—is included in total assets.

Importance: The total assets, although only a bookkeeping figure, enables you to compare that category to the liabilities to make important comparisons. These evaluations help you determine the financial position of the company. (Actually, if the company were to go out of business as assumed in the question above, it most likely would not receive the amount of dollars listed for each asset.)

Solution: Add up all the assets listed in Questions 2, 3, 4, and 5, and all other assets listed on the asset side of the balance sheet.

QUESTION 8.
How much are the total current liabilities? (What is the total amount of money that the corporation will be compelled to pay out in the normal course of its business within one year of the date on the balance sheet?)

Definition: Every debt and obligation that falls due within one year of the date on the balance sheet is referred to as a current liability. The total of all such debts are called total current liabilities.

Importance: Compare the total current liabilities with the total current assets. This lets you determine both the amount of working capital that is or will be available and to set up the all-important current ratio (discussed more fully in Question 17), which is a primary method for determining the financial strength of a company. When total current liabilities exceed the total current assets, the company is usually in deep trouble because it has no working capital and may be declared bankrupt. Most analysts prefer that the amount of total current assets be at least double the company's total current liabilities.

QUESTION 9.
Aside from the bonds and the total current liabilities, how much money does the company owe its creditors that is not repayable within one year from the date on the balance sheet?

Definitions: Long-term debts comprise all debts or liabilities—other than bonds—that need not be repaid within one year from the date on the balance sheet that lists them.

Importance: The long-term debt and respective due dates of each obligation, as well as the amount of interest incurred and to be paid, are important factors. Any of them can affect profits. Also, by learning the amount of long-term credit that has been extended to the company, and by whom, you can get an idea of the company's credit worthiness. During inflationary periods, some speculators seek out companies with large amounts of long-term debt to derive the benefit of the extra earnings that can be secured through the use of leverage. However, leverage can be dangerous if profits or interest rates have a rapid decline.

As used herein, leverage refers to the percentage of debt to equity in an investment, or the financial principle of using less cash to increase the percentage of profit on the cash outlay. For example, if a person purchases a $100,000 item for $10,000 cash down and the balance on credit, and then immediately sells the item for $110,000, the percentage of profit on the amount of cash invested is 100 percent. If he had paid $100,000 in cash, the percentage of profit would be only 10 percent.

Analysis: The amount of the long-term debt should not be disproportionate to the total assets. If a lien or mortgage is given at the time that the liability is created, then that respective creditor possesses a prior claim over the stockholder to the specific item liened, together with a general claim on the total assets. General claims against assets are similar to those possessed by creditors who do not possess secured liens or obligations. Railroads and utilities usually have higher long-term debts than industrial companies.

Solution: Check liabilities in the balance sheet or see the statement of earnings.

QUESTION 10.
What is the amount of accrued federal income tax at the date of the balance sheet or earnings statement?

Definition: Any taxes due the federal government and unpaid are considered accrued. Deferred taxes refer to special savings affected by tax devices.

Importance: In addition to being a major liability that should be included under total liabilities, accrued taxes, such as unpaid federal income taxes, constitute a first lien against the company.

Analysis: Taxes may be accrued or deferred. When the fiscal year for the company has been completed, the corporate tax is computed, which becomes a liability as of that date. Interim financial statements should also make provisions for federal income tax liability, which should appear as "accrued federal income taxes payable." Many investors confuse "accrued" with "deferred" because they are under the false impression that deferred means that the actual payment of the taxes has been deferred until a future date. However, this is incorrect because accountants say "deferred tax" when they refer to a tax savings effected by special tax devices such as accelerated depreciation, investment credits, and installment sales. These tax savings devices actually reduce income taxes for the year paid and produce additional profits.

QUESTION 11.
What are the total liabilities? (What is the grand total of all of the money that the company owes to all its creditors excluding stockholders and bondholders?)

Definition: Liabilities consist of any claims against the company.

Importance: The financial strength of a company is determined by the ratio of total assets over total liabilities. After you establish the size of the total debt, you compare it to the net worth (as described with Question 30) to determine how much of the business is actually owned by creditors and how much is owned by the company.

Solution: Look for total liabilities in the balance sheet, or total the answers from Questions 8, 9, and 10.

QUESTION 12.
What is the capitalization of the company from bonds? (How much money has been loaned to the company in the form of funded debt such as bonds?)

Definition: Interest-bearing bonds or long-term bank loans are referred to as "funded debt." Capitalization refers to all of the securities issued by the company, such as bonds and preferred and common stock. (A bond, or debenture, is much like a promissory note, and its holder is a creditor, not an owner of the company). Short-term loans are not included under capitalization. Usually, short-term loans are due in one year or less.

Importance: The interest on bonds must be paid before dividends are paid on either the preferred or common stock. When the bond interest is too heavy, a company may have a large volume of sales without earning any money for the stockholders. If the corporation has borrowed too much money in the form of bonds, then the value of the preferred and common stock is weakened and the corporation may experience difficulty in securing additional capital.

Usually no more than 25 percent of a corporation's capitalization should be in bonds, although the capitalization of railroads and public utilities can exceed 50 percent. This is because of their unusually high investment in fixed assets, such as tracks and real estate.

Solution: Capitalization figures are usually derived from liabilities in the balance sheet under the categories of "long-term liabilities" or "long-term debt."

QUESTION 13.
What is the common stock capitalization of the corporation? (How many shares of common stock are outstanding that will share in the net proceeds after the owners of the bonds and the preferred stock are paid their respective interest and dividends?)

Definition: Ownership shares of stock that do not have any special rights or obligations are usually referred to as common stock. Even so, there may be two or more classes of common stock with one class having special rights. One class of common stock may be referred to as "par value," another as "no par value," and another as "stated value" stock. Literally, any stock with a preference should be called a preferred stock, but the type of common stock referred to above would not be termed a preferred stock. If you encounter these classes of common stock, check their rights carefully.

Importance: The common stock capitalization is necessary to:

- Calculate how much money each share of common stock earned when you divide the total amount of shares into earnings (Question 40)
- Determine the respective ratios of common stocks to preferred stocks as well as bonds.

If management does not own at least 20 percent of the common stock, the company is exposed to being taken over by other companies that can secure control by a procedure called a "tender offer." If there are any convertible bonds that can be converted into common stock, anticipate that the amount of outstanding common stock will be increased. This will reduce the equity of the common stockholders.

Solution: Look under liabilities on the balance sheet for either stockholders' equity, capital stock, or shareholders' equity.

Analysis: Corporations that have issued large amounts of common stock may earn millions of dollars but each stockholder's share of declared dividends may be negligible because of the great number of stockholders that must share in the profits. Unless the earnings of the corporation are exceptionally high, the common stock should not constitute less than 50 percent of the capitalization. But utilities, such as electric and gas companies which have steady earnings, may have as little as a 25 percent to 30 percent common stock and surplus ratio to the total capitalization (Question 27).

On some balance sheets, par value per share is used to compute the dollar amount of capitalization. The "par value" of a stock is set by the issuing corporation at the time that the stock is originally sold as part of the capitalization process. The "market value" is the price that a buyer will pay for the stock on the open market.

Companies that issue a "no par value stock" give a stated par value on the balance sheet.

QUESTION 14.
What is the amount of the preferred stock capitalization of the corporation? (How many shares of stock have a preferred claim on the company's earnings before payment can be made on the common stock?)

Definition: Preferred stock consists of any class of stock that has a claim against the company's earnings before dividends can be declared on the common stock, together with a priority over the common stock if the company liquidates.

Importance: Check the company's earnings to determine if a sufficient amount of money has been earned to pay a common stock dividend after the preferred stock has been paid. Common stock dividends may only be paid out of an earned surplus. Thus, if no money is left over after paying the preferred dividends, then a common stock dividend may not be declared.

Solution: See the liabilities side of the balance sheet under stockholders' equity or capital.

Analysis: Most preferred stock is cumulative, which means that if the dividends on the preferred are in arrears, no dividends can be declared on the common. The rights of preferred stockholders are determined by the contract of sale, but any payment thereon must first be declared by the Board of Directors. A dividend cannot be declared if the current or accumulated earnings are insufficient.

Ordinarily, preferred shareholders do not receive any voting rights but, in some instances, such as if their dividend is omitted, they are granted a vote. Some preferred stocks are convertible into common stock and some may be redeemed by the company. When the stipulated preferred dividend is much higher than the current prevailing rate of interest, corporations are tempted to redeem any preferred stocks that are subject to recall. According to the terms under which the preferred stock was issued, the corporation usually reserves the right to purchase ("redeem") the preferred stock at a premium or par price at or before the maturity date. This is advantageous to the corporation if prevailing interest rates are much lower than the amount of interest it is paying on the preferred stock.

QUESTION 15.
What is the net worth of the total of the stockholders' equity? (Assuming that on the date on the balance sheet the corporation was liquidated and every asset was sold for its balance sheet value, what dollar value would the stockholders receive after all liabilities were completely paid?)

Definition: The net worth of the total of the stockholders' equity is the equivalent of the sum total of the following:

- The dollar value of all of the classes of stock
- The capital surplus (surplus and reserve accounts)
- The accumulated retained earnings

Importance: In addition to revealing the stockholders' equity in the company, the answer should also be used to determine if the company transacts too little or too much business for the amount of capital invested in it. Also, the answer may be compared to the net worth and the amount of business transacted by similar companies in the same industry, or to the net worth record of the same company for prior years. In Questions 34, 43, and 48, you also use net worth to compare it to fixed assets, percentage of profits, and net sales.

QUESTION 16.
What is the annual amount of total interest payable on the bonds and dividends on the preferred stocks? (How much money is required each year to pay both the prescribed dividend rate for the preferred stock and the interest rate on the bonds?)

Importance: The common stockholders cannot receive any cash dividends until the above requirement is met. Therefore, when compared to the earnings, if the combined interest and dividend payments are too high, the dividends (if any) remaining for the common stockholders will be limited or omitted. On the other hand, if the company has a surplus of net earnings, which may amount to much more than the amount of interest and dividends in question, then the Board of Directors has the option of declaring a larger dividend.

Solution: Multiply the number of outstanding bonds by the interest rate and add that number to the sum of the outstanding preferred stock multiplied by the dividend rate.

Analysis: The safety of both the company and its securities is contingent on the size of the difference between the earnings and the amount that must be paid out for bonds and preferred stock. This ratio is discussed in Question 33 (overall interest coverage).

Net earnings cannot be determined until bond interest is paid. Preferred stock dividends, which may only be paid from net earnings, are the earnings after interest and taxes are paid.

QUESTION 17.
What is the net working capital—net current assets? (If all of the current liabilities are paid off within one year from the date on the balance sheet, how much money would be left?)

Definition: If all current debts are paid off, the amount of current assets that would remain would be referred to as net working capital or net current assets. When economists discuss assets, they usually refer to working capital as distinguished from net working capital.

Importance: A company without net working capital cannot pay its obligations or expand unless it secures new financing. This may be difficult to procure when there is a shortage of working capital. Hence, the company's growth potential may be limited.

Solution: Subtract the total current liabilities (Question 8) from the total current assets (Question 2).

Analysis: An industrial company is considered to have sufficient net working capital if its total current assets are at least twice as much as the total current liabilities.

In Question 24, divide current assets by the total liabilities to obtain the current ratio, which is one of the most used ratios. Use it to evaluate comparative amounts of working capital when comparing ratios of similar companies in the same industry.

QUESTION 18.
What is the amount of the accumulated retained earnings—earned surplus? (How much money has the company retained out of its past earnings, including money that may have been used to purchase new machinery or equipment, etc., that has not been paid out in dividends?)

Definition: The difference between the total assets of a company and the liabilities, including outstanding stock and any capital surplus, is the equivalent of earned surplus or accumulated retained earnings.

Importance: The answer reflects the amount of money that currently belongs to the stockholders. This is money that the company has been able to accumulate from the net profit of prior years after paying dividends on preferred and common stock.

Solution: The answer can be obtained from the statement of income and/or the accumulated retained earnings statement.

Analysis: An earned surplus is not necessarily a tangible amount of money or an amount on deposit in a bank. The figure obtained helps to indicate the past success or current financial strength of the business operation. It does not include capital surplus, which results from an overpayment of stocks, etc.

QUESTION 19.
After paying taxes—but before paying any dividends—how much profit did the company earn in each of the last three years?

Definition: The amount of money earned in the last fiscal years or the earned surplus accounts that are available for dividends are referred to as net earnings or net profits.

Importance: Earnings plus the comparison of annual earnings records form a basis for creating both important ratios and evaluations about management and the future.

Although the major interest is in future net earnings, it is sometimes helpful to derive your estimate using the net profit figures of a few prior years. Some people compare the prior 3 years, some compare 5 or 10 years, and some use a 15-year period for comparison.

Solution: See the statement of income.

QUESTION 20.
What are the pre-tax profits? (Without considering income tax obligations, how much money did the company earn?)

Definition: The amount of money earned after deducting all costs but before deducting taxes and dividends.

Importance: It is an important base figure that is used to make evaluations of management and to establish subsequent ratios.

Solution: The answer can be either in the statement of earnings or in the cash flow statement.

Analysis: The answer will tell you how much money the company earned after paying all interest but before paying taxes and dividends. When internal management is evaluated, it is important to consider the amount of profits before taxes, because changes in the tax rates or in the accounting methods of figuring taxes may unfairly reflect for or against management, particularly when making comparisons with the records of prior years and of similar companies. Without comparisons, pre-tax profits are not very meaningful.

QUESTION 21.
What is the company's cash flow from operations? (How much additional working capital could the company show if all of the bookkeeping deductions were added to the reported net income?)

Definitions: Cash flow from operations consists of the reported net income of the corporation, plus any amounts that have been charged off as depreciation, depletion, amortization, or extraordinary charges to reserves.

Cash flow from operations should not be confused with a statement of source and application of funds. The latter emanates from the income statement, when by converting the income statement from the accrual to a cash basis, accountants show *how* the cash was acquired and expended. Under the accrual basis of accounting, each item is regarded as an earning or as an incurred expense without regard to when payments are received or made. These statements consider non-income items such as funds obtained from the sale of fixed assets, long term borrowing, the reduction of long term liabilities, and expenditures for plant equipment.

Importance: Cash flow from operations is important because it reflects the corporation's ability to pay dividends. Net earnings by themselves do not always reflect the company's actual, usable assets because of the large amount of funds that may have been deducted in bookkeeping procedures in the form of depreciation, depletion, amortization, or extraordinary charges to reserves. Those deductions are considered a source of income for the company, even though they may not be in cash. The funds from depreciation, if in cash, may be saved to replace the equipment, or spent at will.

Solution: From the income statement and the statement of application of funds, add the net income to all of the funds on the financial reports that have been charged off to depreciation, depletion, amortization, and extraordinary charges to reserves.

Analysis: Companies with large non-cash deductions may, if they have the cash, pay larger dividends or finance expansion, even though their net income does not seem to warrant any expenditures.

QUESTION 22.
What is the book value of the common stock? (If the company were to be instantly dissolved as of the date on the balance sheet, how much money would each share of outstanding common stock be worth?)

Definition: The book value of the common stock (the net tangible assets per share) is the figure derived by adding all assets, not including intangibles, deducting all debts and other liabilities, then adding the liquidation price of all preferred issues, and finally, dividing the amount by the number of shares of common stock.

Importance: This answer is required to make comparisons with the book values of similarly priced stocks in the same types of companies in the same industry, as well as to learn and evaluate how much of the company's earnings for each of the past few years were consistently put back into the business.

Solution: Add the stated or par value of the outstanding common stock (Question 13) to the capital surplus account (see balance sheet) plus the earned surplus accounts (Question 18). Then divide by the number of shares of common stock (Question 13).

Analysis: The net book value of the common stocks of banks and investment and insurance companies is a better value indicator than the net book value of the common stocks of most industrial companies. This is because the assets of financial institutions are usually in the form of securities that can be more easily converted into cash than the plant and equipment assets owned by industrial companies.

The net book value of the common stocks of public utilities is usually supported by a stated guaranteed fair return on the amount of the stockholders' investment. A constant loss of book value is a warning signal that the firm's asset values may be too low for its outstanding obligations.

It should be noted that the book value of the assets of a corporation may not have any significant relationship to market value. This is because investors may be keenly interested in the possibility of large future profits and may pay more than the book value for that privilege.

QUESTION 23.
What is the percentage of net income to net worth? (What is the percentage of net profit that has been earned by the company, compared to the value of the investment that has been made by the stockholders?)

Definitions: Net income means net profit, whereas net worth indicates the value of the stockholders' interest in the company.

Importance: A low percentage of profit could indicate that the amount of money invested by the stockholders in the company could be invested elsewhere in a more profitable venture.

Solution: Divide the net income (Question 19) by the net worth (Question 15).

Analysis: The ratio of net income to net worth is related to and dependent upon two factors:

- The combined percentage of profit earned on each sales dollar (Question 44) together with
- The number of dollars of sales volume transacted with respect to each dollar of its invested capital (Question 48).

QUESTION 24.
What is the company's current ratio? (What is the proportion of working capital—current assets—to current liabilities?)

Definition: The current ratio is the figure arrived at by dividing the current assets by the current liabilities.

Importance: The answer may be expressed as a proportion ratio or as a percentage, which is an accepted major guide for evaluating the company's financial position (also see Question 36). The answer also indicates how many dollars of current assets there are for each dollar of liabilities.

Analysis: To change a current ratio into a percentage, multiply the current ratio (the first number) such as the 2 in a 2-to-1 ratio by 100.

A low ratio can indicate that the company may experience difficulty in paying its debts. Although not conclusive, a 2-to-1 ratio is considered satisfactory. However, a company that collects cash and has few accounts receivable, or a company that collects its receivables before it pays for what it has received and sold, may not require a 2-to-1 current ratio.

When comparing the current ratios for prior years, a gradual increase is usually a healthy sign. On the other hand, too high a current ratio, such as 3 or 4 to 1, may be a signal of bad management, because it may disclose an improper use of working capital (see Question 43). There may also be an imbalance in the amount of business being transacted which can be determined from the earnings statement (Question 49).

QUESTION 25.
What are the quick assets of the company? (Out of the current assets that can be converted into immediate cash, how many dollars will there be for for each dollar of current liabilities?)

Importance: The answer to this question provides us with a ratio that tells us how well the company could meet its current obligations if it was forced to discontinue its sales immediately.

Solution: Subtract the inventory (Question 4) from the current assets (Question 2) and divide by current liabilities (Question 8). This is a quick ratio. You can get the same answer by totaling cash, accounts receivable, and marketable securities and dividing by liabilities.

Because merchandise inventories cannot be readily sold, they are not considered a quick asset and are therefore subtracted from the current assets.

Analysis: Current assets should always exceed current liabilities by a reasonable margin, but a ratio of one time is considered satisfactory.

QUESTION 26.
What is the company's liquidity ratio? (What is the ratio of the amount of total cash, U.S. Government securities, and marketable securities owned by the company when compared to its total of current liabilities?)

Definition: The liquidity ratio is the yardstick that reveals the extent to which current liabilities can be met if all of the firm's marketable securities were converted into immediate cash.

Importance: Even though the company may have a high current ratio, this answer might disclose the company's inability to immediately meet current obligations or to pay higher dividends.

Solution: Refer to the asset side of the balance sheet. Total the cash and government and marketable securities, then divide by the total current liabilities (Question 8).

Analysis: The answer is best expressed as a percentage ratio. In comparing the current liquidity ratio with those of prior years, signs of a decline may be a signal that the company requires additional capitalization. However, a decline in the liquidity ratio may also be normal if it is caused by a combination of expansion moves and a concomitant increase in capital expenditures.

QUESTION 27.
What are the company's respective capitalization ratios for bonds, preferred stock, and common stock? (What percentage of the company is owned respectively by the bondholders, preferred stockholders, and common stockholders?)

Definition: Capitalization refers to the total dollar amount of the various securities that have been issued by a corporation.

Importance: Sometimes the strength of each type of security may be determined by its proportionate size to each of the other types of securities issued by the corporation.

Solution: For bonds, divide the face value of the bonds by the total capitalization. For example, total the value of the bonds, the preferred stock, the common stock, the capital stock and then divide into the face value of the bonds (Question 12). For preferred stock, divide the value of the preferred stock (Question 14) by the total capitalization. For common stock, total the common stock, the capital stock, and the accumulated retained earnings, then divide by the total capitalization.

Analysis: Railroads and public utilities usually possess large fixed assets and therefore a correspondingly large bond ratio. But, if the bond ratio of an Industrial company exceeds 25 percent, the banks that loan the money and the new investors may become scarce. Ordinarily, bonds and preferred stock should not exceed 50 percent of the liabilities. A common stockholder must consider how much interest on bonds and dividends on preferred stock must be paid before dividends are declared for the common stock out of the surplus.

QUESTION 28.
What is the ratio of the total stockholders' equity to debt? (Compared to the stockholders' total equity, how much are the total liabilities?)

Definition: The stockholders' equity, net worth, and stockholders capitalization are the same.

Importance: The net-worth ratio is similar to the current ratio in that it is an important indicator of the company's credit strength. The ratio indicates the relationship between capital owned and capital borrowed.

Solution: Divide the total of the stockholders' equity (Question 15) by the total liabilities (Question 11).

Analysis: If the company requires additional working capital at a time that the ratio of debt is too high for the amount of net worth, then the additional capital must be secured from creditors rather than from new capitalization. This is because most investors do not like to buy shares of stock in a debt-ridden, losing venture. However, creditors may provide short term-funds if the security and interest rates are satisfactory.

A stock with a high ratio of equity to debt reflects strength. If the worth-to-debt ratio is too low, the apparent strength of the current ratio (a company's ability to pay its current liabilities out of current assets, Question 24) may not be as valid as it first appears to be. Therefore, if there seems to be a conflict between both ratios, you should compare the worth/debt ratios of similarly capitalized companies in the same industry.

QUESTION 29.
What is the ratio of debt? (What is the amount of debt for each share of stock?)

Importance: The amount of debt attributable to each share of stock is a valuable indicator of the basic value (not market value) of the stock and is based on the liabilities it carries with it. The debt ratio rationalizes owning the stock.

Solution: Divide the amount of the total liabilities (Question 11) by the number of shares of common stock outstanding (Question 13) to secure the correct Ratio of debt.

Analysis: If the debt ratio is too high, a company or its stock should be carefully evaluated before making a decision to purchase it.

QUESTION 30.
What is the ratio of total liabilities to total net worth? (Does the company owe too much money in proportion to what the stockholders own in the company?)

Definition: Tangible net worth is the total of all stocks plus the surplus and undivided profits less the intangible assets.

Importance: A comparison between liabilities and the tangible net worth is another good guide for evaluating companies or their common stocks.

Solution: Divide the total liabilities (Question 11) by the tangible net worth (Question 6).

Analysis: A disproportionate amount of debt requires that you make a comparison with prior records of the same company and with the ratios for similar companies in the same industry. It is normal for some some firms, such as profitable transportation companies, to be heavily indebted because they may have a continuing policy of updating expensive equipment.

QUESTION 31.
What is the ratio of the funded debt to tangible net worth? (Is there too much bond indebtedness for the amount of the company's tangible net worth?)

Definition: See Question 6 for tangible net worth. Funded debt usually refers to bonds that will come due after one year.

Importance: This is an extremely important ratio. It indicates a company's endangered position whenever the company's business declines at a time that the tangible net worth is low and its bond position is high.

Solution: Divide the dollar value of all of the bonds (Question 12) by the tangible net worth (Question 6).

Analysis: The interest on bonds is an obligation that must be paid whether or not the company earns a profit. If the company does not have the funds with which to pay the interest, it is also precluded from paying dividends which may make it difficult to borrow additional funds. When a company increases its funded debt for expansion, it may be able to use the surplus funds that were earmarked for expansion for dividend purposes. If the ratio is too high, it may indicate that the company should procure more invested capital rather than outside funding.

QUESTION 32.
What is the ratio of current debt to inventory? (Is the company's debt too high when compared to the amount of inventory it has on hand?)

Definition: Inventory consists of merchandise or stock on hand, raw materials, goods in process, finished goods, operating supplies, extraordinary maintenance materials, and parts. Current debt, which is the equivalent of current liabilities, is an obligation that must be paid within one year of the date on the balance sheet.

Importance: The inventory of a manufacturing company should be neither too high nor too low. Thus, a comparison of the debt/inventory ratios for prior years is in order.

Solution: Divide the total current liabilities (Question 8) by the total current liabilities (Question 4).

Analysis: If the debt is high and the inventory is low, then an attempt to increase the inventory to its proper level may cause the debt to be increased to dangerous proportions. On the other hand, if the inventory is too high, you may have an indication that goods are not moving or that the company suffers from poor management.

QUESTION 33.
What is the company's overall coverage? (By how many times did the company's adjusted operating profit—profit before paying interest on bonds but after taxes—exceed the combined total paid out for interest on the bonds and the dividends on the preferred stock?)

Definition: The overall coverage is sometimes referred to as combined coverage. It refers to how many times, if any, that the total of both the interest payable on the bonds plus the dividends payable on preferred stocks have been earned as part of the adjusted operating profit. Adjusted operating profit is the profit before interest but after taxes. Operating profit is the profit before both interest and taxes are taken into account.

Importance: Your answer enables you to appraise the strength of the securities. If the combined interest charges on the bonds, together with the dividends on the preferred stock, are completely absorbed by the operating profit, a company could earn very high operating profits without creating the surplus that is required to pay dividends on the common stock.

Solution: Combine the interest on the bonds with the dividends payable by the preferred stock. Then divide that sum into the adjusted operating profit.

Analysis: Professional analysts usually prefer a five-year comparative review. An industrial company should normally earn an operating profit of about five times its bond requirements, whereas about three times bond requirements would be satisfactory for a public utility. The operating profit of an industrial company should be about four times the requirements of the preferred stock. To give soundness to the preferred stock, the common stock should have consistently earned three to four times the preferred dividend requirements.

QUESTION 34.
What is the ratio of fixed assets to the tangible net worth? (Does

the company have too much of its net worth—as asked in Question 6—invested in fixed assets—as asked in Question 3?)

Definition: Net worth is the total of the preferred stocks, the common stocks, the surplus, and the undivided profits.

Importance: Establishing the value of net worth is necessary to evaluate management and to determine if the stockholders' interest is invested as wisely as possible.

Solution: Divide the fixed assets (Question 3) by the tangible net worth (Question 6).

Analysis: Compare this ratio with that of similar companies in the same industry. If the ratio is unfavorable, investigation may reveal that some of the money now invested in fixed assets could have been used for more productive purposes, such as acquiring a larger inventory to increase sales, paying current debts without late penalties, or carrying receivables for more customers.

QUESTION 35.
What is the ratio of miscellaneous assets to net worth? (What is the quality of the assets that comprise the net working capital?)

Definition: All of the assets of the company that do not give it a direct benefit may be referred to as miscellaneous assets. Examples are loans to officers, club memberships, and good will. Net worth (stockholders' equity) is described with Question 15. Net working capital (net working assets) is described with Question 7.

Importance: Too much of the company's impressive assets may not be of any direct benefit to the company.

Solution: Check the balance sheet for miscellaneous items, such as loans to officers or affiliated companies. Then divide that total by the net worth (Question 15).

Analysis: The miscellaneous assets ratio should be low. Not all assets are of the same quality. Inventory and receivables are not as good as cash and government securities. Thus, if the company lists as assets such things as loans to officers or employees, or investments in or loans to affiliated companies, these items would be considered the company's weak or miscellaneous assets. The company, or a prospective buyer, could consider whether the company should liquidate the miscellaneous assets and invest the proceeds to promote their business. Be wary if the miscellaneous assets are too high compared to other companies in the same business.

QUESTION 36.
What is the quality of the working capital assets in relation to the net worth ratio? (How much of the current assets consist of the type of inventory and accounts receivable that are not easily collectible?)

Definition: Net working capital or net working assets refers to the difference between the total current assets and the total current liabilities.

Importance: The ratio obtained is excellent for comparing prior records of the same company as well as against the ratios of similar companies. If too large a proportion of working capital consists of inventory and credit, the current ratio should be higher.

Solution: Subtract from the working capital (Question 17) any of the assets on the balance sheet that are not easily collectible, then divide that answer by the net worth (Question 15).

Analysis: If the working capital is not liquid enough, even a company with a satisfactory current ratio may experience difficulty in paying its bills. A company with a small Inventory and a small amount of accounts receivable has a better quality of working capital than a company with heavy Inventory and a large amount of accounts receivable.

QUESTION 37.
How much money was paid as a dividend on each share of common stock for each of the past three years?

Definition: Dividend means the payment, as designated by the

Board of Directors, to be distributed pro-rata among the outstanding shares. The answer is used for ratios with Questions 38 and 39.

Importance: Dividend comparisons for the past three years may indicate the consistency of the quality of the company's operations, provided that you also check the earnings. (See the following Analysis.)

Solution: Look at the balance sheet for each of the past three years, or at the latest balance sheet if it contains comparative records. Then divide the total of dividends paid on the common stock by the number of outstanding shares. You may also want to refer to *Standard & Poor's Stock Guide* or *Moody's*.

Analysis: Although dividends cannot be declared unless the company has a surplus, a company may declare dividends even if it has lost money during the year. The reason for this is because it is possible for a company to lose money for a few years and still pay dividends, provided that it has an accumulated surplus. Thus, earnings are more important than dividends when determining the strength of a company. This is because if the company has been paying dividends, it does not mean that it will continue to pay them in the future. It may go into the red ink if it does not improve its earnings in the near term.

QUESTION 38.
What was the percentage of dividend payout from earnings? (How much of the income was paid out in dividends?)

Definition: Earnings equal net profit.

Importance: The percentage that was paid out plus the amount that remains as accumulated retained earnings are important factors when used by themselves as a ratio for comparison with other companies.

Solution: Divide the amount of the dividends paid on the common stock (Question 37) by the earnings available to the common stock (Question 19).

How to Understand Financial Statements 287

Analysis: A company that can continue to pay large dividends that amount to a small percentage of its earnings is a stronger company than one paying a similar dividend that amounts to a larger percentage of its earnings. A company that can continue to pay fair dividends while accumulating a surplus is strengthening its financial position. This can lead to larger profits in the future.

QUESTION 39.
What is the percentage of yield? (What percentage of profit is returned to the stockholder for the amount of money paid for the stock?)

Definition: The percentage of yield is the dividend or interest payment paid by a company. It is expressed as either a percentage of the current price you paid or the price that the stock and dividends are anticipated to be in the future. It is also referred to as a percentage of return.

Importance: Both analysts and sophisticated investors use the percentage of yield method. It offers the quickest way to determine how the various yields compare with each other.

Solution: Divide the annual dividend per share (Question 37) by the price of the stock.

Analysis: The percentage of yield lets you make comparisons with investments other than stock. When using the percentage of yield as a comparison with other stocks, the best results are obtained by making comparisons with similar types of companies. It is not wise to compare the yield of a public utility with that of a growth company that is reinvesting its earnings in itself.

QUESTION 40.
What is the earnings ratio per share of common stock? (What percentage of money did each share of common stock earn?)

Definition: The earnings ratio is the percentage of net income earned compared to that of the security to which it is being compared.

Importance: This is an excellent ratio for comparative purposes because of its unusually close relationship to the market price of the stock. Thus, past, present, and future ratios should be evaluated to determine the sound market price that should prevail. However, do not rely on earnings alone.

Solution: After the preferred dividends (see alternative part of Question 16) are paid from the net income (Question 19), divide the balance by the number of outstanding shares of common stock (Question 13 or balance sheet).

Analysis: The earnings ratio is more important than the earnings alone. This is because if two similar companies each earn a million dollars and one of the companies has twice as much outstanding common stock as the other, the company with fewer shares of stock has better earnings ratio.

QUESTION 41.
What was the preferred dividend coverage? (How many times were the preferred dividends earned?)

Definition: The number of times that the preferred dividends have been earned is referred to as preferred dividend coverage (or earnings coverage) per share of preferred stock. (Also refer to Question 33.)

Importance: This ratio helps to establish the quality of the preferred stock or to evaluate the common stocks' chances of continuing to receive dividends.

Solution: Divide the net income after interest and taxes (Question 19) by the preferred stock (Question 14). Then divide that figure by the rate paid on the preferred stock (see balance sheet) to obtain the number of times that the dividends were earned.

Analysis: Buyers of preferred stock like to know how easy or hard it is for a company to pay the preferred dividend. Buyers of common stock require the same information because, by law, they cannot receive dividends until the obligatory dividend payments are made on the preferred stock. A stock that earns four times its dividend is better than a stock that earns two times its dividend. The preferred stock dividend to net income ratio should be evaluated in comparison with similar companies.

QUESTION 42.
What was the percentage of profit on the stockholders' equity—net worth? (What was the profit percentage on the total amount of money invested by the stockholders?)

Definition: Since profit equals net earnings, stockholders' equity equals net worth.

Importance: You can evaluate management by finding out if the company's profit is sufficient for the amount of money invested in it by the stockholders.

Solution: Divide the profit (Question 20) by the stockholders' equity (Question 13).

Analysis: Here we are using profits before the payment of taxes. If the profit percentage is too low, compared to similar companies, then the subject company should be investing its money in a more profitable enterprise as should the prospective stockholder.

QUESTION 43.
What was the ratio of net profits to net working capital? (Is the company making enough profit for the amount of working capital that is available to it?)

Definition: Net profit, net earnings, and the past year's surplus accounts are the same. They are the amount of money earned in the last fiscal year that is available for dividends.

Importance: This ratio enables us to evaluate both management and operating conditions. It lets you make comparisons not only for prior years but with similar companies as well.

Solution: Divide the net profit (Question 19) by the net working capital (Question 17).

Analysis: The amount of net profit that is currently being earned by the working capital of a company should not be disproportionate to the amount of money that has been earned in prior years by the working capital of the subject, or similar, companies.

If the net profits are disproportionate to the working capital, and if efficiency cannot be increased, then good management would find a better and more profitable use for the working capital.

If the ratio of profits to working capital is too low, this company may not be a good investment. However, if there is a sound reason to believe that the future profit picture will materially improve, investing may be cautiously considered.

QUESTION 44.
What is the ratio of net profit to net sales? (What percentage of profit does the company earn for each dollar of sales?)

Importance: This is a very important ratio when compared to similar companies in the same industry. It enables you to evaluate both the profit picture and management.

Solution: Divide the net profit (Question 17) by the sales (Question 1).

Analysis: The percentage of profit may show an increase due to additional sales, a reduction in the cost of making the sales, or a combination of both. Conversely, the percentage of profit may decrease due to fewer sales, an increase in the cost of producing sales, or both.

Note: You should only make comparisons with similar companies in the same industry. Companies with the same industry name in their corporate names are not necessarily similar. For example, there might be two oil companies—named A Oil Co. and B Oil Co.—both with the same amount of capitalization, but one company may only sell oil products while the other company might be limited to oil exploration. For these two companies, the percentages would not be alike. A Oil Co. might be earning $.03 on every dollar of sales and be in good comparative condition, whereas B Oil Co. could be earning $.10 on each dollar of sales.

QUESTION 45.
What is the pre-tax profits-to-sales ratio? (How efficient is the management?)

Definition: The ratio of profit to sales before bond interest and taxes is also referred to as the pre-tax profit-margin-to-sales ratio. Operating profit also refers to the profit before interest and taxes are deducted.

Importance: Nothing is more important than good management. This is what you are purchasing when buying stocks or a company outright. Although this ratio provides an excellent insight into internal control, it is not recommended for comparisons with other companies.

Solution: Divide the operating profit (Question 20) by the sales (Question 1). Please note that Question 44 refers to net profit and not pre-tax profit. The operating profit is also obtained from the statement of earnings on the line prior to where bond interest and taxes are deducted.

Analysis: If this ratio is too small, find out why; then evaluate the management accordingly. The percentage increase or decrease of profit is extremely sensitive to the sales volume because fixed costs, such as rent, interest, and real property taxes remain constant regardless of the amount of sales (excluding percentage rents). Usually, once the overhead is met, the extra sales should dramatically increase the profit ratio and provide some evidence of an efficient operation.

QUESTION 46.
What is the ratio of sales to fixed assets? (Is the money that has been allocated by management to enlarge the productive facilities of the company being spent wisely?)

Importance: Bad management can permit a company to overspend on unnecessary fixed assets, sometimes merely for reasons of pride of ownership or prestige reasons. Such reasoning does not improve either sales or profits.

Solution: Divide the annual sales (Question 1) by the gross value before depreciation and amortization of plants, equipment, and land at the end of the year (see Question 3, or total the fixed assets on the balance sheet).

Analysis: If the company has too much money invested in fixed assets compared to the amount of sales it produces, then the management is weak. For example, a profitable company may have a long-term, low-rent lease on a commercial building. Then for pride-of-ownership reasons, the company decides to buy land next door and build its own building, which it does at a prohibitive cost. Unfortunately, after completion, the sales in the new building do not equal the sales in the old, leased building. The management may then be accused of using bad judgment and misuse of assets.

Note, however, that "heavy" industries may have a smaller volume of sales in relation to fixed assets than "light" industries.

QUESTION 47.
What is the ratio of net sales to inventory? (Is the company buying too much inventory for the amount of sales that it is transacting?)

Definition: Other than supplies, inventory consists of raw materials, materials in process (often called work in process), and finished goods.

Importance: If the money that is tied up in inventory can be put to better use elsewhere, the management could be more efficient.

Solution: To obtain the correct ratio, divide the annual sales (Question 1) by the year-end inventory (Question 4). To calculate the actual turnover of inventory, you should determine the cost of the goods sold and divide that cost by the total inventory amount in the statement.

A company that has purchased an excessive amount of inventory can suffer heavy financial losses if there is a big drop in either sales or prices. A "low inventory turnover" might reflect that the company is placing too high a valuation on inventory that is not salable or of poor quality. The remedy for such situations is a sacrificial disposal of the inventory to raise cash to invest in better inventory.

QUESTION 48.
What is the ratio of net sales to net worth turnover of tangible net worth? (When compared to the amount of money that the company is worth, is the sales volume too high, too low, or adequate?)

Definition: Tangible net worth equals the combined total of the outstanding preferred stock, the common stock, and the surplus less the intangible assets (see Question 1 for net sales).

Importance: A company might be trying to do more business than it can finance, or be doing less business than it is financially capable of handling. Too high a ratio might require short-term financing. If the company is doing more business than it can finance, it is taking a chance of ruining its credit reputation. This may occur whenever its customers do not pay their bills on time. The subject company is thus prevented from paying its bills on time. On the other hand, if the company does not transact an amount of business that is commensurate with its capitalization, then its assets or capital are being wasted and might be better used elsewhere.

Solution: Divide the net sales (Question 1) by the tangible net worth (Question 6).

Analysis: Paradoxically, even though the goal of business is to make big profits, a company should not overtrade. The correct amount of trading volume (net sales) is determined by the amount of net worth that supports the sales volume. To avoid the problems explained above under the heading of importance, the volume of sales should neither endanger the company's financial position nor waste the company's assets and available capital.

QUESTION 49.
What is the ratio of net sales to working capital or turnover of net working capital? (Is the company making enough sales for the amount of working capital that it has available?)

Definition: The figure obtained after subtracting current liabilities from current assets is the working capital or the net current assets.

Importance: The ratio of net sales to working capital refers to the company's efficiency. If the ratio does not compare favorably with the subject company's prior ratios and those of similar companies in the same industry, the management may be at fault.

Solution: Divide the net sales (Question 1) by the net working capital (Question 17).

Analysis: If the answer is negative, the company may not be spending enough money on advertising, merchandising, professional sales assistance, or quality control. A company with a limited amount of working capital cannot afford to advertise as much as a company with an ample amount of working capital. Accordingly, the use of the net-sales-to-working-capital ratio in making comparisons might help tell a valuable story. In Question 48) we were concerned about not properly using the net worth of the company. In Question 49 we are concerned with not making the best use of the available working capital. The reasons for this deficiency must be determined and corrected. Sometimes a product becomes obsolete or overpriced without management being aware of it. When this situation occurs, it is usually because management may still have enough working capital to pay all of the company's bills on a timely basis.

QUESTION 50.
What is the ratio of inventory to working capital? (Does the company have more money invested in inventory than is warranted by the amount of its working capital ratio?)

Definition: The inventory-to-working-capital ratio highlights the percentage of working capital that is tied up in inventory. Net working capital means the excess of the current assets over the current debts and is referred to as net current assets.

Importance: This ratio is only important when considering companies that carry large inventories as a normal part of their business operations.

Solution: Divide the inventory (Question 4) by the working capital (Question 17).

Analysis: On the balance sheet, inventory is that part of the assets from which working capital is derived. When a company's inventory is too large, and it becomes necessary to mark down the inventory in order to dispose of it, the value of the working capital may be drastically impaired through shrinkage. Management must be held responsible for the proper control of the company's inventory. It is frequently tempted to buy more than what the company needs. Volume discounts often tempt managers to buy large quantities of materials to achieve lower unit costs. Endangering a company's liquidity by tying up too much capital in inventory is not considered to be good management.

QUESTION 51.
How much backlog is there? (What is the dollar value of unfilled orders for future delivery?)

Importance: The answer to this question provides an important insight into future operations of the subject company and the amount of profit that it can look forward to earning.

Solution: If you cannot find the backlog in the company's financial statements or *Standard & Poor's* or *Moody's*, write to the company and ask for it.

Analysis: Both future business and profits may be prophesied from the company's backlog of orders. However, a heavy backlog could also indicate that management was not alert enough to anticipate the excessive volume of business obtained or to provide sufficient fixed assets, personnel, or management to consummate the available business and absorb the backlog.

Backlog can also result from a shortage of parts from a supplier. In this case, delays in filling orders could cause excessive cancellations. Even when there is a true backlog, it cannot be relied upon too heavily because of cancellation clauses—particularly if the company is involved in defense orders. If you are contemplating buying stock because of the backlog, consider that the current price may already be based on the backlog.

From an economic point of view, some analysts believe that

large backlogs, especially in durable goods, portend good business conditions, particularly for producers of durable goods.

QUESTION 52.
What is the ratio of price to earnings? (If you want to buy the stock, how many times what it earned per share—not dividends—will you have to pay for it?)

Definition: The price-to-earnings ratio (PER) establishes how many times earnings must be paid for the stock.

Importance: The answer provides a comparative guide to the fundamental market value of the investment. It also affects the public's trading judgment, which can affect the future price of the stock.

Solution: Divide the price of a share of stock by its earnings (Question 19). If the stock is listed on an exchange, check it in the papers.

Analysis: The selling price of any income-producing business or income-producing real estate is usually determined by how many times the annual income other buyers are paying for similar businesses. Frequently, the value of goodwill, franchises, fixtures, fixed assets, and inventory may be added to the price of the business. Based on the type of business and the amount of investment and supervision required, the purchasers may pay one, two, or three times the annual net income. Real estate may sell from four to ten or more times its annual gross income or it may sell on the basis of a 7 percent to 10 percent or 12 percent net return on the money invested plus equity growth.

Some stocks sell at a very high earnings ratio. Sometimes ten times earnings is considered reasonable, while at other times people may pay 20 times earnings. The economic factors of the moment can also affect the price-to-earnings ratio. During bear markets, the price-to-earnings ratio is lower than during bull markets. Stocks in glamorous industries seem to command higher price-to-earnings ratios than ordinary stocks. The ratio is higher for those stocks that seem to promise higher projected earnings and better dividend prospects than for other comparable stocks.

QUESTION 53.
Could a proper evaluation of the financial report have been affected by a change in the company's accounting procedures, the inclusion in the report of non-recurring profits or losses, or an extraordinary income derived from the sale of a plant asset or some other unusual deferment, such as a tax?

Importance: Even though financial statements are usually prepared by Certified Public Accountants (by Chartered Accountants in Canada), there can be a wide degree of variance in the manner in which the books of similar companies are kept. It should be noted that for many years accounting boards and interested critics have been attempting to standardize corporate reports to reduce areas of divergence as well as unethical, deceptive practices in order to make them more easily compared.

Solution: Examine the balance sheet for any extraordinary gains or losses, or for a statement reflecting a change of accounting methods or fiscal years. An extraordinary gain or loss might appear in the surplus account or in the income statement.

Analysis: Accounting changes or improvements may seriously change the net earnings per share of stock. A tax refund or the sale of a plant at a profit might appear to increase the net worth of a company, even though the company might have operated its regular business at a loss.

QUESTION 54.
Will the earnings be affected by the company's contemplation of (1) a new major product, (2) an acquisition of another company, or (3) the discontinuance of an unsuccessful part of its business?

Importance: If the corporation is successful in accomplishing any of these three expectations, its future earnings may be enhanced. This should increase the value of the stock.

Solution: You can get this information from financial reports, trade or financial papers, financial sections of newspapers, or try a letter to the company's president or public relations director.

Analysis: The first problem is to try to find out if the news has already been acted upon by other investors. Even if it has, you may still be early enough to buy the stock and make a profit if all of the other factors are also favorable.

However, both new products or acquisitions are speculative and may result in losses instead of profits. Also, many companies only know how to run their own or a similar type business. It may take a few years until they acquire the correct management or the know-how required by the new company or product. In the interim their cash position could diminish.

QUESTION 55.
Is it contemplated that any major amount of money derived from either additional capitalization or accumulated retained earnings will be used for capital expenditures?

Definition: Capital expenditures usually refer to money expended for plants or heavy or expensive equipment. Such expenditures are similar to fixed assets.

Importance: The answer can drastically affect the company's earnings and the value of its stocks and bonds.

Solution: Read the financial statements of the company in financial or trade papers or write a letter to the president of the company.

Analysis: New capitalization may unfavorably affect and upset the debt ratio or the dividend schedule. If new bond obligations are created, this means that additional interest will have to be paid before the stockholders receive a dividend. On the other hand, part of the new funding may be used to pay off present obligations that carry a higher rate of interest than the new funding. If this occurs, the stockholders may benefit from increased dividends. Also, if the capital expenditures keep the company's equipment modern, the company will not likely suffer from not keeping pace with newer, more modernized companies. Thus, you may possibly look forward to a future increase in earnings.

QUESTION 56.
If the company in which you have been invited to invest is not a stock company, will your capital contribution be used to pay off debts such as back salaries or part of the company's excessive obligations, or can you control your investment so that it will be used to enhance future growth?

Importance: As an investor, you must protect and control your capital. Unless you can afford losses, do not agree to pay off such items as old debts or back salaries. Look for a financially healthy company that wants to use your money to expand a successful business. Preferably, look for a healthier company and a better investment. If in doubt, contact your attorney and ask for help. He may be able to negotiate for you and get your proposed associates to give you independent collateral and collectible personal guarantees.

About the Investment Analysis Chart
Now that you have an understanding of financial statements, you should have confidence in your ability to x-ray any business. You can ferret out the salient facts behind most of the investments that are presented to you. Also, you should use the following analysis chart to both record the information that you acquire and to help you make comparisons between the different companies that you want to check out before investing. For your convenience, the questions and numbers on the chart correspond to the 56 questions and answers just covered.

INVESTMENT ANALYSIS CHART

		# 1 Co. Name	# 2 Co. Name	# 3 Co. Name	# 4 Co. Name	# 5 Co. Name
	Name of Company					
	Industry					
	Statement Date					
	Analysis Date					
Question	1. Net Sales?					
	2. Total Current Assets?					
	3. Fixed Assets?					
	4. Inventory?					
	5. Intangible Assets?					
	6. Tangible Net Worth?					
	7. Total Assets?					
	8. Total Current Liabilities?					
	9. Long Term Debt?					
	10. Accrued Income Tax?					
	11. Total Liabilities?					
	12. Capitalization (Bonds)?					
	13. Capital (Com. Stock)?					
	14. Capital (Pref. Stock)?					
	15. Net Worth?					
	16. Total Int. & Div. on Bonds & Pref. Stock?					
	17. Net Working Capital?					
	18. Earned Surplus?					

Use M for Million, T for Thousand (Example: 100M or 100T)

INVESTMENT ANALYSIS CHART (Continued)

Question		Co. Name	Co. Name	Co. Name	Co. Name	Co. Name
19.	Net Income Last Three Yrs.? 198____ 198____ 198____					
20.	Pre-Tax Profits?					
21.	Cash Flow?					
22.	Book Value? A. Common Stock B. Common Stock C. Common Stock					
23.	% Net Inc. to Net Worth?					
24.	Current Ratio (Times)?					
25.	Quick Assets Ratio (X)?					
26.	Liquidity Ratio?					
27.	Capitalization Ratios? A. Bonds B. Preferred Stock C. Common Stock					
28.	Ratio of Total Stockholders' Equity to Debt?					
29.	Ratio of Debt to Each Share of Stock?					
30.	Ratio of Total Liability to Tangible Net Worth?					
31.	Ratio of Funded Debt to Tangible Net Worth?					
32.	Ratio of Current Debt to Inventory?					
33.	Overall Coverage (X)?					
34.	Fixed Assets to Tangible Net Worth Ratio?					

Use M for Million, T for Thousand (Example: 100M or 100T)

INVESTMENT ANALYSIS CHART (Continued)

Question		Co. Name	Co. Name	Co. Name	Co. Name	Co. Name
35.	Misc. Assets to Net Worth Ratio?					
36.	Quality of Working Capital Assets to Net Worth Ratio?					
37.	Dividend Per Share of Common for Past Three Years?					
38.	Percentage of Dividend Payout from Earnings?					
39.	Percentage of Yield?					
40.	Earnings Ratio Per Share of Common Stock?					
41.	Preferred Stock Dividend Coverage?					
42.	Percentage of Profit on Stockholders' Equity?					
43.	Net Profits-to-Net Working Capital?					
44.	Net Profits-to-Net Sales Capital?					
45.	Pre-Tax Profits-to-Net Sales Ratio?					
46.	Sales-to-Fixed Assets Ratio?					
47.	Net Sales-to-Inventory?					
48.	Net Sales-to-Net Worth?					
49.	Net Sales-to-Working Capital Ratio?					
50.	Inventory-to-Working Capital Ratio?					
51.	Backlog of Orders?					
52.	Price-to-Earnings Ratio?					
53.	Did Acounting Changes Etc., Affect Statements?					
54.	Will Company Policy Changes Affect Results?					

Use M for Million, T for Thousand (Example: 100M or 100T)

INVESTMENT ANALYSIS CHART (Continued)

Question	Co. Name	Co. Name	Co. Name	Co. Name	Co. Name
55. Will New Capitalization or Retained Earnings be Used for Capital Expenditures?					
56. Can You Control Your Investment?					

Use M for Million, T for Thousand (Example: 100M or 100T)

Section 5:
The Different Types of Investments

Chapter 23: Syndications

Syndications

A syndication consists of a group of people who combine some of their money or assets to finance and/or operate a specific project.

The purposes of a syndication may vary greatly. They include venture capital projects, esoteric financing plans, business ventures such as fast food chains, the purchase and sale (purchase and lease-back or construction and lease-back) of a project or real estate, or the underwriting of an issue of stocks or bonds.

Six Kinds of Ownership

The legal entities under which syndications may operate include:

- Individual ownership
- Joint ownership
- Corporations and S corporations
- Real Estate Investment Trusts (REIT)
- Limited partnerships
- General partnerships

Individual ownership refers to a sole proprietorship with only one person owning the business (which includes owning all of its assets and assuming all legal responsibility).

Joint ownership is a common ownership and common liability by two or more people. Each owner assumes full legal responsibility for the payment of all debts, obligations, and liabilities.

Corporate ownership refers to a legal entity that is authorized by a state or government to issue shares of stock to its legal owners. Stockholders do not assume any personal legal liability for the actions of the corporation.

The term *S corporation* refers to a type of corporation that was authorized by subchapter S of the Internal Revenue code. It authorizes corporations with 25 or less stockholders to be taxed similar to a partnership, thereby avoiding the double taxation that affects regular corporate stockholders. The stockholders of regular corporations pay taxes on their dividends after the corporations have already paid taxes on their earnings. Additional tax advantages that are enjoyed by S corporation shareholders include the use of corporation tax credits and the deduction of any operating losses on a pro rata basis against personal income.

REITs are *Real Estate Investment Trusts* that were authorized by Congress to issue shares that may be publicly traded and provide special tax benefits to the shareholders. These tax benefits are available only if 90 percent of the income is derived from dividends, rents, interest, and gains from real estate sales and if the shareholders receive 95 percent of the income. Besides the income, the benefits derived from REIT ownership are the avoidance of double taxation and limited liability for losses. On the other hand, losses suffered by REITs cannot be assumed by the shareholders as with the S corporation or as with limited partnerships.

There are two types of partnerships, *general* and *limited*. Neither kind of partnership pays any state or federal taxes, but all taxes must be paid by the individual partners in the year in which the partnership earns the funds. The general partnership agreement, which need not but should be in writing, is controlled by the Uniform Partnership Act which, with minor variations, has been adopted by all states except Louisiana. Each general partner may possess different percentages of ownership, but their liability is equal for all partnership debts.

Limited partnerships, to be valid, must file a Certificate of Limited Partnership with the respective states in which they operate. Except for Louisiana, most states adhere to the "Uniform Limited Partnership Act" or the "Revised Uniform Limited Partnership Act," with minor variations. If they are public partnerships and have 35 or more partners, they must register with the Securities and Exchange Commission.

Each limited partnership requires at least one general partner. The general partner usually assumes all responsibility for management and all liabilities that occur. Also, some states have different laws with respect to liability and management. Therefore, before you become involved in a limited partnership, consult with your attorney and your accountant for guidance. Unlike the general partnership, limited partners do not have any liability other than the amount of their investment.

In recent years, syndications have been used to raise funds to purchase the land and then construct a specific type of building for business organizations. These businesses may prefer to limit their cash outlay for capital construction and pay rent for the use of the property that has been built to order for them. Also, the rent that they pay is a tax-deductible expense, whereas the money invested in a building is not deductible as an expense item.

Some large real estate ventures formed by syndications buy land, build commercial office buildings, and then rent them to major tenants. Sometimes the general partners of the syndication can make arrangements to rent the space before the limited partners join the venture. But occasionally it takes a few years to rent the property, which can materially reduce the projected cash flow of the syndication and the limited partners.

Small syndications may escape regulation by the government. The larger ones—those that usually advertise or use brokers to secure syndicators—may be subject to state and federal regulations. These regulations often restrict the participation in the syndications to people who meet certain financial qualifications. Some real estate syndications have been sold by either state licensed brokers or stockbrokers subject to the rules of the respective state of origin and the Securities & Exchange Commission.

You should know that the states and the Securities & Exchange commission rarely pass upon the "adequacy or accuracy" of the prospectus about the securities offered. That injunction also applies to funds that invest in government-sponsored or insured investments. These include such investments as Treasuries or "Ginnie Maes" (GNMAs, also known as Government National Mortgage Association mortgage-backed securities).

Despite that lack of assurance, there are many reasons for the popularity of syndications. They frequently fit the financial requirements of so many investors. First, the accumulated funds from individual investors or firms make larger sums of money available for multiple investments. This permits diversification into more than one property or project, which helps to minimize the risk. Second, the investors can rely on the expertise of experienced principals in the syndication, who, of course, should possess a good track record.

Therefore, you will not have to contribute any time to either the formation, creation, operation, management, or bookkeeping of the syndicate. If the syndication involves real estate, which appeals to many investors, the investors can secure income tax advantages by taking advantage of depreciation. They can increase their assets and wealth through capital appreciation of the property through inflation. If the investments are properly set up, the investors can secure a guaranteed or insured income. By buying unleveraged investments, they may protect their investment from loss through foreclosure.

Evaluating Investments in Syndications

Syndications constitute an excellent investment medium that fulfills many investment objectives. However, they should always be approached with caution. You should thoroughly investigate a syndication for:

- The current and anticipated future economic climate
- The finances, integrity, experience, and track record of the entrepreneurs
- How much money the syndicators put up, and the percentage of profits they will keep for themselves in comparison to other similar types of syndications
- The details concerning the types of investments to be made
- What the present or anticipated future money-making status is of the specific projects or businesses that the syndication is considering as investment mediums

If the syndication is mortgaging its property, make sure that the financing is for a long period at good terms. Also consider how much of your investment could be lost if the project is unsuccessful.

For example, assume that a proposed syndication plans to finance the construction of office buildings that will be leased to tenants. You must find out the vacancy rate in the area being considered. If there is a high vacancy rate, the building may take a few years to become fully occupied. If you require immediate income, then look for another type of syndication.

If the proposed investment meets your criteria, determine:

- What percentage of your investment will be used for organization and sales expenses?
- How much profit will be made from brokerage commissions or building fees?

- How much is the percentage of operating and management fees?
- How much will be left for you?
- If a business and leases are involved, will they include a "cost of living index" and a "minimum percentage of gross income" clause?

Any legitimate syndicator will be glad to answer these questions for a bona-fide investor.

There are also a few types of cost-of-living clauses and indexes you should investigate. Basically, what is the difference in cost between filling a basket of consumer goods today and filling a similar basket at a previous base period? Ordinarily, such clauses provide for adjustments in rents and wages based on the new costs. Cost-of-living clauses are supposed to compensate for the effects of future inflation or deflation.

A "minimum percentage of gross income" clause adjusts the rent or other payment according to the total amount of income received from a business or income property. This does not include the deduction of operating expenses, such as wages, commissions, depreciation, taxes, and utilities. Also, the preferable leases are always Net Leases. This should mean freedom from management expenses other than light bookkeeping and supervision. The tenant pays all of the expenses, such as repairs, taxes, and insurance.

If one of the stated purposes of the syndication involves real estate depreciation for tax purposes, bear in mind that depreciation is limited to the buildings because land cannot be depreciated. Some syndicators plan short-term depreciation schedules. However, the conservative syndicators, especially since the Tax Reform Act of 1986, use long-term depreciation (see Chapter 21). Whenever possible, syndicators strive to include personal property such as furniture or business fixtures as part of the investment package, and try to use a short depreciation schedule.

Some fast food or restaurant chains, usually franchises, use syndicators to buy the land and build to their specifications. The restaurant chain will then lease the premises on a net basis. This means that once the property is completed, either the restaurant-lessee, the franchisor, or his franchisee pays the taxes and all expenses for upkeep and repair. Some of these syndications stipulate that the tenant must pay an amount of rent that will assure that the investors receive a guaranteed percentage on their investment. They may also receive an overage if a certain percentage of the lessee's gross income exceeds the guaranteed minimum. Also included is a cost-of-living clause that provides for increased income if the federal Cost Price Index increases.

Conservative and Speculative Syndication

Syndications, regardless of their merit, are usually devised to appeal to either the speculator or the conservative investor. The latter pays all cash for his share because the syndication is set up to be free of indebtedness.

The speculator, who usually uses leverage, joins a syndication that is based on making a small down payment and borrowing a substantial amount of the funds required to complete the transaction. Hence, he pays some cash down, receives a smaller equity interest, and takes the chance of losing the property and his investment. This position is not without risk, especially if the tenant fails or economic conditions deteriorate and the payments cannot be met and the property cannot be refinanced.

The conservative investor figures that even if something bad happens to the tenant, or if the economy goes into a tailspin, he cannot lose his equity in the property as long as he pays his share of the taxes. Because he has paid cash, he can only lose his share of the revenue that he had anticipated receiving. Some investors believe in leverage but, because of their age or the desire to limit their risks, only invest in full equity syndications. (Refer to Chapter 5 for further information on leverage.)

An important distinction must be made between private and public syndications. Private syndications are similar to a partnership of a limited number of people, who usually get together through the recommendation of friends. Most public syndications are offered—and possibly participated in—by brokerage or investment firms that advertise and sell a syndication idea. These are put together and operated by a professional syndicator.

Syndications are usually long-term investments for which there is typically no immediate resale. Accordingly, many states require that purchasers of interests in these major syndications have a specified net worth or a certain minimum annual income, or both, before they may buy an interest. The syndication's prospectus usually states the risks that are involved. Unfortunately, many do not understand the risks because they are overwhelmed by the large size and impressiveness of the expensive brochures that describe the exciting purposes for which the money is to be used.

The Meaning of Insured

Frequently, the word "insured" appears in the prospectus or on the cover of the accompanying brochure. A closer reading may reveal that only a percentage of the lease payments and none of the equipment are insured. Further, the word insurance does not mean that the investors are guaranteed a profit or that their investment money will be returned. Usually, the insurance will be paid directly to the partnership and not to the individual investors. Then, too, the payment of insurance depends on the financial stability of the insurance company (something on which you should not always rely).

If you are concerned that the insurance coverage is not adequate, discuss it with the syndicators and ask them for an explanation. If you are not satisfied with their explanations, ask them for the name of their insurance broker. Contact that person, tell him what concerns you, and get his or her reaction to your dilemma. If you are still not satisfied with the answers, contact your own insurance firm or check the yellow pages of the phone book and call any of the large firms that might handle that type of insurance. If you are still unhappy, contact your lawyer, secure his or her professional opinion, and then abide by it.

The prospectus can state that the syndicator will receive substantial fees and profits even if the venture is unprofitable. Remember that whenever a franchise is involved, the success of the individual franchisee—not the presumably well known, well financed franchisor—will determine the profitability of the syndication and your investment in it.

If there is a profit, a portion of it will be paid for operational expenses. Another portion of the proceeds will be used to cover organizational and offering expenses.

Because of their multiple benefits, syndications may be an excellent medium for many investors. However, each syndication must be selected with great care according to the investment requirements of each investor. Even if you have had satisfactory experiences with the same syndicator, you must carefully review the details concerning each new syndication that is offered to you. This is especially true whenever the tax laws change.

What to Look for: Advantages and Disadvantages

In order to derive the usual desired benefits—such as capital appreciation, a safe investment with a minimum of risk, a fair income return on the investment, an absence of management problems, and a depreciation schedule that will not be disallowed by the IRS—the investor should limit himself or herself to syndications that offer some of the possibilities itemized in the next paragraph.

If the syndication is involved in the franchise industry, make sure that:

- Both the franchisor and franchisee have good credit ratings.
- The franchisor has a successful franchise.
- The syndication deals with the franchisor and not the individual franchisee, unless the franchisor guarantees the franchisee's obligations. Preferably, the franchisor's name should be on the lease.

You can secure a credit rating from the tenant company, from a credit-rating agency, or from your bank. You can judge their success by asking for and reviewing audited financial statements for the past few years and making comparisons. You should also visit a few existing locations and check out their style of operation.

Many of the major syndications raise money without revealing the specific locations or the names of the proposed lessees. It is preferable to know in advance the locations, the names of the lessees, ownerships, and the types of and quality of their management. Again, do not hesitate to request this type of information from the syndicator, together with a copy of the latest credit report on both the franchisor and franchisee, if there is one. If the syndicator fails to cooperate with you or gives you incomplete answers, look for another investment. If they seem cooperative and provide you with answers, check out existing locations, the type of operation, and the product.

Remember that the operation must be successful or the franchisee, if undercapitalized, may fail. The syndication will be stuck with a one-purpose building that has been designed for one type of franchise.

It is disconcerting to walk into the premises of a poorly managed property or business in which you possess a syndicated interest as a limited partner (an investor without a voice). As a limited partner, bear in mind that regardless of the size of your investment, you have given up the right to have any say in the selection and/or management of the property or syndication. You relinquished that right in exchange for your not being additionally liable beyond your agreed investment for any of the debts that are incurred by the syndication.

For example, you may have an interest, via syndication, in a business that is located in a 100 percent location (maximum amount of exposure to potential customers) that is not doing as well as their competitors. You may notice that the signs are inadequate and that better signs could help the business and your ultimate profits. As a limited partner, you can only voice your opinion, but no one is obligated to act on anything that you suggest.

One of the tax breaks afforded by some syndications is that they treat part of the distributions as a return of capital until the capital investment is reduced to a zero basis (when your investment is fully returned). Prior to the Tax Reform Act of 1986, heavy equipment was usually depreciated on a five-year basis, which approximates the 150 percent declining balance basis. However, since the new Tax Act, both factories and equipment are depreciated at a slower rate.

When a syndication plans to invest in improved real estate, such as commercial buildings, it has two options: The first is to purchase completed buildings. The second is to purchase the land and construct the buildings. If the buildings are constructed, it may take three or more years until the properties are rented and a cash distribution can be made to the partners. If the buildings are complete when purchased, the rental schedule is set and the distribution should be quicker.

However, the syndication that contemplates construction of a building will probably have larger tax write-offs than can be secured through the purchase of a completed building. If you are inexperienced in these matters, show the formats to your accountant, and ask which type they recommend for you.

In many syndications, a few different entities may be involved with the partnership. Frequently, there is an admitted conflict of interest, which can work to the detriment of the partnership. For example, through the imposition of management or other fees, a part of the syndication can earn money even though the partnership may be losing money.

Basically, an accredited, experienced syndication can be very beneficial to those investors who do not possess the experience, time, or capital to plan and successfully accomplish the proposed goals of the syndication. Syndications enable investors to participate in money-making ventures with many benefits. Those benefits include: limited liability for losses, capital appreciations of assets, and not paying the double taxes on profits that stockholders of a corporation pay when the corporation pays taxes before it pays dividends.

A final word of caution: If you do not have any experience with the syndicators, first investigate their track record for experience and success. If you cannot check yourself, ask your lawyer to check them for you before examining the syndication agreement. Then, if you feel confident that the syndicators are honest, experienced, and usually successful but you do not actually know someone who was successful with them, begin with a small investment. If that investment is successful, they will undoubtedly have future investment opportunities. Then you can invest additional funds with greater confidence.

Chapter 24: Franchises

Franchises

Franchises have become very popular with both the retail public and entrepreneurs who want to manage, operate, or own a business. Today, the public shops or eats in franchised establishments with a great deal of confidence. This is because people are familiar with the type of management, service, and merchandise offered, even when shopping in a new or unfamiliar location.

Today, franchises account for as much as one half of all retail sales in the United States. From 1983's $383 billion in retail sales, it is estimated that approximately 6.3 million employees in 478,000 outlets accounted for about $560 billion in sales in 1986.

But, as with any other business or investment venture, the con artists are having a boom with franchises. According to reports linked to the North American Securities Association and the Council of Better Business Bureaus, every year prospective franchisees get taken for $5 billion. The public must be unaware that the Federal Trade Commission requires that all franchisors disclose information on both their business and litigation history to their prospective franchisees.

The Canadian Imperial Bank has issued a franchise booklet that describes franchising as "a system of distribution in which one party (the franchisor) grants to another (the franchisee) the right to distribute (sell) products or perform services and to operate a business in accordance with an established marketing system. The franchisor offers its technical expertise, trademarks or other designations, along with initial and ongoing operational support, in exchange for a continuing right to royalties from the franchisee. The aim is to receive benefits for both parties by combining the strength and expertise of centralized buying and merchandising with the energy and ingenuity of local ownership and management."

There are many kinds of franchises. They should be viewed from the point of view of the franchisor, the franchisee, and the public's acceptance of their operation. The major benefit to the franchisors is that they use the capital of the franchisee to help them (the franchisor) increase their distribution, expand their base of operations, or make a quick profit.

Benefits of Franchises

For the franchisee, there are a number of advantages inherent in the franchise arrangement. In starting a business, it is often safer and less expensive for an entrepreneur to use the franchisor's expertise and support than it is to be an independent entrepreneur. That is because in a legitimate operation, the franchisees may derive a combination of benefits. Benefits include:

- A trademarked name
- Goodwill that can bring business to their door with a minimum of low-cost advertising
- Business training
- A tested product or services
- Approved accounting systems
- A better chance of experiencing success with the franchisor's guidance than without it

That guidance includes:

- Finding the proper location
- Helping the franchisee lease and/or construct the proper type of building
- Securing and installing the necessary fixtures and specialized equipment
- Providing training for the franchisee and his employees
- Tested advertising and promotional ideas

Ninety percent of non-franchise start-ups fail within 5 years; only 10 percent of franchised start-ups fail.

A good franchise can benefit both the franchisor and the franchisee. However, the prospective franchisee must be alert to the franchise that is only intended to benefit the franchisor. Franchisors sell franchises for many reasons.

Areas to Investigate

Some sell franchises just to make money for themselves. All they offer is a good idea that sounds like a winner to inexperienced people who have a strong desire to become their own boss. Even if the franchisors are legitimate, they may not have the training facilities that are required by inexperienced entrepreneurs (franchisees). Unfortunately, too many prospective franchisees are unaware of the many facets of buying and operating a franchise. Before you sign a franchise agreement, investigate the following items with your attorney and accountant.

- The terms of the franchise agreement
- The initial and follow-up costs
- The proposed price structure of the merchandise to be bought from the franchisee and the suggested selling price
- The royalties
- The costs involved in securing, leasing, and constructing a building
- The equipment costs
- The costs of training the franchisee and employees
- Advertising and promotional costs
- Potential revenue at various levels of business activity
- Cash flow
- Break-even

Generally, franchisors may derive many benefits other than franchise fees from franchising. Some franchisors are not interested in franchise fees as much as they are interested in securing and expanding outlets for their products. They make a profit from merchandise that is used by the franchisees to carry on their business. Basically, franchisors benefit from shared advertising costs, greater identification of their name and logo, and greater distribution of their products. Further, by increasing sales, the franchisor not only reaps greater profits, but also lowers the purchasing costs for materials that are bought in bulk or larger quantities. Then, too, every new location helps to advertise the franchised name and promote sales.

In some instances, franchises are not bought for profitability. Many sports franchises, such as baseball, football, and basketball teams, are bought to nurture a wealthy person's personal ego or for advertising and promoting products or trade names. Frequently, the losses are written off as tax deductions against personal income taxes. But under the new tax laws, deductions are limited to the amount risked. If the loss is passive, its deductibility may be restricted to being offset against passive income. (See Chapter 21.)

A large company that owns its own retail outlets may at any time, for any of a variety of reasons including labor, management, or profitability problems, decide to franchise a large number of its existing outlets. In one such case, many of the employees and store managers took an early retirement and then bought franchises for themselves. Consequently, the franchisor received the benefit of securing experienced franchisees who did not require too extensive training. The franchisees had the advantage of being familiar with the worthiness of the franchisor and the profit potential of their own franchise.

You can encounter many difficulties when involved in buying or setting up a franchise. Following is a lengthy list:

- The franchise salesmen may be action-oriented achievers with "superb closing" skills and an ability to think on their feet. Consequently, they may rush you into a bad deal before you can investigate or get proper advice.
- The franchisee seldom becomes the actual owner of the goodwill. The term "goodwill" has many meanings: It is an asset that includes the expectation of future public patronage, either from past good service, the lack of competition, a unique location, or the business name. The franchise agreement may state that on a sale of the franchise by a franchisee to a third party, the goodwill may revert to the franchisor. This disadvantage may not have been disclosed in the prospectus or information sheet that was originally offered to the franchisee or his vendee. Thus, the purchaser of a franchise from a franchisee, if not careful, also may be compelled to pay the franchisor for the goodwill. This is one of the reasons you should consult your attorney before you make any business arrangements.

- When the franchise is in operation, the financial reporting must satisfy the franchisor (which may involve more cost), even if the franchisee is satisfied with less accounting.
- After a franchisee opens, too much local competition from the franchisees of other franchisors or from individuals in the same business could seriously affect profits. This is true of non-franchised businesses as well.
- In order to bolster their financial statements, some franchisors may count as capital some of the funds that were advanced for the advertising fund by prior franchisees.
- The franchisors' purchasing agents may get kickbacks from vendors—with or without the knowledge of the franchisor—causing products to be overpriced.
- Sometimes the major product being sold by the franchisor, which must be stocked in large quantities and paid for by the franchisee, may soon become obsolete and bankrupt the franchisee. This can happen in franchises involving electronics.
- The franchisors may be going into bankruptcy, even if their business seems to be booming. This occurs when their administrative expenses are too high for the number of franchises they have sold or are operating.
- Some franchisors may not provide the required type of marketing, support, and training that is promised in the franchise agreement.
- Some franchisors may keep and operate the good franchises for themselves and only franchise the marginal locations.
- Sometimes franchises call for leasing equipment and fixtures when buying might be preferable (or vice versa).
- In some franchise arrangements the franchisee may have insufficient capital. When the franchisor loans the franchisee money, the arrangements of the loan may not be in the best interests of the inexperienced franchisee. For example, repayment schedules for the early part of the franchise may not provide the franchisee with sufficient working capital to keep the business afloat. Further, the terms of the franchisor's loans should be compared with bank loans or those available from the Small Business Administration.
- Some franchisees complain about not having a voice in the type of advertising being used by the franchisor.

Before you invest in a franchise, there are many questions that you must investigate. Among these are:

- The background of both the franchisor and its principals
- The pitfalls in the franchise agreement
- The quality of the product or services being franchised
- The present and future need for these services
- The ability of the franchisor to meet changing trends
- The future competition from improved products or services offered by similar franchisors
- The appropriateness of the location or territory.

With regard to investigating the background of the principals, the franchise itself, and all other matters about which you are inexperienced, consult an attorney and an accountant to help you.

The franchisor will want your financial statement. In return, and regardless of how big or how well-known the franchisor may be, it is more important that you acquire the franchisor's financial statement and have it professionally analyzed for present and future financial stability. As previously mentioned, the franchisor's income may be excellent, but their expenses might be greater than their income.

Do not measure the franchisor's success by the amount of money they may have accumulated from selling franchises. If you depend upon those figures, differentiate between the amount of money that has been collected and what is still due. A high volume of sales of franchises for a fee is not as important as the post-sale business performance of the franchisors and franchisees. The mere fact that franchisors were able to get franchisees to sign agreements and give them a down payment does not make them successful. Moreover, they may be using the uncollected balance due from the franchisees as part of their assets, even though they may be uncollectible.

It is imperative that you talk to a few of their other franchisees. Find out the failure rate of their franchises so that you can consider the undesirable problems that can arise. Meanwhile, watch the operation at a few locations to see if they operate as promised. Also, be sure that the type of operation is compatible with your needs and lifestyle. Experience indicates that operating a successful franchise requires hard work.

To avoid heavy financial risks, prospective franchisees looking for bigger profits should avoid becoming general partners in the franchisor's deal. It is unlikely that a successful franchisor will offer a partnership to an inexperienced partner. Moreover, the financial risks that you must assume to become a general partner are too many and too great for the average person seeking a franchise. If you insist on considering such a partnership, please contact your lawyer.

Termination

With respect to the franchise agreement, nearly everyone pays close attention to the initial amount of money required and how it will be used, the amount of royalties to be paid out, the duration and terms of the agreement, and the required operating procedures. However, very few prospective franchisees pay attention to the termination aspects of the agreement until it is too late. Check the renewal clauses and what rights will be retained by the franchisee if there is a willful or unwillful termination.

An unwillful termination might occur in many ways. For example, the building that houses the franchise might burn down. Because of a change in zoning regulations, the local authorities might not permit a similar building to be constructed in that location again. The cost of erecting a new building in that precise location might be too expensive. Or, for some reason, the insurance company will not pay the claim.

Another example of unwillful termination occurs in the event of the unexpected, sudden death of a franchisee. According to the terms of some franchises, the lawful heirs may be prevented from continuing the franchise without the approval of the franchisors, whose approval may not be forthcoming.

Questions to Ask

While considering the present and future need for franchised products and services, and the ability of the franchisor to meet changing trends and future competition, the franchisee must also consider:

- Is there any special uniqueness to the product or service?
- Will there be a long-term need for the product or service or will it just be a fad?
- Is the product or service a repeat item that can be sold to the same people frequently?

- Will it be a difficult or expensive product or service to introduce?
- Is the product or service something people come to see and discuss, like a home improvement, sporting goods, clothing, a car, etc.?
- Is the product or service an impulse type of item that can be bought on the spur of the moment by pedestrians without prior planning (like a quick snack, a shoe shine, or books)?

The answers determine the amount of traffic that your item requires to sell well. This in turn dictates the type of location you will need and the rent or cost of the property if you buy it. The most competitive business is probably the food business, which may require both foot and car traffic. If you get into a cookie business, for example, you will require pedestrian traffic because it is an impulse (spur of the moment) item. This is why most large malls already have a cookie franchise. But, therein lies the problem. Most good locations are already taken, and a cookie, no matter what you do to it, is seldom unique. Thus, if you have a cookie franchise in a mall and another franchise operator moves into the mall and offers cinnamon rolls, you might receive stiff competition.

You should determine if the product or service you are considering is a fad. Then, you must determine if the franchisor and you can successfully combat and outlive the fad aspects of the product. Usually, the ability of franchisors to remain competitive depends not so much on the original creator of the franchise as it does on experienced, visionary personnel and the effectiveness of their promotional programs.

In review, the purpose of a franchise is to extend benefits to both parties by combining the strength and expertise of centralized buying and merchandising with the energy and ingenuity of local ownership and management.

In starting a business, it is often safer and less expensive for an entrepreneur to use the franchisor's expertise and support than it is to be independent. He starts off with a trademarked name, goodwill that can bring business to his door with a minimum of low-cost advertising, business training, a tested product or service, approved accounting systems, and a better chance of experiencing success with the franchisor's guidance than without it. That guidance includes finding the proper location and then helping the franchisee lease and/or construct the proper type of building, securing and installing the necessary fixtures and specialized equipment, providing training for the franchisee and his employees, and offering tested advertising and promotional ideas.

However, the prospective franchisee must investigate the character, reputation, and success record of the franchisors. Even if the franchisors are legitimate, they may not have the training facilities that are required by inexperienced franchisees. Unfortunately, too many prospective franchisees are unaware of the many pitfalls encountered while buying and operating a franchise. Be sure to discuss all the terms of the franchise with your professional advisors and the franchisor before you invest.

Additional information about franchising may be obtained from: *The United States Department of Commerce's Annual Franchise Opportunities Handbook* at a cost of $15 from the Superintendent of Documents at the U.S. Government Printing Office, Washington, D.C. 20402 or The Secretary of the Federal Trade Commission, Washington, D.C. 20580.

In Canada, the Canadian Imperial Bank of Commerce has a Franchise Section at Commerce Court, Toronto, Ontario, M5L1A2, or contact your local manager.

Chapter 25: The Lure and Risks of Venture Capital Opportunities

The Lure and Risks of Venture Capital Opportunities

Every investment of capital may be referred to as a venture. But those investment funds that are furnished to a company by outsiders to develop a technological idea or prototype are referred to as *venture capital*. Because of the high profitability potential, there has been a considerable growth of venture capital funds and partnerships. It has been estimated that they have contributed about $19 billion to the venture industry. Most of these funds were secured from institutions and wealthy people.

High Risk—High Reward

Because of the many risks involved, furnishing venture capital may be very rewarding. This is why so many new investors are anxious to learn about it. It has become a standard method of equity financing throughout the world. Equity financing has achieved a high degree of success in the United States, particularly in the Silicon Valley area just south of San Francisco. This is because of the rapid growth of computer-related technological advancements by firms in the area, most of whom required an extensive amount of seed money. Current indications are that the field of medical technology will also become a major user of venture capital.

Ordinarily, venture capital investments are different from conventional investments in two respects. Usually, they are only an investment vehicle for persons or companies that possess large amounts of expendable funds, vast amounts of patience, and the knack of picking winners from a multitude of exciting, promising, novel, but untested ideas. The ideas may be revolutionary and make fortunes or they may never work and result in heavy financial losses for the participants.

But small investors with a flair for risk-taking need not be disheartened. They, too, may participate in venture capital projects, hopefully after they qualify themselves. Even though venture capital investments have many drawbacks, under the right circumstances, qualified investors should invest some of their investment funds in them. If you are interested in a venture capital project, you should first understand the various types of venture capital opportunities that are available, how they work, and the risks involved.

Most of the ideas that are funded by venture capital are usually too speculative for banks. As a result, special investors or investor groups, called venture capitalists, fill the gap by patiently assuming the risk. They provide the money to the bright engineers who give birth to the idea but who usually lack the required business experience and organizational acumen.

Venture capital is also referred to as risk capital. Some venture capitalists use their funds to finance start-up companies or to restart what were start-up companies that have failed, but still have promise, and now need additional funds. "Start-up" is a technical phrase that is used in the venture capital industry. It connotes that the company has more than an idea; it already has established a plan providing for management, marketing, sales, financial possibilities, and various applicable projections. Some venture capital may be used for companies that are not prepared as well as start-up companies. But most venture capital investors will not put up their capital—usually referred to as seed money—until the above-described plans are complete.

Mostly, large venture capital companies form partnerships with the start-up companies to whom they provide the venture capital. On occasion, however, large, well-established manufacturing companies compete with the venture capital companies because they desire to become partners. Usually these competing companies are in the same business or, if the new company is successful, they desire to be in a position to either furnish raw materials or to become exclusive distributors for the new product.

S.B.I.C.s and Limited Partnerships

Usually, the only way that the small investor can get a piece of the action is by becoming involved with a Small Business Investment Corporation (SBIC)—which is very difficult. He can also become a limited partner in what is referred to as a venture capital limited partnership. SBICs are licensed and funded by the Small Business Administration (SBA) of the U.S., which will gladly provide you with additional free information about SBICs.

Venture capital limited partnerships are usually unlisted companies. They are often formed by brokerage houses who offer shares in these venture capital limited partnerships to the public. There are also a few venture capital investment funds, but their names might not reveal in what, or how, they invest. All of these may be referred to as investment funds, but some are conservative and do not speculate. Others may indicate that they are involved with venture capital investments but actually, because of the high-risks and long waiting periods, may only use a small portion of their capital for venture capital purposes. If you want the risk, the funds you should check are those that only use their capital for venture capital investments. However, you should also be aware of some of the recent developments that have been reported and that might be adopted by some of the investment funds.

Some venture capitalists now believe that owning a chain of established businesses, without incurring heavy start-up costs, can be much more profitable than sponsoring esoteric engineering firms. Also, recently, venture capitalists have been seeking profits that could be secured from consolidating successful businesses in the same industries.

Based on the high profits that were originally available, the management fees that were charged to the investors were very low. Today, however, as yields have declined, some of the annual management fees have increased to somewhere near three percent of the invested capital or assets.

But, a word of caution. If you decide to invest in a limited venture capital partnership, contact the large brokerage firms and make comparisons between the various partnerships and what they offer. Then, reserve your judgment until you finish this chapter.

What Venture Capital Buys

It is important that every venture capital investor understand that the venture capital that is advanced is not a loan, does not draw interest, and need not be paid off. Venture capital buys an equity interest in the company. That equity interest provides the investors with many combinations of ownership and profits, depending on the skill of the negotiators and the needs of the parties. In many instances the profits may exceed 50 percent.

The Operation

Regardless of the venture capital source or terms that accompany it, the recipients of the funds usually operate within the following parameters.

When they think that the product is ready for marketing, they usually offer shares to the public to secure additional funds. Sometimes the capital fund investors do not invest their cash until immediately preceding the public offering of the company's shares of stock. But their pre-acknowledged backing provides a form of stability to the public offering. In other instances, particularly if seed money is involved, the limited partners may receive shares of stock through the company going public.

By now you must be asking, "If I invest, what are the risks, what are the problems, and what rewards can I look forward to if I invest?"

Although some venture capital investments in computer-related industries in California's Silicon Valley were very rewarding, knowledgeable sources in the venture capital industry estimate that 40 percent of the companies that are funded by venture capital lose money, that 30 percent provide a meaningful return, and that about 30 percent return one to two percent on the original investment. Reportedly, some returns were about five times the investment. That means that a $1 million investment returned $5 million.

Risks and Problems

Undoubtedly, there are many interrelated risks and problems. These are:

1. The idea you are backing may be bad, impractical, and never succeed.
2. You may have to wait seven to ten years to find out if the idea will succeed.
3. In the interim, many other companies may be working on the same type of project. For example, at one time 33 companies were working on an idea for the same type of computer. Even if all of them had successfully completed their projects, the competition would have prevented any of them from making a profit. Thus, 33 well-intentioned projects were a waste of both the capital venture funds and the valuable time of the involved technologists.
4. Even if the basic idea is successfully developed, the firm's management, sales, and promotion departments might not be able to sell it. Remember, even if the firms that furnish the

capital reserve the right to participate in management, they may not possess the expertise required to manufacture the product, manage the company, advertise, promote, sell the product at a profit, and keep it up-to-date and competitive with new innovations.
5. Even with the best planning, the expenses might exceed the start-up capitalization funds that were originally projected, and the idea might require large infusions of extra capital to salvage the original investment. Research and development is rarely susceptible to accurate planning and never cheap. Because of their bad history, efforts to rescue re-start companies (sometimes called burnout turnarounds) are considered very risky. To secure venture capital, they must give up more equity than would be required from a start-up company. Accordingly, the equity that is left for the entrepreneurs is very small, and even the interests of the original venture capitalists are diluted.
6. The owners of the project might not be able to secure the high type of engineering skill and scientific brain power that the venture might require. The best engineers are usually attracted by large companies that have large, modern experimental facilities, lots of funds for research, and a variety of good engineers and scientists with whom they can exchange information.

What to Look for

If you ever consider investing with a venture capital group, first try to find one that, in addition to management know-how, also has technologically experienced partners or personnel that are able to help start-up companies when they get into trouble.

The major profits from venture capital investments are made from the sales of stock or from the sales of the companies themselves after they become successful and establish an interesting record of sales and net profits. On the other hand, a successful product may produce many sales and profits. This causes the entrepreneur and the venture capitalists to retain the company, let it grow, retain their interests, and enjoy the dividends.

In exchange for the venture capital, the entrepreneurs might give up from 40 to 60 percent of the equity in their companies. It has been reported that re-start companies have given up as much as 85 percent of their equity to venture capitalists. Following are some basic types of venture capitalists arrangements:

- Entrepreneurs accept the investment capital with the understanding that they will give up an equity interest in the company, but will continue to experiment and work on their project without any help or interference from the venture capitalists.
- As part of the deal, entrepreneurs give up a part of their management and development authority so that they can receive the benefit of the venture capitalists' technical assistance in developing and marketing the product.
- The entrepreneurs may prefer to first perfect the product, complete their business development program, seek and hire their own management, and be in an independent position before soliciting funds.

New Opportunities

Recent developments in the venture capital industry have included the creation of a new type of venture capital firm in Palo Alto, California. This firm is prepared to consider highly sophisticated technological ideas, and if it approves of them, it is prepared to build prototypes, organize a management team, create a business plan, and furnish the venture capital needed. Reportedly, companies that it has already helped seemed very satisfied. When venture capital companies like this start looking for additional funds from small investors, which seems likely, be prepared to investigate them.

Other opportunities for investment may well arise in the medical field. Efforts to combat the fatal disease of AIDS will require a tremendous amount of equity capital to do the required research. Undoubtedly, even small investors will be invited to participate by venture capital firms that will help capitalize the medical researchers. If this should happen, do not be swayed by your emotions. Carefully investigate the principals and the researchers. Take nothing for granted.

Moreover, if you are attracted to any form of venture capital proposition, please remember this: even though the rewards may be great, the risks are unknown and high, the waiting period is long, and you must be prepared to lose your entire investment. Therefore, only participate in venture capital propositions if you will not miss the money you invest.

Chapter 26: Real Estate as an Investment

Real Estate as an Investment

Real estate, the basis of all wealth, has offered the average person more opportunities to make a living or become wealthy than any other form of investment. It has provided investment income and profits for every conceivable class of person, syndication, or corporation.

Many uneducated people with a poor grasp of the language and without any experience in real estate matters have used real estate to become financially independent. With or without skilled hands that could reduce maintenance fees, they have used either the buying, selling, financing, or renting of various types of real estate to make or supplement their living and have frequently amassed great wealth. Sometimes, without buying real estate, but appreciative of its value as a sound collateral, they saved their money and loaned it to real estate buyers in exchange for a mortgage that paid them better returns than interest on their savings accounts.

Usually, however, they consummated their first real estate purchase with a small amount of cash, sometimes with a partner, and the expeditious use of mortgages or trust deeds. Then, they acquired the practical experience of renting, managing, buying, and selling. Frequently, they found it expedient to alter or remodel the properties, and thus learned enough to become builders and developers. Some of the ambitious entrepreneurs bought vacant land. It was not unusual for developers to secure financing for as much as 75 percent of the value of their finished lots, plus enough money or credit to pay interest on their debt for at least a year. The increased value of the finished lots gave them an opportunity to finance construction of planned improvements.

It is true that during economic slumps many people lose their income property because of a scarcity of tenants and vacant rental units. But, in most instances, those who lost their property had financially overextended themselves with too much debt. Usually, however, judiciously financed real estate has been profitable. This includes all types of real estate in the form of raw land, desert property, farms, ranches, houses, apartments, condominiums, hotels, and industrial or retail complexes.

Fortunately, money-making opportunities in real estate are still available for those who understand the importance of both selecting the correct locations and the right timing for buying and selling.

To appreciate the acceptance of real estate as an investment, consider the 1982 IRS report that "approximately 25% of the assets of estates in excess of $300,000 were invested in real estate." In essence, owners of real estate can derive profits from gains if they sell it, and from rents if they rent it. They can enjoy pride of ownership and the pleasure of not paying the landlord. If they own income property with many tenants, they have the choice of managing it themselves or of hiring someone to manage it for them.

Fundamentals of Property Ownership

The focus of the balance of this chapter is to acquaint potential investors with important fundamental principles before they invest. Thus, we explore the fundamentals of property ownership and how to take title to real estate if you buy it. The emphasis is on how to start investing in residential income property or in land. This type of information provides the groundwork for subsequent investments in other types of income-producing properties.

The crux of understanding the *basic values* that are involved in any real estate investment is that the value of real estate is determined by the value of the right to the present and future use, potential income, sales profit, and tax benefits available from the investment. Do not confuse the basic values with real estate values determined by appraisers. They may use other methods, but most frequently they appraise property on the basis of current market value as determined by previous transactions involving a similar piece of property in the same area.

It is a major mistake not to own real estate that can work for you. In the absence of deflation, real estate will work for you by increasing in value every year without any physical effort on your part. Economic history indicates a steady trend of inflation. We must accept the premise that inflation, even if it takes a respite, will continue. Only its growth rate changes.

In times of rapidly increasing inflation, even people with little business experience who are willing to take a chance with their time, money, and credit can earn large sums of money through real estate. They need only be at the right place at the right time. They must, however, be alert for recessions and sudden dramatic increases in interest rates. And they must be willing to pay for the real estate experience that they acquire.

Function of Escrow Companies

Some states have escrow companies that attempt to protect buyers and sellers alike. They are run by escrow officers who do not pretend to act as attorneys. Basically, the function of an escrow office is to act as a stakeholder of the moneys (the deposit and the final payment). They fill in printed forms with the vital information, issue an order to have the county's real property ownership records searched for ownership and liens, and get the buyer a standard policy of title insurance guaranteeing valid title. Then, they close the transaction by recording the deed and paying the seller. Even if you agree with the seller to use an escrow office, if you are inexperienced, first consult with your attorney before you "go to escrow."

Having the title to property usually means having the recorded rights to ownership of that property. That ownership may be legally described and recorded in various ways. Each type of ownership has different rights, obligations, and liabilities.

Types of Ownership

Basically, there are two types of ownership. The first type is referred to as *separate ownership*. The second type is referred to as *concurrent ownership*.

Separate ownership means that only one person or entity owns the property and that person or entity is entitled to all benefits and burdens (such as taxes) and has the right to sell it without other signatures.

Concurrent ownership embraces tenancies in common, joint-tenancies, community property, and tenancies in partnership. (As used herein, tenancies are legal terms that refer to ownership interests and are not to be confused with tenants who pay rent.)

Tenancies in common refer to two or more persons, including a husband and wife, owning an undivided interest, in equal or unequal shares, in a single estate, with equal rights of possession. It is a troublesome type of ownership that should be avoided. It usually occurs when the deed granting title does not specify one of the other types of tenancies. Each owner may sell his common interest and if an owner dies, his heirs become proportionate tenants in common with the surviving owner.

Joint tenancies refer to two or more people owning an undivided interest in real property. If one of the joint tenants dies, the survivors automatically own the interests of the deceased owner.

Community property refers to equal ownership by a husband and wife, with neither being able to sell it separately unless one of them dies.

A *tenancy in partnership* refers to title being vested in the partnership. Individual partners cannot sell their share in the partnership without the consent of the other partners. If a partner dies, his interest passes to the surviving partner, pending liquidation of the partnership, at which time his share goes to the estate.

Basically, real estate should be evaluated from two aspects: the value of the land and the value of the improvements on the land. Sophisticated investors, however, consider other aspects. For example, the immediate or future potential of the land or property for increased value or higher revenues, with and without additional improvements, is considered.

Equity Sharing

Some inexperienced investors with small amounts of cash get started in real estate investments through a plan called "equity sharing." The plan is also referred to as a "shared appreciation" system. Through "equity-sharing," an investor, instead of loaning money to a borrower to buy a house or a few small rental units and then taking back a mortgage or trust deed, uses the same amount of money to purchase an interest in the property. This way the investor is able to share a portion of the tax advantages and benefit from any increase in the value of the property.

It is presumed that a tenant with an ownership-interest in the property will take better care of the property than an ordinary renter. However, these types of agreements should not be entered into without the advice of a knowledgeable real estate or tax lawyer. To properly deduct depreciation for tax purposes the agreements must conform with the Internal Revenue code.

The "lease-option" plan is another method that helps potential investors with small amounts of cash. The procedure is simple, even if your funds are limited. First, find a house or duplex in which you would like to live, and then purchase it when you are able. Then, offer the owner more rent than he asks, but ask him if he would give you a one- or two-year *lease option* to buy the property at a fair price. The lease option permits you to buy the property within the time specified in the lease option at the price specified. If, within two years, the property has increased in value, you can buy it and make the profit. If it has not increased in value, you are not compelled to buy it. You can either renew your lease or try to renew the lease option.

When acquiring a lease option, it is necessary to give the owner a special consideration for the lease option. This is necessary to be enforceable in a court of law since all contracts, including lease option agreements, must have a consideration (something of value) given in exchange for the promise. It is also important to secure the advice of a lawyer to properly prepare the documents.

Real estate can be bought with or without a broker. But regardless of how you buy it, if you are inexperienced, get an attorney to represent you. Do not part with any money or sign any documents without your attorney's permission.

Mistakes to Avoid When Purchasing Real Estate

When buying property for income, there are several mistakes you can make. Here is how to avoid some of these:

1. If you find the property through a real estate broker, ask whether he or she represents the seller or you. If the answer is, "the seller," be alerted that the broker is not obligated to tell you the lowest price that the seller would accept for the property.
2. Be aware that one of the major mistakes made by investors when considering the value of most types of income property is that they look over a statement of income, expenses, and profits without understanding it or checking the arithmetic. Even on established properties that should have actual figures to back up the sales representations, some brokers and sellers furnish estimated statements instead of using the actual figures. Make sure that you get the actual figures and that you understand them.
3. Make sure that you acquire clear title to the property. Even if all of the arrangements and terms seem satisfactory to you, do not sign any documents until your attorney, preferably someone who specializes in real estate, checks them for you.

4. Even though you might like to enjoy the pride of ownership, if you have a choice between two properties—one that offers higher net profits and one that offers lower profits but that will give you pride of ownership—treat the transaction like a business. Regardless of your preferences, if the value is there, take the profits and forget the pride.
5. Both sellers and brokers may minimize losses from vacancies as well as proper expenses for maintenance and repair. The investor may be led to believe that the premises are always 100 percent occupied. Determine free rent concessions and any lost rent due to the time required for redecorating after a tenant vacates the premises. Check the area to see how many vacancies similar properties have. By finding out if there are any other properties for sale and comparing their statements with the one given to you, you will get a much better idea of the true picture of your potential purchase.
6. Paying cash for investment property usually is not recommended. Therefore, your method of financing becomes very important. Even a fraction of a percent of interest, like half of one percent, makes a big difference over a 30-year mortgage or trust deed. It is not only the extra one-half percent that mounts up in 30 years. If that one-half percent could have been used to reduce the principal with each payment instead of being used for interest, the overall interest would be materially less. By way of comparison, consider a 30-year $500,000 trust deed or mortgage with 10 percent interest. There would be 360 monthly payments of $4,390 per month, totaling $1,580,400. If the interest were one-half percent less (9½ percent), the amount paid in 30 years would be $4,205. per month, totaling $1,513,800 and reflecting a savings in interest payments of $66,600. But the amount saved actually exceeds those savings. The $66,600 that was saved could have been used to earn additional income.
7. Check whether you can assume the current financing and how much extra, if at all, your assumption of the current financing will cost you. Also, check the cost of refinancing and the amount of the new interest rate and new monthly payments, based on the amount of cash you desire to invest. Try more than one source of financing. Then make comparisons between the existing and the best proposed financing.

8. Learn about the intelligent use of *leverage* to enable you to increase your profits with a minimum of risk. In real estate transactions, using leverage refers to making the most amount of money that you safely can from your real estate investment without increasing the size of your investment. To understand how leverage works for you, assume that you had $200,000 cash that you wanted to invest in an apartment house that showed an undisputed annual net return of $30,000 a year if you bought it for cash. That would mean that you were getting a 15 percent return on your investment. If, however, you decided to buy the same property for $200,000 with $140,000 in cash and the buyer taking back a 30-year mortgage or trust deed for $60,000 at 9½ percent payable monthly, the amortized payments (those that pay off the principal) would be $504.60 a month, or $6,055.20 a year. If you deduct those amortized payments from the scheduled net profit of $30,000 on an-all cash investment, the profit would be approximately $24,000 a year. Then, to get the correct yield on your investment, you would divide your cash investment of $140,000 into the net profit of $24,000, and your yield would be 17.1 percent, or 2.1 percent higher than if you had paid all cash. And with every payment you would be paying off your principal. Moreover, you would have an extra $60,000 to invest elsewhere or to keep as a cushion for protection.

   The only problem that is encountered with leverage is that some people try to use an excessive amount of it. If there is a downturn in the economy, these people may not then be financially able to cope with the new economic circumstances.
9. Do not buy property when money is tight and interest rates are too high. Although rates can go higher, experience indicates that when interest rates get too high, they always drop because of the lack of demand for money at those high rates. You cannot afford to be stuck with income property that carries long-term financing at high rates. Whenever your fixed expenses are too high, you take the risk that your competition, with less expense, will rent for less than you. When that occurs, you will have too many vacancies and you may not be able to pay your obligations and taxes.

10. Check your potential profits by allowing for a 5 or 10 percent vacancy factor. (Take a percentage of the gross rental—divide the gross rental by the vacancy factor—and subtract the answer from the gross rental.) If you are unfamiliar with vacancy factors or what they are in your area, check with the managers of buildings with similar units in the area and find out how long it usually takes to secure a solid tenant. (A solid tenant is a person who is either working, has an income, or has money in the bank, and will sign a lease.)
11. Allow a sufficient percentage for maintenance, repairs, janitorial services, and periodic redecorating and recarpeting. If you are inexperienced and unfamiliar with these types of statements and figures, make comparisons with those of other buildings that are for sale. Again, if you do not understand them, get professional assistance.
12. Do not take on the burdens of owning and managing an apartment house unless you can visualize a large increase in the value of the property. You should also anticipate a net return on your money of at least 15 percent plus the amortization on the mortgage or trust deed.

Before You Give a Deposit

After you are satisfied with the stipulated income and expenses and agree on a price, then before actually giving a deposit or signing any papers or making the purchase of any type of income property, there is no substitute for:

1. A physical, walk-around examination of the neighborhood combined with a conversation with a few local brokers or landlords in the community. Try to find out what property is for sale that is comparable to the property you are evaluating.
2. An inquiry to local shopkeepers and real estate brokers as to what new developments may occur that could affect either the tenancy or the value of similar neighborhood properties. At the same time, inquire about what the normal rentals are for the type of property you have in mind.
3. A physical examination of both the interior and exterior of the building with special emphasis on the type of care and maintenance it received. Find out if it requires attention and how much it will cost to maintain or restore it to good condition.

4. Getting an idea directly from the tenants as to what their future plans are, even though the seller may not approve.
5. Inserting protective clauses in the first document signed by you. Regardless of whether it be the deposit receipt, contract of sale, or escrow agreement, your first document should state that the purchase is subject to your examination and approval of the alleged leases. It should also be subject to your approval of a report, by a qualified engineer of your choice, of the results of an inspection of the boilers, elevators, roofs, equipment, and fixtures within the building.
6. Securing a good real estate lawyer, selected by you, to provide the additional protective clauses that will protect your deposit and investment.

Buying Undeveloped Land

Buying undeveloped land offers both poor and rich investors the best opportunity to increase their wealth and protect their future. Both can use a maximum amount of leverage (described earlier in this chapter) when purchasing land. And, when they are ready to sell, both can benefit from permitting other people to also use leverage when buying the land from them. Another wonderful part of making money out of unimproved land is that it increases in value without you doing anything. The only requirements for success are that you buy land that is in the path of growth, and then just hold on to it patiently. Fortunately, the rewards are worth the waiting. Although making profits out of land investments is not a "get rich quick business," you can shorten the waiting period if you observe the following suggestions:

- Try to buy land that is in the path of growth before the growth gets there, and before everybody learns about it. You may still make money if the area you select is developing or is being promotionally exploited, but you can usually afford to buy more land and make more money if you buy before it is exploited. Whether or not you like the land or from whom you buy it is unimportant. Liking the land is only important if you are going to live on it. Many people live on, work on, and have sold for large profits, land that you would not like. Even the price is not as important as being able to buy it with a small down payment, such as 10 or 20 percent down, and long-term, easy monthly payments that you can afford. It is

wiser to overpay for the property and have the terms fit your budget than it is to purchase property that might be a better buy but could endanger your financial position.
- Also, no matter how little land you buy, try to purchase parcels that are large enough to split up into smaller parcels. This gives you the choice of selling part of it immediately to help you pay for what you bought, while retaining part of it for the future. Or you may want to keep it all and sell it later in one piece or in smaller subdivided lots. Finally, you might want to build income property on it.

Putting a selling price on a parcel of undeveloped land may be compared to "pricing" commodities such as sugar. Just as a 100-pound sack of sugar is cheaper per pound to buy than a one-pound bag of sugar, 640 acres of land is usually much less expensive per acre than a single acre. This is why the owner of a large tract of land can afford to sell smaller parcels at a fair price and make a fair profit.

For example, assume you bought an acre of land (43,560 square feet) at a fair price. Then later, as the area becomes more desirable, you have two choices: Sell the acre as is for the going price. Or, legally subdivide the acre, subject to zoning laws, into four or five lots, and sell them at a price that will make you and the buyers happy. If you sell your acre on time, you can collect interest on the balance due, which could be 100 times more than the amount of the down payment that you made when you bought the property.

In 1963, 10-acre parcels of undeveloped desert land in Southern California sold for $200 an acre ($2,000 for 10 acres) with $400 down and monthly payments of only $16 per month including 6 percent interest. In 1987, that same property sold for $20,000 with $2,000 down and a balance of $18,000 payable at the rate of $180 per month at 10 percent interest!

The reason that the land business has been so successful for most of the people who have participated in it is that it is possible for the buyer to get a good buy while allowing the seller to make a profit.

Usable vacant land is a good asset because it does not deteriorate, go out of style, or require management other than paying the taxes, which are usually low. Unfortunately, you cannot depreciate land for tax purposes. However, subject to changes in the tax laws, you can deduct from your federal income taxes the local property taxes and, in some instances, a limited amount of the interest that you pay out.

As a prospective real estate investor, you must be aware of some of the traps. The owners of both improved and unimproved real property have the burden of paying taxes and improvement assessments on their property in the district in which the property is located. Assessments may be for improvements that offer no benefit. Frequently, tax assessments are levied for improvements that are made in a part of the assessment district that will not materially benefit the assessee. For example, the district in which the property is located might be assessed for a sewer, water, or fire district. The property may be unimproved, vacant, and not require a sewer, water, or fire protection. Or if it is improved, it might not be near water or sewer lines for many years. Also accompanying land ownership is the possibility of becoming liable in damages for accidents that may occur on your land, even if it is vacant and you were not personally negligent or at fault.

About Taxes

Investors must always be concerned with tax considerations. In addition to garnering the benefits of inflation, all types of property ownership may yield some tax benefits, subject to the Tax Reform Act of 1986 and expected revisions in the future. Even without depreciation, benefits are obtained through the deduction of the local property taxes and a limited amount of interest payments.

Property that qualifies as income property, which may even include a resort or second home that is rented or leased out under conditions that satisfy the tax authorities, may also use depreciation of the property as a benefit and tax shelter.

The words "tax shelter" instead of tax savings are used for real estate depreciation because a portion of the savings are sometimes only temporary. This is because the money that is saved may have to be paid to the government at a later date. This can occur whenever the selling price of the property exceeds the amount of money that has been depreciated or, in some events, if the depreciation schedule was for too short a period of time.

Most improvements to income property, including fixtures that are permanently attached, are considered real property. For tax purposes they are treated differently than personal property such as trade fixtures, furniture, and removable carpeting. Also, they may be depreciated in a shorter period of time.

Because of alternative minimum tax provisions in the Tax Reform Act of 1986, the same property could have different tax consequences for different buyers. Accordingly, the tax regulations that pertain to investment interest and the restrictions on deductions that apply to passive and non-passive income should be discussed with a professional tax adviser before you invest.

Now you know about many of the benefits available from owning real estate. You may possess a strong desire to own some yourself, especially since you have learned how to get started in income-producing properties. The information provided in this chapter (showing you mistakes to avoid) should give you sufficient confidence to start your own investment program. Based on this information and the practical experience that you will acquire after you start investing, you should be able to invest with relative safety in any of a number of property types.

Chapter 27: Stocks, Bonds, and Commodities

Stocks, Bonds, and Commodities

It is not the function of this book to tell you how to get rich in the stock market or to suggest that you play the market. There is no shortage of books, financial advisers, or stock brokers professing to do that. However, all informed investors should possess an understanding of the various types of securities, different stock exchanges, stock markets, and how to protect themselves against them. All adults should learn the difference between stocks, bonds, commodities, and the various other types of securities. Even if you are not inclined to play the markets, someday you may form a stock corporation, inherit securities, or receive an irresistible "hot tip" about a promising stock issue.

What are Securities?

The term "securities" refers to documents that evidence a debt-relationship between the issuer and the owner and in which the owner is the creditor. Stocks, bonds, options, and futures contracts on commodities are referred to as securities.

Every corporation begins its life through the capital funds that it collects from investors. In return, the investors receive shares of stock which are evidence that they own a capital (equity) interest in the company. An equity interest refers to an ownership interest as distinguished from the interest of a lender in a bond.

Although bonds are also used to raise capital for the corporation, they cannot be issued by the corporation until it is formed and has issued stock. Basically, a corporation bond is a promissory note from the corporation, usually issued in multiples of $1,000 (but it can also be $50, $500, or $5,000). The bond specifies that the corporation will pay a certain rate of interest at specific times for a set number of years, after which it will pay off the debt.

The difference between a share of stock and a bond is that the bondholder lends his money to the company and does not own an equity interest. A stockholder buys a percentage share of the corporation. Thus, any profits or increases in the value of the corporation benefits the stockholders (as owners) but not the bondholders, except for gaining confidence in the safety of their bonds.

When the corporation makes a profit, the board of directors may declare a dividend. This means that all shareholders will receive an equal share of those profits. Bondholders never receive a dividend. Instead of a dividend, they receive a specified interest payment even if the corporation does not earn a profit. However, when the company operates at a loss, the value of its stocks and bonds usually decrease.

Occasionally, corporations do not want (or cannot afford) to disturb their assets. However, if they want their company to appear active, they issue additional shares of stock as a dividend instead of cash. When this occurs the stockholders' percentage of ownership remains the same. They do not derive any tangible benefit until the corporation prospers or the value of the stock increases.

Classes of Stock

Corporations may issue more than one class of stock, usually called class A, class B, preferred, or convertible stock. One class of stock may have more rights or preferences than another. For instance, some classes may have voting rights and others may not. Some stocks, called preferred, may entitle the owners to a specified dividend before the owners of the common stock receive theirs. Cumulative preferred stocks have an advantage over regular preferred stock. When a company does not earn a sufficient amount to declare a dividend for the preferred stock, the missed dividend is lost. However, with the cumulative preferred, if the specified payment cannot be paid, it is not lost. When the corporation has sufficient funds to pay dividends, the owners of the cumulative preferred stock are entitled to receive the total of all the specified cumulative dividends that were missed.

You should never buy any shares in any corporation until you check the types and quantities of stock that were issued. Also, ascertain what special rights each class of stock grants or takes away. A stock that is called preferred may, in fact, have fewer rights than the ordinary common, but it is legal to call it preferred.

As an enticement to purchase their preferred securities, some corporations issue warrants with their preferred securities. They are called subscription warrants and permit the holder to purchase a specified amount of stock at a certain time in the future at a specified price. This can be advantageous if the stock rises in price.

Bonds, preferred stock, and debentures (any instruments other than a mortgage or trust deed that evidences corporate debt) may be convertible. This means that they may be exchanged in accordance with the terms of the issue and at a specified date or occurrence, for a certain amount of shares of common or preferred stock. Convertible instruments usually sell for a premium because they offer their owners certain rights. At their will, owners may convert their stocks to another type of stock that pays higher dividends than their convertible stocks.

Quality Rating

The quality of corporate bonds traded in the stock market is evaluated by rating services such as Standard & Poor's, Moody's, and Fitch. Standard & Poor's and Fitch use AAA as the designation for their "top rated" bonds. Moody's top rating for the highest quality bonds is Aaa and their lowest rating is C. The bonds are rated according to a system that divides them into four groupings (Moody's only has three) based on their quality. Each grouping contains three classifications. As the quality of the bonds decline, their alphabetical ratings in each classification also decline alphabetically. The A's drop to the D's (except Moody's) and change from triple letters to single letters. Thus, in the top group, AAA is the highest quality followed by AA, a high quality bond, and then by A, a medium quality bond. The next group starts with BBB for a medium grade, declines to BB which mostly refers to speculative bonds, and down to B for low grade and highly speculative bonds. The last two groups are the C's and D's, which should not merit your attention.

All bonds are considered extremely interest-sensitive. For example, a bond that is rated AAA and paying 10 percent interest, will drop in value if similar bonds are issued at 11 percent. Conversely, this bond will increase in value when the interest rate drops.

Listing on the Stock Exchanges

The stocks or bonds of ordinary corporations cannot be sold on the stock market. The various stock markets only sell securities in corporations that have been approved by them. The major stock market in the United States is the New York Stock Exchange (NYSE), which has been in existence since 1792. The requirements for listing stocks on the NYSE are stricter than for the other exchanges.

Membership in the NYSE is limited to those brokerage firms that meet its requirements and who own what is called "a seat on the Exchange." There are about 1,366 Exchange seats. Seats are usually purchased from other members for considerable amounts of money that vary according to the current volume of stock market activity and potential profits. Stock brokerage firms that do not possess a seat on the Exchange must clear their buy and sell orders with a member firm. The other major exchange in the United States is the American Stock Exchange, whose requirements are not as rigid as those of the NYSE. The NYSE only accepts companies that meet its extremely high financial and performance requirements, which eliminates any speculative companies. This forces them to be traded on the other exchanges.

To be listed on the New York Stock Exchange, companies must first prove their acceptance by the public on the other exchanges. Then, if they meet the NYSE specifications, they might be listed on that exchange. Even IBM did not get started on the NYSE. It worked its way up through the smaller exchanges. Stocks are also sold and traded on the "over the counter" market and by other minor and foreign exchanges.

On both the New York and the American Exchanges, stocks are bought and sold on a "bid and asked" auction basis. The price that you see in the paper is usually the last price for which 100 shares of stock in a particular company was traded. But first, the owner of the stock places an order with his broker to sell a certain quantity of stock at a specific price. The buyer, through his broker, offers to buy a certain quantity of the same stock at a specific price. Each order is promptly relayed to the floor of the respective exchange that trades in these stocks. Then the respective brokers, who make a market in these stocks on the floor of the exchanges, act as their trading agents. At times, however, in order to stabilize the market, the floor brokers may buy stocks in their own account.

Most small corporations usually begin the sale of their stock on the "over the counter (OTC) market" or other types of markets. The OTC is not referred to as a stock exchange. Its trading is usually done electronically by stock and bond dealers who are supervised by the National Association of Securities Dealers (NASDA).

The stocks of many small companies that are not listed on the OTC market are listed and quoted in the "Pink Sheets" issued by the National Quotation Bureau (NQB). These sheets list bonds on what is called a "Yellow Sheet." The prices quoted in the Pink Sheets are usually determined by specialists. Every company is represented by one or a few specialist brokers who "make a market" in the stocks of the companies in which they specialize.

For example, if you are interested in the stocks of one of these companies and want to learn the "asking price" for a specific number of shares, your broker will contact the specialists who "make a market" for the stock. He will obtain their "bid-and-asked" prices for the stock. It is important to contact more than one specialist broker because the asking prices are seldom the same.

When stocks are listed on an exchange, they are usually assigned a three- or four-letter symbol to identify them. When you ask for a price quotation on a stock, brokers prefer that you use the specified symbol for the stock because this is what they refer to when checking it on their computer.

Buy Low—Sell High

There's no doubt that the most logical investment advice that you can receive is "to buy low and sell high." Although this advice leads to success in most ventures, it's really a joke—an elusive dream shared by millions of unsophisticated investors who do not realize that anything connected with the stock market is a big gamble. That includes some blue chip companies and municipal bonds. Experienced investors understand the gambling aspects of their investments. They would also like (but don't know how) to buy at the lowest price and sell at the highest price. They are satisfied, whenever possible, to find a safe investment that will return a reasonable profit when they sell it.

The original purpose of the NYSE has been overshadowed by the inclination of most of its investors to turn it into a gambling arena. The original purpose of the stock exchange was to help corporations raise capital funds through the sale of stocks. The basic idea was to encourage the investment of capital in new corporations by making their stocks more liquid and attractive. The Exchange provided a central area in which the original owners could sell their stock, through brokers, without undue delay.

Market Price

In 1792, when the NYSE was formed, the value of most stocks was not dependent upon supply and demand. It was based on the capitalization (assets) of a corporation, the experience of its directors and management, its capital appreciation potential, and its ability to make a profit and pay dividends.

Today, the market price (not the intrinsic value) of a corporation's stock is not as much dependent on its capitalization, assets, and potential to make money. It is more dependent on the opinions of a select group of unrelated money managers of billions of investment dollars who seem to follow each other's financial inclinations like so many sheep. These are the managers who control vast sums of pensions funds, mutual funds, and IRA and Keogh funds.

It is unfortunate that the whims of this small group of people have taken control of the market from the general public. Because they control stock market activity and volume, they are able to influence the economic climate of the United States. Meanwhile, the general public sits by helplessly. For example, the various organizations that collect and administer pension funds usually place them in the hands of investment houses whose money managers are expected to know enough to earn the highest return. When interest rates are high, the managers tend to loan out the money (the riskier the loan, the more interest they can charge). Those who want to show a high percentage of profit, loan the funds to poorer risks. When the loan is endangered, they still carry it on their books as an asset; the interest due may be shown as an account payable asset. More importantly, if one of the managers gets an idea—not necessarily scientific or correct—that interest rates will decline, the available loaned money and cash reserves are quickly switched into stocks which are probably priced low because of high interest rates. When the other money managers, who watch each other like hawks, learn of the switch, they also switch. This creates an unusual demand for the stocks and an increase in their prices.

Thus, an individual investor who may have been checking out

certain stocks and deciding to buy them on their merits receives a sudden, disheartening surprise: the cost of the stocks have increased and, therefore, the percentage of return on the investment will be smaller than expected. And, yet, while this investor is still investing in the same corporation, the underlying fundamentals of the stock will not have improved.

Price Determined by Supply and Demand

Since the manager of a large pension fund can increase the price of a stock, even though its basic, intrinsic value may not have improved, an auxiliary lesson can be learned. In the marketplace, the true asset value, current earnings, or earnings potential of a stock may not be as important as the price that is created by the supply and demand for the stock.

By extension, any similar and equally unwarranted decisions that cause a money manager to dump stocks to accumulate cash can seriously affect the values of all stocks regardless of the merits of either the stocks or the manager's decision. These decisions may be based on wrong guesses, incorrect interpretations of economic indicators, undue pessimism, or unfounded hunches on the part of money managers. Consequently, an investor who does his own analysis and becomes familiar with economic trends may find many undervalued or overvalued stocks at any given time.

Even if the proper stock selection is made at the right time, there is always the necessity for selling the stocks at the right time. This means that your stock transaction does not end when you make the purchase. Your constant supervision and personal follow-up are always required until the transaction is completed through a subsequent sale.

Unless you are prepared to follow the company's business and financial activities, as well as the fluctuations of its stock in the market, do not buy any stocks. The exception is if you plan to put them away and forget about them for an indefinite period. In past years, this was not a bad idea. But in today's modern world, where a high degree of technical innovativeness contributes to a high rate of obsolescence of industries and products, the prices of your stocks must be watched vigilantly. This is particularly true since the Black Monday of 1987, when it was established that stocks could drop as much as 508 points in a single day. Because of the plethora of computerized trading and the constant explosion of up-to-date business and stock market information disseminated by the media, the investment markets are not as stable as they were two or three decades ago.

Today, the various markets—and some of their stocks—are subject to too many unpredictable variables. These include the effects of the latest reports of unemployment, inflation, and up-to-the-minute, computerized governmental and private reports about important changes in the economy. The markets' extreme sensitivity to these factors, combined with fluctuations of both foreign and domestic interest rates, can change the value of your assets before you know it.

Sophisticated Trading Techniques

There are many other factors that contribute to the instability and occasional high volatility of today's stock markets. Among these are:

- Short selling
- Programmed trading
- The triple witching hour

Many investors now engage in short sales. A short sale is a sale of borrowed stocks by an investor who expects their price to drop. If they do drop, the investor buys them at the reduced price, replaces the borrowed stocks with the stocks that he purchased at a reduced price, and retains the profits from the difference in prices.

For example, an investor knows of a stock that is selling for $100 a share and believes that the price of the stock will drop to $90 a share. He effects a short sale using the following technique: He borrows 100 shares from his broker by giving the broker an order to sell short 100 shares of the stock for $100 a share. Regardless of what happens to the price of the stock, the investor is obligated to purchase and replace the borrowed stock. If the price of the stock goes higher, he loses money. If his prediction about the reduced price materializes and the stock drops to $90 a share, the investor orders the broker to buy 100 shares at $90. Then, he repays the 100 shares to the broker and, before deducting commissions, his gross profit becomes $1,000. This is the difference between the $9,000 for the shares he bought and the $10,000 for the shares he sold.

Programmed trading is a prearranged plan used usually, but not necessarily, by financial institutions. The plan calls for buying or selling options and/or futures in commodities or financial instruments, such as stocks. For a fraction of the cost of actually buying the securities themselves, the institution can buy either a call or a put option. An option is a right that is granted by an option writer (a person or financial institution) to a buyer for a fee (premium). The option entitles the buyer to either buy or sell commodities, stocks, or stock indexes at a fixed price before a specified date. An option to buy is referred to as a "call option." The option to sell is referred to as a "put option." These options provide buyers with a tremendous amount of leverage at a very low cost.

Another advantage for the buyers is an opportunity to speculate, be wrong, lose their premiums, and still make an overall profit. The options may be exercised at any time within the prescribed periods, which are usually for 3, 6, or 9 months. Most options are exercised before they become due.

There are many variations of these options. All are controlled by the Options Clearing Corporation (OCC). The OCC, upon request, will provide you with a free prospectus that describes the details and risks that are involved in buying or writing the various types of options. You may secure this information by writing to them at 200 S. Wacker Drive, 27th floor, Chicago, Illinois, 60606.

Futures contracts are agreements created and traded at commodities exchanges to buy or sell a definite quantity of commodities or securities at a set price at a specified future date. Unlike options, the contract must be fulfilled.

Programmed trading can create heavy swings in the market on two occasions. One occasion is called the *triple witching hour*. The other is when a large amount of buy or sell orders are issued automatically by computers and professional traders. The swings occur as soon as a large disparity in prices between stock index futures and current prices are spotted.

The triple witching hour is the last hour of trading that occurs four times a year: on the third Friday of each March, June, September, and December. It is a by-product of the popularity of "stock index contracts." Contracts such as "options," 'futures on stocks," and "stock indexes" usually expire at the end of the witching hour. Prior to these quarterly settlement dates, the market is flooded with a huge avalanche of expected orders. The resultant up or down volatility of the market in those quarterly closing hours, which produces vast uncertainty among investors, created the term triple witching hour.

Mutual Funds

The mutual fund industry is very large and complex. Here, our discussion only covers the important highlights. It does not pretend to be a thorough review of a complex subject or to qualify you to select the best one for your purposes. Further sources are recommended at the end of the discussion.

Mutual funds, formerly referred to as Investment Trusts, have become popular investment vehicles. Mutual funds provide the investor with a care-free opportunity to invest in securities and commodities. A major benefit is that mutual funds are supervised by professional management. They also offer a diversified portfolio of securities.

Mutual fund companies constitute an industry that caters to every type of investor. The funds enable an investor to select and invest in a fund whose investment goals are the same as those of the investor. Their objectives may be conservative, speculative, or both. They may be oriented towards capital growth, the payment of regular dividends, gains from short- or long-term trading, investing in other mutual funds, other unlimited purposes, or combinations of each. Also, the funds spare the investors from becoming involved in the mechanics of buying, selling, and supervising a variety of their own stocks.

Another advantage for investors whose capital is limited is that mutual funds enable them to save extra commissions whenever they purchase less than 100 shares of many different securities.

According to a mid-1985 Associated Press report, 47 million Americans were stockholders; 63 percent had an Individual Retirement Account (IRA) or Keogh Plan (HR10), and there was an increase in investors who were participating in mutual funds. Recently, a Merrill Lynch director of Marketing Services estimated that nearly 24 percent of all new investors chose mutual funds.

It has been estimated that there are about 2,000 different types of mutual funds. Most use varying percentages of their funds to buy different types of securities, including a large percentage of stocks (called equities). When the managers of mutual funds do not feel that it is timely to invest in equities, they invest their reserves in liquid, safe, interest-bearing instruments or accounts.

It is not easy to select the mutual fund that will serve you best. The major problems connected with selecting the correct mutual fund involve:

1. Securing undistorted facts relating to performance, fees, and undisclosed charges
2. Finding one in which the the buy-in charges do not reduce your investment too drastically. For example, on a "load-fund," if you invest $5,000 and the buy-in charge is 8 percent, your net investment will be reduced to $4,600 without considering other fees.
3. Finding one that matches your investment objectives

The performance records of mutual funds vary from good to bad. Many investors have been disappointed by some of their poor results. Unfortunately, many of their statements regarding profits are not always accurate or based on acceptable accounting standards.

For example, a recent report on a mutual fund indicated a high percentage of profit. It stated that it only used profit percentages from the amount of money invested. The managers of the fund did not average their alleged profit with low profit from a large uninvested reserve. Moreover, the profits occurred when most stocks were increasing in value. Such deceptive tactics and reports make it difficult for the average investor to select a satisfactory mutual fund.

The two types of mutual funds are called *load* and *no-load*. The load funds, usually sold by brokers, can cost as much as 8 percent or more of the amount invested in the fund for commission fees. Adding the 8 percent commission to 3- to 4-percent annual inflation rate means that the load fund must make an 11- to 12-percent profit per year to break even. Of course, when we have double-digit inflation, the break-even point is about 18 percent. You should also know that the commission rates may be considerably lower for large dollar investments.

The no-load funds, usually sold by mail without a broker, do not have any commission or brokerage fees. This is because most of the selling business can be transacted by mail. However, the management fees and sometimes withdrawal or other hidden fees that come with the no-loads can be more than you bargained for. The no-load management fees vary, of course, but usually range between ½ to 1 percent of the fund's asset value.

Recently, a *Wall Street Journal* article stated, "Consumer groups charge that some companies are selling alleged 'no-load' products that actually contain hidden fees."

One mutual fund letter refers to some mutual fund practices as deceptive, citing 4 percent redemption charges. Sometimes the charges (or loads) are on the back of an agreement instead of the front. Some new funds that pose as no-loads charge about 1 percent of the value of the fund's assets annually, plus a redemption fee and an advertising fee. All of these fees may be listed in the prospectus but you will have to be a careful reader to find them. It is difficult to interpret how they will affect your investment and whether the fund's profit figures take into account the fees that will be deducted from the assets.

Look at the following solicitation copy found in a newspaper: "No set-up fees, yearly maintenance fees, or sales commissions." You still have to find out if there are withdrawal, advertising, or management fees. If there are, you should compare the solicitation with those of equivalent type funds.

Some investment advisers feel that the performance of a mutual fund is more important than their commissions, withdrawal, or management fees. In other words, if a mutual fund loses money, you might have been better off paying the loads for a company that made a profit. Although this type of reasoning sounds good, it is fallacious. There is no reason why a no-load fund cannot be as profitable or even more profitable than a load fund.

If you want a mutual fund to make your market investments for you, first carefully compare the literature on such funds. Learn about the claims and expenses associated with the funds and the types of investments being made by the managers of the funds. Then invest in a fund whose investment philosophy seems to be compatible with yours.

Some funds offer a variety of specific goals while others try to combine growth, income, and safety. Mutual fund growth refers to its capital appreciation. Income refers to earnings. Safety refers to concentrating on risk-free investments. But remember, the mere fact that one of these mutual funds had a good record in recent years does not mean that it will have a good record next year.

Aside from the economy, which can help or harm any investment, the performance of individual mutual funds depends on three factors: the investments selected, the amount of capital that is kept invested, and the timing used to get in and out of the investments. After mutual funds managers have determined the industries in which they will invest, their biggest challenge is to remain underinvested until the market starts to boom. Then, they must avoid being overinvested when the market starts to drop.

Even though there are many reputable mutual funds, you must always examine the various performance claims. For instance, if a mutual fund has made a larger profit than most others in the same type of market, it may mean that the fund's managers took extraordinary risks that paid off. Remember, if you invest in such a fund, changing conditions may cause the fund's risky investments to lose an extraordinary amount of money. And it is always possible that some mutual fund companies are so badly managed that they can lose money even when the market is in a steady rise.

A major problem experienced by pension and mutual funds is that the managers get into and out of too many transactions too quickly. This generates an excessive amount of commission and management fees. You can check if a mutual fund has had too much turnover by securing statements from a few mutual funds that have the same investment goals. Then, for each fund ascertain its assets and the number of transactions in which it was involved. That way, you can make easy comparisons. If, by comparison, a firm's transactions are too high for its asset value, then its management may be poor. However, if its earnings were higher than those of the other companies, the management might be using good judgment. There are also situations in which the disadvantages of high fees and undisclosed charges can be ignored. An investment is justified if it shows a net profit that is at least equal to the interest earned from high quality bonds or savings accounts.

Because of the poor performance of their money managers, some funds companies have gone into "mechanically investing" their funds according to various stock indexes. For our purposes, an index is a measure of the value of a group of stocks, other interests, or securities. The indexes are compiled and disseminated by various sources on a frequent basis. An index may be based on either all or only a sample of the stocks whose value it is intended to represent. All indexes must start with an index base level, as of a certain date. There is no set standard for creating an index base. Setting the base involves selecting the stocks, determining the number of stocks to be used, and then deciding how to evaluate them. After the base is established, the index may be assigned an arbitrary level, such as a number 100. This makes it easier to understand and work from. Once the index level of the base is established, it becomes the reference point for future activities and comparisions.

In essence, private investors and mutual funds, instead of buying stocks, place a wager in the form of an order on what the future value of the index will be at a certain date. They also place buy or sell orders that are automatically fulfilled when the index reaches a specified index level. That is a form of "automatic" or "mechanical" investing.

This kind of trading is conducted under the general framework that is referred to as trading in the options or futures market. "Mechanical investing" (automatic trading) ventures have become quite successful in recent years. Some of the large financial institutions are offering investors the opportunity to participate in the use of "extended market funds." Some of these funds have from a few to several thousand stocks as the basis of their index. Some use Standard & Poor's variety of small indexes and the Wilshire 5,000 Index. Also, individual investors may now use an option or a futures contract to buy or sell a quoted value of a stock index. (The futures contract is a commitment and must be exercised by a set date; but the options contract may be exercised by the expiration date or ignored.)

There are many mutual fund investment letters that are widely distributed. Among the companies that evaluate the performance records of mutual funds are Lipper Analytical Services, Inc., a Wall Street Research firm.

Advisors and Planners

If you cannot select your own securities or other investments, obtain the assistance of an independent investment advisor. An investment advisor is sometimes incorrectly referred to as an investment counselor or a financial planner. Get a recommendation from someone whose opinion you respect. Investment advisors are required to register with the Securities & Exchange Commission (SEC). They are not permitted to have a conflict of interest in whatever they recommend to you. They may charge you an hourly fee or a percentage of the amount that you invest.

Some advisors maintain a brokerage license from the SEC and may be satisfied to advise you without charge in exchange for the commission they earn if you buy or sell through them.

To avoid a possible conflict of interest, it is preferable to pay for advice. If you trust the advice, purchase your investments through a reputable brokerage firm that will give you prompt service and understandable bookkeeping.

Some investors prefer the services of Certified Financial Planners. They must pass a tougher qualifying test than Registered Investment Advisers. The latter should not be confused with the registered representatives who work for the broker/dealer with whom you trade. These representatives are also authorized to advise you but receive a part of every commission that you pay to their employing broker. You may also have your own independent representative who is capable of giving you good advice. Nevertheless, a conflict of interest may exist because if he works on a commission basis, which most representatives do, his income is increased by every order that you place with him.

In spite of professional advise, remember that no one can guarantee success in the stock market. All anyone can do is to help you get started, enable you to derive some experience, and try to prevent you from making avoidable mistakes. If your advisor is successful, stay with him. If his advice becomes too costly for the results obtained, and you feel that you could do better on your own, you can use the services of your broker.

If you want to learn more about a company or industry, ask your representative to supply you with the available prospectuses and any information that will help you to evaluate a company or investment. Chapter 22 helps you evaluate both the information and the company. Just remember that when you are in the stock market you are involved in a gamble.

Margin Accounts

In order to increase their potential profits, many investors purchase securities, such as stocks, on margin. In the stock market, margin is the amount of money an investor deposits with his broker to finance his purchase or to make a short sale. The broker usually borrows the money that he loans to the investor. The amount financed is usually the difference between the amount deposited by the investor and the cost of the transaction. In effect, the broker opens a separate margin account for the investor and retains the purchased securities as security for the unpaid amount.

The minimum margin requirements—and the stocks that cannot be margined—are delineated by Regulation T of the Federal Reserve Board. For a purchase or short sale of marginable stocks whose price exceeds $6.75 per share, the initial margin (frequently referred to as a deposit) must be 50 percent of the amount of the transaction. It may be paid in cash or with approved securities of equivalent value. Thereafter, the margin account must be maintained at a certain level, subject to the rules of Regulation T, the National Association of Securities Dealers, the New York Stock Exchange, and the brokerage firm with which you are trading. These regulations usually require that investors maintain a minimum of $2,000 in cash or securities in their brokerage accounts. Each customers' equity (ownership interest) in the assets of his account cannot drop below 25 percent of the current market value of the securities that are held in the margin account. To protect themselves further, the margin agreements of some brokerage houses require that customers maintain a higher percentage of equity (frequently 40 percent) than is required by the regulatory bodies.

Sometimes the actions of the market cause the amount on deposit to fall below the required maintenance or minimum level. When this happens, the broker issues a margin call to the investor to replenish the margin account so that it complies with the various regulations. A margin call, frequently referred to as a maintenance call, is a demand by the brokerage firm for additional funds or securities to comply with the minimum margin requirements. Upon a failure to comply with the margin demand, the brokerage firm is entitled to sell the stocks to protect its own interests.

In a typical example, let's assume that your brokerage firm has $5,000 worth of your fully owned securities in a "street name" (street name refers to stock that is held in the brokers name but in your account). Somehow, you learn that a certain construction company, whose stock is selling for $12 per share, is going to receive a multimillion dollar construction contract. Because of the large profits that you expect the construction company to earn, you believe that the stock will be worth $20 per share. Accordingly, you would like to buy 1,000 shares at $12 per share. Unfortunately, you have just paid your taxes and only can spare approximately $4,000. With this amount, you can only afford to buy about 350 shares. Believing in the principles of leverage (as described in Chapter 12) and desiring to increase your potential profit, you discuss your dilemma with your broker. He checks to see if the stock is marginable. After verifying that it is, he then explains that by using the $5,000 value of your stock that is already in his custody and adding the $4,000 in cash that you have available, your account will be worth $9,000. This amount will enable the broker to loan you 50 percent of it or $4,500. This will enable you to buy on margin approximately 700 shares of the stock you desire for $8,400, plus commissions. If you agree and he buys the 700 shares, you will own 700 shares of the stock plus your original stock. However, all of it will be on margin. You will be charged interest on the $4,500 balance that you have just borrowed from your broker.

Unfortunately, a week later the entire market and all of your stocks decline in value. The value of your portfolio in the margin account drops below the minimum allowable balance. Compelled to comply with regulations, your broker issues a margin call requesting that you bring in funds or securities to bring your account into compliance with the minimum balance regulations. Because the market is still dropping, you are afraid to borrow more money elsewhere or to sell some other assets to add to the account. Also, you are aware that even if you bring in the cash, the stocks and the market may continue their decline. You might receive another margin call. Moreover, the drop in the market tightened the availability of money. This made it harder for you to either borrow money or sell your assets. The deadline passes, your broker sells your stocks, collects what is due him, and credits your account with the balance.

The lesson to be learned here is that unless you are the type of gambler who doesn't mind losing his shirt, don't use margin. Although I endorse the use of margin, it should only be used by people who can afford to back themselves up financially or afford to lose their investment. Very frequently, the financial ability to hold on to margined stocks during a decline can result in a healthy profit after the value of the margined stocks increase to their normal values.

The Securities & Exchange Commission does not determine the amount of brokerage commission that you pay for the margin purchase. Nor does it control the amount of interest that the brokerage firm charges you for the amount loaned. These are determined independently by each brokerage firm. In some instances, when the account is large enough, commissions and interest rates are subject to negotiation. Also, brokers profit from margin accounts because they borrow funds at a lower percentage rate than they charge investors. The interest rate charged by the broker is only a few points above the prime rate, (the lowest rate that banks charge their best customers).

There is another possible benefit that may be derived from the use of a margin account. The percentage of the interest paid on the margin account may be deducted from income taxes. However, the interest that an investor receives from keeping his money in a bank instead of using margin, is taxable. Prior to the Tax Reform Act of 1986, interest paid on margin accounts by the average investor was deductible against earnings. Beginning in 1988, however, interest paid on margin accounts can only be deducted from passive (unearned) investment income. Because of new limitations on the amount of interest that is deductible, consult your accountant.

Naturally, when your money is at risk, you must carefully watch the performance of your margined stocks. If you cannot afford to back them up and they begin to drop drastically, take your loss and sell them before you get wiped out. If you like buying on margin, diversify your purchases and, if possible, try to buy securities with a limited downside risk.

Convertible Securities

All investors should become familiar with the advantages offered by owning convertible securities. Convertible securities are usually preferred stocks or bonds that can be exchanged for a definite amount of common stocks at a definite future date. Convertible securities are popular with those investors who want to combine a fixed income with the opportunity for capital appreciation (profits). Investors usually pay a premium (more money) to buy "convertibles." This is because they are granted the opportunity to exchange them for a fixed number of stocks that may have materially increased in value.

Some convertible preferred stocks are cumulative and some are not. Those that are not cumulative do not receive any dividends if their dividend date passes without the corporation's ability to pay the dividend. However, most preferred stocks are cumulative. Owning convertible, preferred cumulative stocks can offer many advantages.

First, convertible preferred stock offers a non-guaranteed, fixed dividend, that is usually higher than the common stock dividend. This means that the dividend on the convertible stock must be paid before the dividend on the common stock can be declared and paid.

Second, if the dividends that become due on the convertible preferred cumulative stock are not paid, they accumulate and must be paid before any common stockholders can receive a dividend.

Third, if the common stock increases in value and/or its dividends exceed those of the convertible, preferred cumulative stocks, the exchange for stocks provides double benefits.

Owning convertible, preferred cumulative bonds also offer many advantages.

First, they offer a fixed rate of interest that is usually higher than the anticipated dividend of the common stock. The bond is like a loan and does not pay dividends.

Second, they are considered senior securities. This means that no dividends on the common stock can be paid until whatever interest due on the bonds is paid.

Third, at a future date the rate of interest being paid on the bonds may become lower than the then going rate and the stocks may have increased in value and be paying good dividends. The opportunity to exchange the bonds for stocks can be very profitable.

If you are interested in convertible securities, you must become familiar with the following three terms: conversion ratio, conversion value, and conversion premium. The ratio is the number of common shares into which the convertible can be exchanged. The value refers to the dollar value of the common shares in the ratio. This is derived by multiplying the specified (ratio) number of common stocks by the current price. Convertibles usually sell for a higher price than their market price. The extra price that is paid is referred to as the conversion premium. For example, if the stock is trading at $100 and the security is convertible at $90 but is selling for $100, the conversion premium is $10. But some analysts refer to the conversion premium as the percentage by which the convertible's purchase price exceeds its conversion value (the current value of the convertible). To find out the conversion premium (the percentage ratio) for any convertible security, you can use the following three-step system:

1. Multiply the price of the common stock by the number of shares to determine the present market value of the convertible security.
2. Deduct the present market value of the convertible security from its par value (face value) for the amount of premium that you pay in dollars.
3. Then, to find out the percentage of premium, divide the premium (2) by the present value of the convertible (1).

If you don't like math but want to find out the conversion premium, just ask your broker.

Some analysts will not pay more than a 10 percent premium for convertible bonds and insist on at least a 9 percent interest rate, although these securities may be hard to find. Most analysts consider that if the conversion premium is above 15 percent, the risk is too great. Rates change according to the the value of the dollar, its availability, and the safety of the underlying securities. Therefore, the investor should find out what rates are being offered.

Most convertibles have a specified "call date." This is when the issuer can retire the stock or bond at a specific price. Actually, preferred stocks are a sophisticated investment with many variations. Buy them with the guidance of an advisor who specializes in them and has a computer to help him compare their advantages and disadvantages.

Municipal Bonds

The subject of municipal bonds requires a special investor alert. The Alternative Minimum Tax provisions of the Tax Reform Act of 1986 have changed the tax-exempt status of municipal bonds. Even before your accountant can advise you, he must use two different formulas before he can tell you if your municipals are tax exempt.

Because municipal bonds are referred to as "tax exempts," they have become popular with investors seeking fixed incomes with minimum tax liability. The term "municipal bond," does not just refer to an indebtedness issued by a city, town, or other district having a corporate charter. It also includes bonds issued by state agencies. But, both the federal government and insurance companies may back municipal bonds.

There are many types of tax-exempt municipal securities that are available to sophisticated investors. However, the average investor is usually interested in the two major types—the general obligation bond and the revenue bond. The general obligation bond is secured by the full faith, credit, and taxing power of the issuer. The revenue bond is backed by a promise from the issuer to pay the interest and repay the principal from the revenue derived from a special project financed by the bond.

Municipal bonds are usually issued in $1,000 denominations and are popular for two reasons. First, the interest derived from them is exempt from federal taxes. When the residence of the taxpayer is in the same state as the municipal authority, the interest income may also be exempt from state taxes. Second, many people are under the false impression that municipal bonds are their safest investment.

According to an investor's tax bracket, municipal bonds can appreciably increase an investor's after-tax spendable income. However, the safety and worthiness of a municipal bond is no better than the issuer's ability to pay all obligations when due. Munis, as the bonds are frequently called, have defaulted on many occasions. In recent years, some municipal bonds have been guaranteed. However, there are times when the guarantees were worthless. See the story in Chapter 5 about the municipal bond issue in Washington state.

Municipal bonds that are highly rated, such as AAA, yield less than lower rated bonds. Likewise, insured municipal bonds yield less than uninsured bonds. You should know that insurance only guarantees that the principal and interest will be repaid in case of a default. Insurance does not guarantee that you can sell your bonds before their maturity date and get back what you paid for them. The maturity date refers to the date that the obligation must be repaid in full. It is different from the due date. The due date usually refers to a specified payment date for interest and sometimes a portion of the principal.

The net asset or cash value of municipal bonds can decrease or increase. Some of the factors that affect the net asset or cash value of a municipal bond are inflation, deflation, and general interest rates. Accordingly, municipal bond holders must pay constant attention to these economic factors. They can affect their after-tax income or the net asset value of their investment.

A general obligation municipal bond, which is the safest type, pays less interest than the revenue municipal bond. It is safer because the general obligation bond is backed by the full faith, credit, and taxing power of a state or municipality. The revenue bond depends upon income from the financed project for which it is issued. This can include such projects as a tunnel, transportation system, or electrical power plant. Most municipal bond defaults have occurred with revenue bonds used to finance business-oriented, revenue-producing ventures such as tramways, toll bridges, utilities, and nuclear power plants.

Investment advisers usually advise municipal investors with less than $15,000 to purchase insured municipal bond funds. Shares in these funds must usually be purchased through a broker and can be subject to an annual management fee.

If you want to invest in municipal bonds, learn enough about economics, interest rates, and taxing authorities to purchase good government obligation municipal bonds within your own state. Be sure to select bonds that mature within a period of time that meets your financial needs. The time is important because it determines when the principal is returned to you without a penalty.

Incidentally, in the stock market, a point is the equivalent of $1, but in the bond market, one point equals $10. So, if you read that bonds dropped two points, this means that each $1,000 bond sold for $20 less than before it dropped in price.

A U.S. Treasury bond is the most secure type of bond that you can buy. Yet, like other bonds, it can drop a few points from face value whenever analysts and the public anticipate that the government will issue a good economic report. Applicable examples are when either a higher employment rate or a tightening of credit is announced. A tightening of credit leads to higher interest rates.

If the interest rate on newly issued bonds increases, then the market value of all unmatured bonds decreases, and vice versa. An anticipated loosening of credit plus higher unemployment figures cause the market value of bonds to increase.

Whenever it looks like interest rates are about to decrease, some brokers urge investors to purchase long-term bonds to "lock in" high yields. But, before buying such long-term bonds, investors should check them for "call" or redemption clauses. These clauses are used by certain issuers who want to reserve to themselves the right to redeem their bonds after a certain number of years. This is sometimes at a lower price than was paid by the investor or, in the event that they can refinance their long-term debt, at lower interest rates. Redemption clauses can be complex and favor the issuer in many ways, such as limiting the future appreciation of the bonds and the continuation of the high yield. Therefore, avoid buying bonds with redemption features.

Every one who invests in securities should become familiar with the difference between bearer bonds and registered bonds. Registered bonds can be traced because the investor's name is on the bond and registered in the books of the issuer.

Since July 1983, federal law requires that all new bonds be registered. In prior years, most people preferred bearer bonds which, because they did not name the owner, helped the bearer to avoid taxes. Another advantage to buying bearer bonds was that ownership of the bonds could be transferred by simply delivering them to a new owner.

Taxable municipal bonds are those that are not issued for essential purposes. Bonds for an amusement park or a new shopping mall are examples. Even though their returns might be greater than tax-exempt municipals, professional traders consider them to be too risky for the average investor who might want to sell them before they mature. Because they are not tax exempt, an increase in interest rates following their issue means that the non-tax-exempt bonds would have to be sold at a large discount for a big loss.

In recent years we have seen the advent of what are called *junk bonds*. The name given to high yielding, frequently unsecured securities that are rated BB or lower by the security rating agencies. Recently, they have been used as collateral by people or corporations to finance the acquisition of new companies. While their use is controversial, many of them may be worth the risk and may survive the fears of the investment community that the increasing number of junk bond firms in bankruptcy may cause the junk bond market to collapse.

Zero Coupon Bonds

As you learn more about the securities market, you are bound to encounter *zero coupon securities*. These securities derive their name from the fact they do not pay interest. In effect, undeclared, unpaid interest on these securities accrues in the form of capital appreciation. As a result, the security is bought at a very low price—much lower than its face value. But, at a specific future date, it can be redeemed for its full face value. This security appeals to a person who wants to know that at a certain date the security can be cashed in for a set amount of money. The deterrent to zero coupon bonds is that in an inflationary period the purchase value of the cashed-in security may be seriously eroded.

Commodities

As mentioned many times, the basic purpose of this book is to provide you with investment information. Just as important, the book is intended to help you avoid unnecessary financial losses.

Beware of commodities. Commodity futures are considered investments, and there are several commodities exchanges. But commodities are only recommended to two specific types of business people. The first could be a manufacturer who seeks protection from the increased costs of commodities used in his business. These increases are usually due to future shortages or higher prices. Accordingly, the manufacturer seeks a guaranteed normal supply of the commodity at a predetermined future date and at a predictable price. For such a manufacturer, the buying of commodity futures might be judicious.

The second category includes the farmer or producer who can furnish the required amount of the commodity in the future at a specific time but wants the protection afforded by a guaranteed price. In the event that there is an oversupply of the commodity when the farmer is ready to ship his, he is able to lock in his anticipated profit in advance.

Through a process called hedging, or going long, the manufacturer buys a futures contract for the commodity. The farmer or producer, in a process called selling short, contracts to sell the commodity at a specific future date at a set price. In effect, each of these people, unknown to the other, executes independent contracts with a commodities exchange broker who receives a commission.

If, at the predetermined date, the price of the commodity goes up, the manufacturer pays the increased price to his regular sources of supply. He also sells the futures contract for a profit. This helps to pay for the increased cost. If the price drops, he buys the commodity at a lower cost. He uses the profit from the lower cost to offset losses on the futures contract.

Meanwhile, if the price goes down, the farmer or producer sells his commodity for less than anticipated but makes up the loss by selling the futures contract at a higher price. If the price goes up, he makes a profit on a cash sale that helps to pay the loss on the futures contract.

This is definitely a speculator's gambit. You must buy either the long or the short futures contracts according to your information or inclination. As a speculator, you could sell the contract whenever you could make a profit.

All investments involve some degree of gambling. But the field of commodity futures involves too much gambling on too many contingencies. Experts have calculated that over a period of time, from 75 to 95 percent of commodity speculators lose money. The rewards of being successful in the commodities field can lead to immense profits. However, the chances of losing money greatly exceed the chances of making a profit. Even the promise of immense rewards cannot justify commodity trading for the investor who does not use the commodity in his business.

Investment Tips

Investment tips refer to private or secret advice or special information that you may receive about investing your money. Unfortunately, these secret tips are usually widespread. Nevertheless, all of us are susceptible to responding to them. Be forewarned that many of them are created to enrich someone other than yourself. Unless you check them out carefully before investing, the results may be financially disastrous.

It is not likely that any of the tips that you receive are really *inside information*. This is because people who receive, use, or disseminate actual inside information about a corporation are subject to severe penalties under the federal law. Accordingly, very few responsible people will break the law. Thus, most tips are probably from unreliable sources and worth what you probably paid for them—nothing.

Even if you pay a professional advisor for investment information, do not expect any unusual advice. You are paying for experience and guidance to improve your chances of making an intelligent, profitable investment without losing money through unnecessary mistakes. Some of the professional advice about general investing follows:

- Dun & Bradstreet's Investment Guide recommends buying on Mondays and selling on Fridays. But that advice can only be recommended for speculators.
- Many speculators only buy stocks that are takeover candidates because, if they buy the stocks early enough, they can usually make a good profit if the takeover takes place. But these speculators are also prepared to take a loss if the takeover does not occur and the stock decreases in value. However, when a proposed takeover does not occur and the stock drops in value, check the fundamentals of the company. There is a strong likelihood that its stocks are a good buy and that the company may still be acquired in the future by another company.
- Some investors like to sell short when they learn through the financial papers that the insiders are selling. (As previously explained in detail, a short sale is a sale of borrowed stock by an investor who expects its price to drop.) But, selling short is also dangerous. Many times insiders sell because they have too much of the stock and either need some cash or want to diversify their investments even though the original company is sound.
- Because the Tax Reform Act of 1986 removed the benefits of capital gains, many believe that dividends will now be more important than capital gains.
- Many investors have become interested in mortgage-backed securities. But they have been disappointed when the underlying mortgages were prepaid or paid too slowly. However, the Federal National Mortgage Association (referred to as Fannie Mae) has begun to issue "stripped" mortgage-backed securities in which the interest and principal payments of the collateral are separated and pay different interest rates. Those with prepayment protection pay less interest. They do provide investors with the opportunity to select securities in which the underlying investment is not paid off too quickly or too slowly. "Stripping" refers to separating parts of the security so that the separated rights may be traded independently of the security.

There is no end to the amount of special advice and good investment techniques that could be given to you here. Unfortunately, none are foolproof. Most investors look for unusual situations. I do not fault this. But, while they are looking for these special situations, they may be ignoring the good, sound, rock-solid securities and other forms of investment that exist everywhere. These are the kind that have good fundamentals such as:

- Five-year records of good management
- Lots of cash
- Low debt service
- Increased sales and profits
- Good potential for future earnings
- Not overpriced

Watch for these fundamentals.

Always remember that there will never be a shortage of securities. Someone will always dream up another method of creating securities, investing, speculating, or "grabbing" an investor's money. Consequently, do not rush into any type of investment without first investigating whether it is a sound investment that fits your personal goals and disposition.

When you learn how to protect yourself, which you should now be able to do, the next most important ingredient is timing. Even with all of the know-how of a professional investor, your financial success depends on correctly timing when to buy and when to sell. This means that you cannot ignore the economic conditions that exist now or in the future. Therefore, stay informed about national and international trends that could possibly affect your investments. Even then, you cannot always be right. But at least you will know that you did your best, provided you observed two other basic investment rules in the process:

1. You did not financially overextend yourself to retain sufficient capital to invest again when the time seems right.
2. You diversified your investments to assure the receipt of income, capital appreciation, and tax relief.

Chapter 28: Buying or Starting a Business

Buying or Starting a Business

This chapter is for you if you are contemplating opening a new business or buying an established business or a franchise. Before you invest your hard-earned money, there are many things you should know before becoming involved in a new business venture. This chapter pinpoints several important issues—hopefully, helping you before you find out the hard way. It cautions you against the potential for overpayment. It includes the answers to a number of questions often asked by would-be business people. And, equally as important, it contains some basic business, legal, and accounting fundamentals.

Every year a new crop of unprepared, nonbusiness people become owners of businesses. They are primarily responsible for the high annual mortality and bankruptcy rate that is characteristic of new business ventures. Too few understand that good business people are usually trained, experienced professionals. In fact, very few inexperienced amateurs become successful business people.

The difference between amateur and professional business people is that professionals prepare, plan, and organize their activities. Conversely, amateurs are usually haphazard in their preparation; they tend to operate by reaction rather than through a thought-out process based on experience and skills. In addition, amateurs are often unaware of how severely they are handicapped by a lack of both business experience and management skills. It has been estimated that the majority of new businesses fail within three years of startup.

What entices so many untrained entrepreneurs into the business world without the fundamental knowledge necessary for success? Here are a number of them:

- A psychological or physical inability to continue to work under the direction of a boss or company policy

- An inability to procure employment that utilizes one's talents and helps one feel creatively fulfilled
- A need to earn revenue before one spends investment seed money
- An inability to find a job that financially rewards for talent, skill, time, and efforts
- A desire to benefit from and earn money through the efforts of others
- An ambition to develop a chain of business ventures or to create a franchise
- Overconfidence in one's ability based on a narrow experience acquired by working in a similar or related business
- Inheritance of a business

Business-Related Statistics

None of the above are good reasons for getting into a business. A look at some business-related statistics are in order. These statistics indicate trends, which are important to serious business people.

- The United States Bureau of Labor Statistics predicted in 1985 that during the following 10 years more jobs would be created by small businesses in the service sector than in the industrial sector.
- According to a Dun & Bradstreet report: in 1984's third quarter, 31,728 new businesses opened in the U.S. with retailing leading the list with 33.8 percent. Only 15.4 percent of the new entrepreneurs entered the service industry.

According to a 1985 *Wall Street Journal* article, the Small Business Administration (SBA) analyzed Dun & Bradstreet Corp.'s business failure data for 1983 and learned that the lowest failure rates were among funeral homes, tobacco wholesalers, fuel oil dealers, laundries and dry cleaners, drug stores, hotels, manufacturers of wood products, providers of personal services, beer and wine wholesalers, and service stations. SBA analysts also found that the highest failure rate was 290 per 10,000 businesses. These included florists, book stores, hobby shops, gift stores, and sporting goods establishments.

The number of businesses that fail is not an accurate indication of how many are doing poorly. Nor do these failures reflect the number of owners who would like to quit. Many are trying to hold on for many reasons. They may not want to lay off their employees.

Some fear financial and contractual liabilities to financial institutions, landlords, and customers. Others may abhor the thought of being labeled a failure by friends. And there are some that simply do not have an alternate plan or interest.

Most successful business people are multidimensional. Besides knowing their product and market, they understand people and their motivations. Unless they have a monopoly on an essential product or service, chances are they are pleasant, understand their customers, and give them what they want at a fair price. Further, they give their customers confidence, deliver what they promise, and rectify their mistakes.

Ingredients Required for a Successful Business

Other ingredients required for success in any business are a complex mixture of the following:

- Correct timing
- Foresight, training, and experience
- Ability to plan, organize, and prepare an operating budget and comply with its limitations
- Ability to make intelligent decisions on time
- Sufficient start-up and follow-through capitalization
- Ability to secure additional financing when warranted
- A good knowledge of the product or service
- Ability and desire to satisfy customers and create good will
- Some knowledge of promotion and advertising and the ability to apply it to the business
- Ability to properly screen and hire employees without legal complications
- Maintaining cooperative, trusting employer-employee relationships
- Ability to control and discourage employee-theft of money, time, and merchandise
- Ability to keep adequate purchasing and sales records
- Ability and willingness to pay suppliers, rent, and taxes on time
- Ability to distinguish between gross profit and net profit after taxes
- Personal devotion to the business
- Ability to refrain from withdrawing necessary operating funds from the business

Unfortunately, many would-be entrepreneurs lack many of these essential ingredients, characteristics, and attitudes. Even when sufficiently capitalized, they may not possess the correct temperament that is required to successfully operate their own business, supervise employees, promote the business, and develop proper customer relations that creates goodwill. They may never have experienced the absence of a regular paycheck or not earning a spendable profit. Further, in the absence of a profit, can they survive the trauma attached to paying rent or meeting a weekly payroll?

It is at this stage, i.e., when they become financially squeezed, that many learn a fundamental business and investment lesson that they should have known from the beginning: Before getting into any venture, no matter how good it seems, take the time to calculate how much it will cost and how long it will take to get out. There are dozens of circumstances that can make it necessary or expedient to give up.

Always remember, it is easier to get into a business than it is to get out of one. The enthusiasm that comes with opening a new business makes it seem easier; the heartbreak that accompanies a failing business makes it extremely difficult to terminate it.

Why Some Fail

Let's briefly investigate some of the major reasons that people fail in business.

Lack of Planning

Lack of planning and perhaps lack of ability to prepare a written, comprehensive, proposed operational plan for the business is one reason for failure. A business plan includes all of the necessary information, including written budgets for either establishing, purchasing, or operating the business and contingency (back-up) plans for whatever aspect of the business becomes unsuccessful.

Lack of Capitalization

The failure to calculate and secure the proper amount of start-up money and reserves required to get the business off the ground is a common mistake. Every proposed or established business should have a financial forecast and someone who can calculate the cost of acquiring capital. It is customary to calculate that one half of the capital will be used for start-up and the balance for operating expenses. For most new businesses, it takes an indeterminate waiting period until the income equals expenses. There should be sufficient funds or enough credit available to carry new customers' accounts until they pay. Sufficient capitalization also includes enough money to pay bills and expenses on time while adequately caring for family and personal needs. Depending on the kind business, it may take many months or even years for a new company to start realizing a net profit.

Part of financial planning involves whether to use equity or debt financing. Equity financing gives up part of the business—and a share of the profits and losses—in exchange for new capital; debt financing is the equivalent of a loan in which the lender usually does not share in either the profits or losses.

Lack of Experience

A person may lack experience in a number of important areas. These include:

- The various aspects of good management, such as being a good manager or being able to hire one
- Securing additional capital and obtaining credit
- Selecting the correct location or locations for the specific business or service
- Executing a lease with favorable terms
- Purchasing merchandise or parts from the best sources
- Understanding business in general
- Properly understanding how to promote, advertise, market, and sell a product or service
- Understanding the heavy cost of pilferage and dead beats and how to avoid both
- Being able to hire personnel correctly and avoid the legal pitfalls that sometimes follow terminations

Unanticipated Events or Circumstances

Many things can cause a business to suffer severe loss. Following is a partial list.

- An economic downturn
- Local factory layoffs
- Plant destruction
- Financial or labor problems of a prime supplier

- A change in import laws fostering high domestic and import prices
- Obsolescence of the major product or service
- Unexpected large increases in interest rates
- The opening of too many competitive stores in the same area

A Lack of Continued Planning and Management

There are many routine functions that should be performed by a business. These include:

- Establishing and maintaining quality control
- Employee orientation and training
- An established labor replacement plan
- A good inventory control system
- A sufficient range of adequate insurance for anticipated and unanticipated claims and losses, including product liability insurance.

The Inability to Maintain Adequate Records

Laws, regulations, and record-keeping requirements permeate nearly every phase of business. Few people can risk not understanding the laws and regulations before entering the world of commerce. Failure to maintain required paperwork and proper payment records connected with unemployment and payroll taxes, as well as other bookkeeping duties, has been the downfall of many entrepreneurs.

Where to Get Assistance

The United States government offers business advice and some financial assistance through its Small Business Administration (SBA). The SBA may also help you to guarantee a loan. The SBA uses volunteers with extensive business experience as advisors. The local telephone numbers are listed in the Government section of many phone books. Aside from the loans offered by the SBA, it also offers qualifying small businesses the opportunity to participate in federal contracts. These contracts are funded annually by a $15 billion allocation. Unfortunately, the red tape required in securing an SBA loan plus the long wait for a reply discourages many people from applying. The red tape and delays, in addition to the fact that many overlook the SBA as a source of help, will likely contribute to cuts in the SBA's budget.

In Canada, however, the situation is different. Aware of the vast amount of help and experience needed by new business people, the Canadian Province of British Columbia inaugurated a student loan program. A few years ago it granted 450 student entrepreneurs $2,000 each in interest-free loans. In 1984, the province claimed, "Only 9 percent of last summer's debts remained unpaid." The cost to the British Columbia government was only $250,000, which was used to pay interest on the loans granted by the Royal Bank of Canada, and to cover the possibility of defaults.

According to *The Globe and Mail*, many of Canada's provinces are also attempting to help both new business entrepreneurs and student business consultants. University MBA and undergraduate business students, in most cases financed by provincial governments, form business consulting firms that offer limited services to large corporations. Most of these new embryonic consulting firms help small businesses by counseling them at low rates ($50 to $150 a day as contrasted to $75 to $275 an hour for professional help). The customary problems discussed are the legal, accounting, and practical basics of running a business. Included is the importance of business plans, budgets, and market research. On the other hand, the neophyte counselors, who have been trained in theory only, get practical experience by observing how different businesses actually operate.

In the United States, according to the Emergency Training Veterans' Job Training Act, wage reimbursement is available to certain employers. The requirements for reimbursement are as follows:

- The employers must be in a growth industry requiring technical skills or in occupations in demand, and they must provide a permanent job and at least 6 months training.
- The employee must be a Korean Conflict or Vietnam-era veteran who has been unemployed for 15 of the 20 weeks prior to his or her application for employment. For further, up-to-date information, contact the Veteran's Employment and Training Service of the Department of Labor, or contact your local Veterans Administration office.

Should I Buy an Established Business or Start My Own?

One of the most frequent questions asked by would-be business people is whether they should purchase an established business or open their own.

Buying a going, profitable business has many advantages over opening a business from scratch. This even applies to a business that is adequately funded and started by an experienced business person. Ordinarily, when you buy a going business, you pay for worthwhile benefits. There are many reasons to support this conclusion:

- First, you buy an immediate established income. Sometimes it takes as long as 3 years for a new business to show a profit, if ever.
- Second, even if you possess sufficient experience and know-how to successfully open your own business from scratch, that same experience will help you to understand and analyze the ramifications of the business that you are contemplating buying.
- Third, you save the precious time and expense involved in locating, renting, equipping, stocking, promoting, and starting a new venture from scratch. This includes the costs of buying fixtures and training personnel. All of these start-up costs can take time and can be very expensive.
- Fourth, if you are expansion-minded, you can either enlarge the business or use it as the base from which to open additional locations.
- Fifth, the going business that you buy is similar to an investment. It should be a valuable asset that you can resell, hopefully, for a profit. Any going business that can show a profit is usually a viable, resalable business that is worth many times its annual net income.

How Much Should I Pay for the Business?

"How much should I pay for a business?" This question cannot be answered without first considering a number of variables—some include personal preferences. One of the most important variables is referred to as the price/earnings (P/E) ratio, frequently called *the multiple*. The P/E ratio is usually determined by dividing the price of the business by its past or expected net earnings. While the answer tells you how many years you will have to wait to get your money back, it does not tell you the book value of the tangible assets of the business (book value equals depreciated cost of items such as machinery). Neither does it tell you the amount that you are paying for goodwill (the amount paid in excess of the book value for the assets).

Thus, how many multiples more than net income the business is worth (or how many times the income you should pay for the business) depends on:

- The length of the lease
- The annual rental schedule
- The amount of money ascribed to inventory and for usable and unusable assets
- The frequency of turnover of merchandise in a year
- Whether the new business requires the new owners to work as if they had a job, or if their main role is only supervisoral or managerial
- If the business can operate profitably without personal supervision (usually not recommended prior to establishing the proper management, behavioral, and financial guidelines)
- Using new buying techniques that permit the parties to arrange the sale so that the seller receives more money than he wanted without extra cost to the buyer. (A specific example is provided in a subsequent portion of this chapter.)
- The value of goodwill, an intangible asset in terms of how much profitable business it will produce.

Selecting the Correct Operating Entity

Every business person must determine whether to operate as an individual, a partnership, or a corporation. Selecting the correct operating entity is important. Making the wrong choice can affect taxes, fail to provide legal protection when expanding the business, and might not properly protect the assets of the business person or investor-associates in the event of a business failure. Review Chapter 13, *Selecting the Correct Operating Entity*. Secure practical advice from experienced business people as well as professional counsel from accountants and lawyers.

Many competent people are flattered and honored when asked to give you advice or to become a member of your Board of Directors if you operate as a corporation. In recent years, however, outside board members are difficult to procure if they are not protected by adequate insurance.

Franchising

Many investors are fascinated with the prospect of owning and running a burgeoning franchise business. The proliferation of franchises is due to two key factors:

1. The franchisors have a special product or service, the distribution of which is vastly increased by having many franchisees and by using common advertising and identical operating techniques. The appeal to customers is that they can get the same service or product at any of the franchisees, no matter where they are located.
2. Many potential franchisees were people who wanted to engage in business but did not have the necessary experience or organizational and management ability. They were aware that they required practical advice concerning personal and personnel training, general guidance, the selection of a location, the quick start-up benefits that would be available from both a well-known, well-used product, and the goodwill attached to the franchise logo.

Many wealthy, experienced business people frequently purchase franchises in which they have no background. They want to take advantage of the experience, guidance, and goodwill offered by a well known franchisor. However, these investors usually employ capable, trustworthy people to take advantage of the training prescribed by the franchisors. This ensures proper management of the franchise. In other words, they view it as an investment and not a business. (For further information about franchises, read Chapter 24.)

How to Find a Business

Businesses can be found in many ways, depending on the philosophy of the investor. Some investors use business brokers, others scan trade or business papers or the classified sections of the daily newspaper, and still others contact salesmen and supply houses. Salesmen and supply houses are very good sources. They know the volume of business being conducted and believe that if you buy a business through their recommendation you will feel morally obligated to continue dealing with them. Attorneys and accountants are also a good source because they often know which businesses are for sale.

Another way to find a retail business is to canvass (personally visit) the type of businesses you like. Many successful business brokers, as well as many individuals seeking a business, walk from store to store to find businesses that are for sale. Doing this gives you the opportunity to buy a business that the owner might not have considered selling. Also, some business people do not like to advertise the fact that their businesses are for sale. They fear that some of their customers will take their trade elsewhere and it can be unsettling to employees. Through canvassing, you can find owners who are ready to sell their businesses. They may be ill, bored, or ready to retire. Many will be happy you approached them because you saved them the expense of advertising or hiring a broker and paying a commission. Occasionally, even if the owners don't want to sell, they may know someone else who does.

When canvassing a store, you have the opportunity to become familiar with the salient details of a business before the owner becomes aware that you are evaluating his business. You can familiarize yourself with actual trade volumes and customary operating methods.

If you are shy, it may be difficult for you to contact owners of businesses by yourself. If you are too shy, you might well reconsider whether you should own a retail business that involves meeting the public. If you are not shy, it is very easy and rewarding to make direct contact with the respective owners of retail businesses. Salesmen do it all the time. Before you walk into the establishment, look at the storefront and windows for the name of the owner. Then, walk in and politely introduce yourself without stating why you are there. Ask to see the owner; use the owner's name if you know it. You should not state your purpose; the average owner does not want his staff to know that he might be considering a business sale. If you are lucky, you might be talking directly to the owner. If not, find out if the owner is on the premises. If he isn't, try to find out when he will be there. When you meet him, introduce yourself and state that you are trying to buy a business and that you want to know if he was interested in selling. If he says yes, ask him for details. A list of essential questions follows:

1. What is the volume of business transacted this year and last year?
2. What are the actual and estimated profits?
3. What are the sales price and terms, if any?
4. Is the facility owned outright, rented, or leased?
5. Who are his suppliers, what is the dollar amount and quantity he buys from them, and what are their credit terms?
6. Will his sales tax records be available for your inspection?
7. Will he open his books for inspection?
8. How long will he stay to break you in after he sells?

Some owners will not provide much of the information you seek on the first visit. They will first want to check you out. If you do get the required information and it seems legitimate, find out how to contact him again, and tell him you will come back. Bring the information to your accountant. If he approves the information, then contact a commercial lawyer. Unless you are very experienced, let your lawyer and accountant do all the work. If you were not successful, continue canvassing until you find what you want. These procedures should be followed regardless of how you find a business you want.

What to Look for When Buying a Business

Some experienced business buyers look for a marginally profitable, poorly managed business that they can buy at a low price. They use their experience to increase the profits and then sell at a large profit. Other investors look for an owner who wants to retire but has no one in the family to carry on the profitable business.

If you find a business that suits you, verify all statements before you sign any documents or put up any money. You must be careful even in progressive states, where licensed brokers and sales people are held professionally and financially responsible for misrepresentations and loose statements. (Progressive states do not countenance business frauds and actively prosecute those who make misrepresentations when selling a business. The unprogressive states will not prosecute criminally without being forced to since they prefer that the victim of a business fraud use the civil courts to sue for damages.)

Before a business is purchased, the owner should verify that the books reflect stated profits and have been properly and honestly kept. The buyer should try and determine if, during the period that the business was offered for sale, the owner puffed up profits or used shills (fake customers) to make the business look profitable. Check also for contracts or orders accompanied by small down payments. These could, after the purchase agreement has been consummated, be easily canceled, even by legitimate, putative buyers.

To investigate or operate any business—and particularly if a manufacturing business is involved—you must consider a number of additional important factors. These are covered in detail in Chapter 22, *How to Understand Financial Statements*.

Also, in evaluating businesses and to avoid overpaying, do not rely on the price for which similar businesses were recently sold. Special circumstances might have distorted the price. The following paragraph provides an excellent example.

The Sophisticated Way to Buy or Sell a Business

Occasionally, through intelligent planning, a sale of a business can be consummated in which the owner can sell his business for about two and one half times more than his asking price. For instance, in a situation in which the owner only asked $3.2 million for his business, but received $8 million. As reported in the *Wall Street Journal*, a buyer wanted to buy a certain business for its book value of $3.2 million. The owner was satisfied with the price but was afraid that if he received the total purchase price at one time, he would have to pay too much income tax. With the help of an acquisition expert, the transaction was arranged whereby the seller would make three separate payments. One payment was for the assets of the business. A second payment was for the owner to be a consultant to the business. The third payment was for an agreement by the seller not to compete with the buyer in the future. The interesting results of this arrangement led to the seller receiving $8 million at a total cost to the buyer of $3.2 million. Specifically, the transaction was structured to pay the seller $1 million at the close of escrow, $200,000 annually for 20 years, and $1 million respectively in 5, 10, and 20 years. The buyer was able to make these arrangements by buying an annuity and zero coupon bonds with 5-, 10-, and 20-year maturity dates. The cost of the annuity was $1.4 million and the cost of the zero coupon bonds was $800,000. The annuity paid the seller $200,000 annually, and the zero coupon bonds were scheduled to make the three respective $1 million payments 5, 10, and 20 years. Inflation protection was also included. (Zero coupon bonds are explained in Chapter 27.)

The payments described above assured the seller of deferred payments (for tax reduction purposes). Supposedly, because the annual payments were compensation to the seller, the buyer could deduct the cost of the bonds and the annuity as a business expense. Thus, both parties benefited from the transaction.

Professional Advice

Don't try to save money by not paying for diversified business advice from experienced outside business people or professionals such as accountants and lawyers. Frequently, assistance can help you develop your business into a public corporation. This is especially true if you learn about preparing a written operating budget, planning a long-range program, and how and where to secure low-cost financing.

There are a few types of budgets. The basic budget is a financial plan that estimates how much the operating expenses and income will be. This type of budget is usually called an operating budget. It alerts you to your need for financing before it is too late. For a new business, you should also have a capital budget. It helps you estimate how much money you will be required to spend for fixtures and improvements before you can open. Many businesses fail because they do not use written budgets and do not anticipate the need for financing before it is too late to secure it. Financing is frequently denied when a business finds itself in financial need. It is always easier to secure a credit line when a business is in strong financial condition.

Production, marketing, and distribution companies usually require a lot of capital, many competent employees, and outside expert advice before they are likely to succeed.

Libraries, various government offices, and the United States Government Printing Office all offer many books that provide good business advice. However, there is no substitute for practical, hands-on, experience. (The government provides a free catalog of their books upon request.)

An easy, inexpensive way to get experience in a business is to get a job in it. This way, someone else pays for your training, experience, and mistakes. If possible, get acquainted with whoever is responsible for budgets, financing, marketing, and planning.

Try to learn the basic principles that they use when making their plans. And use every opportunity to improve your sales and marketing techniques. The importance of salesmanship cannot be overstressed. Every business transaction starts with the sale of either an intangible item, tangible merchandise, or a service.

Location

Never select a location just because the rent is cheap. Do not settle for an existing location because you are in a hurry to get started. Finding and selecting the correct location for your business, whether you open it from scratch or buy a going business, is difficult. Acceptable locations vary according to the type of business and the community for which it is planned. Some important questions about location are:

1. Is the neighborhood changing in a way that may hurt your venture? Be sure to check current zoning and potential changes.
2. Will contemplated construction or building modernization programs in or near your building affect your business potential?
3. Will your business depend on lots of car traffic, foot traffic, neighborhood business, drive-thru, or telephone business? Is the location right for the answer you got? (Interestingly, 40 percent of the business of a major hamburger franchise is derived from drive-thru trade.)
4. Will the allocated parking space for your customers be convenient and adequate?
5. Will you have sufficient interior space to service customers, receive supplies, and warehouse stock?
6. Can you afford the rent? Will the lease be long enough?
7. How does the rent compare with your written operating budget?
8. How good is the visibility of your proposed business from the street? How much sign space can you use?
9. How close is the competition? Will it hurt or help you?
10. What will be the estimated cost of preparing the interior and exterior for business? Does it comply with your capital budget?

It is important that you secure answers to the above questions.

Then discuss them with your accountant. Also, try to check similar businesses. Determine why they are successful. Decide whether you can follow their pattern or if you should blaze a new trail. Usually, it is safer to follow a tested, successful pattern. You should also determine why a business might be failing to look for things to avoid.

Above all, do not select a location merely because the rent is low. Often, the only people that can try low-rent locations are the well-financed retail warehouse-type of operations that do a volume business based on heavy advertising, thousands of memberships, and low, discounted prices. Most experienced business people advocate that you open your business in a well-populated area in which business is already being heavily transacted. Working hard and putting in long hours in the wrong location can be very frustrating.

Competition and Promotion

While you do not want to open in an area that is saturated with your type of business, don't be frightened away by a moderate amount of competition. This is especially true if potential customers are readily available and you have something special to offer. Frequently, competition brings more customers to each store than would have come for a single store.

Too many entrepreneurs open a business as if it were a secret. They open without any fanfare and literally sit and wait for walk-in customers to find them. This is the wrong way to open a business. Sometimes they fail before most of the neighborhood knows that they ever existed.

Advertising costs must be included in the operating budget. The "grand opening" should be well-advertised with special inducements for people to come into the store. The phones should be ordered and space taken in the local Yellow Pages as soon as the lease is signed.

Before you open, learn what your potential customers want that your competitors are not offering. When you find it, satisfy that want. Guaranteeing customer satisfaction and having an easy return policy can keep your clientele coming back—especially if you do a better job of buying and merchandising than your competitors. But to get new customers to come to you for the first time, you must let them know about your policy of guaranteeing satisfaction. Then stick to it, even if it means taking an occasional loss.

Offered benefits are meaningless unless a large number of your potential customers know about them. In other words, you have to toot your own horn through promotion and advertising. In most successful businesses, this is an expected, ongoing expense.

The wrong type of advertising can hurt you. Big companies have lost fortunes by using the wrong type of advertising. Therefore, unless you understand the advertising business, it behooves you to get a good advertising agency to prepare your ads. They will know where to advertise and how to reach the most people at the lowest cost. It may cost you more than if you prepare your own ads, but if agency-created advertising brings you more business than your own ads, then the percentage as a cost of sales will be less expensive. If the ads do not help you, then change the agency without hesitation.

Successful advertising should lead to a greater sales volume. Increased sales should let you purchase larger quantities of merchandise at a lower cost. You can maintain profits even with reduced prices that permit you to undercut your competitors and continue to advertise.

If you cannot afford to pay for conventional advertising, use unconventional methods. Certain businesses succeed when the owner or someone he hires canvasses local homes and businesses in the area. The fact is that many major industries in America were based on cold canvassing (personal, direct solicitation from house to house or store to store). During the Great Depression in the 1930s, many unemployed people became successful business entrepreneurs by canvassing residents and offering daily home delivery of such items as freshly ground coffee, fresh bakery products, and milk. Canvassing is not easy. Not everyone can do it. But when there is a shortage of advertising and promotional funds, direct canvassing offers one way to make a business successful. Neatly dressed owners or paid canvasers need merely offer a business card while introducing themselves to their prospect. They can explain that they are letting people know about the new business, what it offers, and that their trade will be appreciated. Also, on the card, they may offer an inducement, such as a 20-percent discount for any item in the store purchased within a specified period of time.

Goodwill

It is important to budget an adequate amount of money for long-term, preprogrammed, promotional advertising. Such advertising, in addition to promoting the initial business, will contribute towards building goodwill, a salable asset in the future.

Goodwill should be understood. It is often an important ingredient whenever a business is bought or sold. Goodwill is the amount of money paid in excess of the book value of the assets. It is the expectation of continued public patronage. However, it does not include the right to use the name of a person from whom it was acquired. Goodwill does not mean having the advantage of simply occupying a particular building which had been previously occupied by a manufacturer or retailer. It means using every possible advantage established by a business, whether connected with the premises in which the business is conducted, the name under which it is managed, or any other matter carrying with it the benefit of the business. Although goodwill is an asset, it cannot be depreciated.

When capital gains taxes are important, sellers favor allocating a larger amount of the purchase price to goodwill. The payments can then be taxed at the lower capital gains rates.

General Business Tips and Guidelines:

- If you are a business person, you may be interested in taking advantage of a veteran's program which, in certain industries, enables qualified employers to reduce labor costs by being reimbursed for half of the starting wage—up to a maximum of $10,000 for each veteran hired. (See Where to Get Assistance earlier in this chapter.)
- If you are in a production or manufacturing business, you should try to improve on or invent new equipment that can save time, labor, or help in the making of by-products. Many companies owe their success to their use of in-house-invented, cost-cutting equipment that gave them a competitive edge over similar manufacturers.
- Changes in employment laws, particularly those dealing with sex or racial discrimination, have made employers liable for employment discrimination.

- When you purchase a business, make sure that all promises and representations upon which you relied are written into the contract.
- Don't expect to be right all the time. The late financier and statesman Bernard Baruch was quoted as saying, "If you make a mistake, don't live with it. Cut your losses quickly."
- The use of mail for business may be more expensive than telephone calls. But, if you employ many people, you should secure the least expensive, best quality phone service available. Obtain the cooperation of your employees in limiting nonbusiness phone calls. In some companies, phone bills can account for 30 percent of the company's operating expenses.
- If you purchase a business that has good managers, or if you are going to be an absentee owner, it is considered good business to sign them to long-term contracts and to give your managers a share of the profits.
- Even though the financial statement is important when purchasing a business, it does not reveal the value of all assets. For instance, the value of assets that have been depreciated but have increased in value because of inflation are not revealed. Also not revealed are the value of goodwill, marketing, and promotional skills. Undoubtedly, however, the sales price of a business that shows a profit will include a value for goodwill.
- Whether you buy or want to open a business, first check whether the location is properly zoned for the type of business you have in mind. Don't make any assumptions about legality. Check with the local licensing departments as to what their requirements and fees are. Contact the state and local authorities that regulate sales or use taxes and find out what they want you to do or pay before you open and engage in business. Also, contact the local banks and find out from the managers what kind of services they can offer you if you open a business account with them.
- If you do not know the true value of a business you are contemplating buying, find out the name of an accountant who services that type of business. The accountant can help you find out how its performance compares with similar companies in the same industry. Some of these types of business statistics are also available in the reference rooms of certain public libraries. Librarians will be glad to help you.

- With the exception of service businesses, most other businesses are exposed to shoplifters and professional thieves. Experienced shopkeepers look for people who linger in the store, have large pockets, oversized clothing, large purses, and shopping bags. It is dangerous and can be very costly to make any accusations without direct proof while the suspected customer is still in the store. To discourage shoplifting, it is better to give constant attention and service to those you suspect than it is to wait for them to steal.
- It has been conservatively estimated that one out of every ten shoppers is dishonest. The average family overpays $250 a year to make up for pilferage losses suffered by retailers. Thus, when you are in business, you must protect yourself from losses that are caused by different forms of customer corruption, pilferage (shoplifting), employee theft, and credit swindlers. Also, employee theft is on the rise. The September 1987 issue of *Nation's Business* reported that "shrinkage—shortages in inventory have been steadily increasing from an average 1.65 percent of sales in 1983 to 1.98 percent last year." It also reported that 5,000 companies give written honesty tests to their employees and that the biggest employee theft was in stolen time. This amounted to $170 billion of their employers' time.

  It is worthwhile to contact the white collar crime division of your local police department to stay abreast of new developments and to protect yourself from shoplifting, credit, and corruption losses. If you give credit, join a local credit association.
- Even if you own or are offered a fantastic invention, its financial success will depend on a number of things. Included are a combination of adequate capitalization, good management, experienced production, planned marketing, timely distribution, affordable yet profitable pricing, and acceptance by the public.
- Whatever type of business you enter, first determine its current image, such as the type of market it appeals to (age, sex, socio-economic bracket), and whether it is catering to a cash or credit business. Then compare this image with the one you want to create and the market which you want to serve. Try to evaluate the profitability of both—the cash or the credit system—and then decide which one you like best.

- Many different appraisal methods are used to determine the value of a business. They include market value comparisons with similar businesses, replacement costs less depreciation, capitalizing gross sales, and capitalizing net sales. But, a major appraisal method that should never be overlooked involves using the Net Asset Value (described in Chapter 22).
- If you contemplate buying or selling a business, do not overlook the hidden value of intangible assets. These include goodwill, established management, customer lists, special buying contracts, a valuable lease, undervalued property, and other assets listed on the financial statement.
- If you decide to negotiate the purchase of a business, do not sign any preliminary documents without first specifying in writing that, before the deal is finally consummated, the seller must furnish you and/or your accountant with sales tax and income tax records and all books of account.
- If the business that is for sale is in corporate form, contact your lawyer and accountant to determine whether under the circumstances you should purchase the assets instead of the stock of the corporation.
- Most states have a form of the Bulk Sales Act that is intended to protect the buyers and creditors whenever there is a change of ownership. It requires publicly advertising the change of ownership to give creditors the opportunity to present their bills before the sale is completed. By abiding by this Act and the use of an escrow to hold all funds until a clean deal is consummated, you may be protected against all debts and obligations owed by the seller for such things as merchandise, fixtures, and delinquent taxes.
- If the seller wants you to buy his current accounts receivable, try to arrange to collect them for him instead of buying them.
- Although the use of escrows is always recommended, please remember that the escrow company is only a stakeholder. Escrow companies are usually licensed by their respective states and are usually bonded. Escrow officers do not act or substitute for your lawyer or provide legal advice. Their function is to comply with the written instructions given to them by the parties involved in the transaction being escrowed. They collect money for the parties and hold it in trust until all provisions of the escrow agreement are fulfilled. It is advisable that your lawyer furnish the escrow

company with complete instructions that properly protect you against all contingencies.
- In states that do not have escrow companies, do not try to consummate the purchase of a business without a lawyer. However, even when you use an escrow company and a lawyer, it is imperative that you determine the requirements of the local and state laws concerning zoning, licensing, and protecting creditors, and whether you can comply with them.
- Your initial agreement concerning the purchase of a business should specify:

1. The monetary details of the sale together with the closing date and a time frame for you or your lawyer or accountant to review the tax records and all books of account
2. The obligations that you are and are not assuming
3. The amount of inventory
4. The dollar value of the specific accounts receivable that you are receiving, if any
5. The real and personal property and fixtures that are included
6. Any other factors that induced you to purchase the business
7. A reasonable, noncompeting business clause so that the agreement restricting the seller's right to engage in business is not in conflict with local laws (with respect to the distance from the business sold, the time length of the restriction, and, when appropriate, the creativeness of an individual seller)
8. All taxes and fees that are either overdue or that will become due before the sale closes
9. The names and addresses of all suppliers and creditors and the amounts owed to them, including the maximum amount of credit they authorized
10. All existing and potential lawsuits, mortgages, liens, and security agreements that exist against the business. (A false statement of this type, in addition to constituting evidence for a civil action, will subject the seller to criminal penalties.)

A list of creditors may serve you in many ways. It will enable you to verify the amount of business the seller transacted with them as well as the amount owed by the seller. It also enables you to establish your own line of credit with those same suppliers.

By now, you would be correct in surmising that while many people might think they would like to own their own business, there are many reasons why many of them should not. For instance, many are undercapitalized, unqualified, too inexperienced, or unwilling to accept the responsibility and hard work that owning and managing one's own business entails. Most would-be entrepreneurs lack management skills and cannot plan or properly organize for success. Many lack general business experience or direct experience in the specific business in which they intend to become involved.

You now know about many of the problems involved in selecting and running your own business. You should also know how to protect yourself against many of the known hazards. With this background, you might be inclined to try your hand at investing in your own business. Even if totally inexperienced, you may still be successful if you possess the four following essential attributes:

1. The will to overcome obstacles
2. The desire to succeed
3. Sufficient capitalization to allow mistakes while acquiring the necessary experience
4. Management skills or the ability to secure and follow management advice. (Management is the ability to analyze, plan, organize, and execute a plan.)

You may survive in your own business, even without management experience, if you possess the first three attributes. However, with or without business experience, if you do not know how to manage a business, supervise people, or hire competent management, it is unlikely that you will experience a substantial success.

The moment that you try to expand, employ additional help, or open another location, your business will require a manager with the ability to budget, plan, and organize. A good manager will help you analyze your products or services, determine what your customers expect, and how to help them get it.

It is not essential for your manager to have experience in your industry, although directly-related experience is highly desirable. Even without experience in the same business, a qualified, experienced manager should be able to adapt his or her skills and make valuable contributions in planning and organization.

Chapter 29: Investing in Gold

Investing in Gold

Who hasn't been affected by the glamour and romantic notions of raw gold? Think of the poor prospectors who became rich gold miners overnight. Consider ancient objects exquisitely crafted with gold, distinctive gold jewelry, or the aura of people who wear it. Any investment connected with gold seems to have a "value-built-in" or "get-rich-quick" appeal. Thus, this chapter's purpose is to help potential gold investors avoid making common mistakes. It acquaints them with some basic facts about this precious commodity—hopefully, before they take the plunge.

When becoming involved in buying either bullion or gold coins, it is important to understand the basic nomenclature of the trade. Gold is an ore found in streams, in mountains, or on the surface of the earth in an exposed vein. When converted to bullion it is reshaped into 400-ounce bars in the form of gold ingots, assaying at least 0.995 fine (assaying means that it has been tested and weighed for gold content).

An *ingot* is a mass of metal cast in a convenient form prepared for shaping, resmelting, or refining. Bullion is heavy and expensive to shape and there is a cost for melting it down into smaller amounts. The term *fine* refers to the percentage of the total gross weight of the gold that is pure. Thus, 0.995 fine means that five one/hundredths of one percent is not pure gold. Twelve *troy ounces* equals an *avoirdupois* (16-ounce) pound.

The Cost of Gold

Regardless of where gold is found, it has been expensive to find, finance, extract, refine, and distribute. But, because most people believe that gold is usually found or discovered by accident, many investors don't realize that there is an expensive monetary cost attached both to the mining of gold and to its distribution. In most cases, mining gold is more scientific than haphazard. Yet, many companies have drilled 3,000- to 6,000-foot wells that only rewarded them with granite. Sometimes, expensive long-term drilling produces only low-grade ore. Profitability is not normally achieved without 4 to 6 years of development.

The costs of producing gold vary according to deflation, inflation, interest rates, and the export regulations that attempt to control the price by reducing the available supply. A prime example of the volatility attached to gold investments may be garnered from a 1985 press report concerning the Homestake Mining Company, a major American mining firm. Homestake reported that it had a mine in Lead, South Dakota, whose cost to produce an ounce of gold in 1984 was $327. Unfortunately, this is only one of the many instances in which the cost of producing gold bullion has exceeded the cost for which it could be sold at the time.

It is believed that the world's major sources of gold are in South Africa and Canada. Many other countries have gold mines, and some hold huge amounts in reserve. In June 1985, the Canadian newspaper *Globe and Mail* reported that according to statistics published by South Africa's Department of Energy and Mineral Affairs in 1984, South Africa produced more than 60 different minerals at 883 mines; 83 of the mines yielded gold. Additional statistics were that 72 percent of South Africa's exports were gold. The country had more than 20,000 tons of reserve gold—more than half of the world's known deposits.

It was estimated that the worldwide production of gold in 1986 would exceed 42 million ounces, and that South Africa would contribute between 45 and 50 percent of that total. Also, it was estimated that $4 out of every $5 spent on mining exploration goes for gold. It is expected that during the next 5 years, many gold mines will be opened for exploration in the United States.

Ways to Invest in Gold

In the past decade, the desire to acquire, invest in, and hold on to gold has caused both people and countries to lose billions of dollars. Their reasons vary as gold is purchased for purposes of adornment, large potential profits, future security, or protection against weakening monetary systems. Even the greedy OPEC countries, who used their inexpensive oil to raid our pockets, suffered losses as high as 100 percent when some of the gold that they bought at prices up to $850 per ounce plummeted to the $300 to $500 range. Yet, there will always be promoters who succeed in soliciting investors to buy gold.

Investing in Gold

There are many ways to invest in gold, depending upon your preferences. You may purchase gold bullion, coins, or jewelry. You may invest in gold mining companies by becoming a partner in a mining company. You may buy shares of stock in a gold mining company or in a mutual company that specializes in owning mining companies. Or, you may buy put and call options (explained in Chapter 28).

Each method of ownership has advantages and disadvantages. In my opinion, which is supported by various other people, the disadvantages of owning gold by the average investor, in any form, outweigh the advantages. "Why then," you may ask, "do so many people invest in gold?" There is more than one answer. Most of the motivations and supposed advantages that attract the average investor to gold are summarized as follows:

1. It can be used to back a country's currency.
2. There are many ways to invest in it.
3. It is durable.
4. It makes nice looking jewelry.
5. It can be used as a medium of exchange.
6. It has industrial and dental uses.
7. It is a mysterious, fascinating form of investment.
8. It has made some people rich and seems like a good speculation.
9. Exaggerated promotional claims and "get-rich-quick" promises sound good.

Most gold purchasers are motivated for a variety of reasons other than quick speculation. Non-speculators, as a rule, desire to hold gold for the following reasons:

- As a hedge against inflation
- For long-term appreciation
- As a viable, usable asset in the event that the credibility of the regular monetary currency becomes suspect and unstable
- For reserve or emergency funds to escape to another country in the event of political, social, or monetary upheavals

Many political refugees owe their lives to the foresight that prompted them to have gold reserves available when they had to flee for their lives from their native countries.

Outweighing the advantages of investing in gold by the average person are the many disadvantages. Some disadvantages are:

1. It has caused heavy losses for many speculators and investors.
2. In bullion form it is too heavy for convenient use.
3. It costs money to warehouse, guard, and insure.
4. It does not pay interest.
5. It may be counterfeit and must be assayed to determine its gold content, weight, and value.
6. It is a very speculative investment.
7. It is not an investment that is recommended for the average investor.
8. New methods of production, such as "heap leaching" (a chemical process that separates gold from ore), may lower its price dramatically.
9. It is subject to the government's control and may be called in.
10. The Soviet Union may at any time release a lot of gold to pay for its grain purchases. That would increase the supply of gold and lower its value.
11. It may even be subject to state sales taxes.

Other than refugees fleeing a country, all other investors in non-emergency situations who decide to invest in gold should not invest in any aspect of gold for more than 5 to 10 percent of their investment portfolios. However, the various promotional schemes about how to invest in gold confuses many would-be investors. After potential investors become interested in gold, many have difficulty deciding on the type of investment that best suits their financial needs. They may ask, "In what form of gold should I invest? Bullion, coins, gold shares, a direct interest in a gold mine, or options using puts and calls?"

The answer is not easy. It must consider the investors' assets, their other investments, financial requirements, and their ability to cope with the vagaries of each form of investment.

When you purchase gold to make a profit, you are virtually wagering on a number of factors. Will the:

- Demand for gold surpass the supply?
- Cost of locating and extracting gold increase?
- U.S. dollar decrease in value?

- Uncertainty about international events make people afraid of paper money.

Mining Company Stocks

The easiest way to benefit from an anticipated increase in the price of gold is to buy stock in a company that mines gold. This eliminates costs for storage, security, and insurance. However, before investing, attempt to minimize your risk. First compare the assets, potential earnings, and equity values of the various gold mining companies as suggested in Chapter 22. Also, be cautious about believing the promotional literature and claims disseminated by some of the gold companies. Not all stock exchanges employ the same control standards that are used by the New York Stock Exchange. Moreover, be careful before investing in the penny gold stocks offered on the Canadian stock exchanges. Often, the risk in penny stocks seems smaller because of the amounts involved.

Many companies that deal in gold have extremely high promotional (or boiler room) costs. They frequently suffer financial problems. Therefore, before you invest with or through a company that you do not know personally, do a little checking. This advice should be followed even if you think the delay will cost you big profits. Protect yourself by re-reading Section 1 of this book. Contact both the Better Business Bureau and the Securities & Exchange Commission.

Gold Coins

Many people believe that buying gold coins is the easiest way to invest in gold. This approach lets them possess interesting mementos that can eventually be sold for a premium price. Gold coins can be used for jewelry and are easy to handle. Of course, there are many types of gold coins. Because of the minting charge, most gold coins sell at a slight premium over bullion. The Chinese Panda gold coins are among those that sell at a high premium (there are relatively few in circulation). On the other hand, the once popular Krugerrand has been selling below its gold value. Basically, the future value of gold coins depends upon the issuing government's ability to back them up.

In 1986, the United States issued four types of American Eagle gold coins. A reported budget of between $5 and $8 billion was issued to sell 2.2 million ounces in the first 12 months. At the time they were issued, the price of gold was about $422 an ounce.

The gold content and approximate prices of each of the four coins were:

0.10 ounce	$ 48.60
0.25 ounce	$118.00
0.50 ounce	$228.00
1.00 ounce	$443.00

These figures do not include a 1 percent service charge or state sales tax.

The most popular coins have been the Canadian Mapleleaf and the South African Krugerrand. The latter was withdrawn from production after its sales were banned in the United States.

The May 30, 1985, European edition of the *Wall Street Journal* contained an article that demonstrated some of the problems that occur when buying coins. The article reported that thousands of gold coin investors were disappointed when the South African Gold Coin Exchange became the subject of a court-appointed investigation based on allegations of irregularities and potential liquidity problems.

The Exchange had promised 30 percent annual returns to purchasers of "proof Krugerrands," even while bullion prices were falling. Proof Krugerrands are high quality coins that contain one troy ounce of gold (12 troy ounces is the equivalent of one avoirdupois 16-ounce pound, the system of weights used in the United States and Britain). Proof Krugerrands are limited in production and are traded internationally. A gold-industry official said the guarantees of 30 percent annual returns during a time of falling bullion prices would be untenable. "An offer of such returns under present market conditions would be fantastic for the investor and unrealistic for the trader." After the court intervened, the prices of proof Krugerrands dropped 40 percent.

When purchasing gold bullion or coins, the selling companies often offer to hold the coins for you. It is important to check whether or not they actually possess all the coins they allegedly bought for you. Many times they do not! Consequently, ensure that you are doing business with reliable dealers. Ask the Better Business Bureau if your dealer has been the subject of complaints for unfair dealing.

A major disadvantage of purchasing bullion or coins for investment is that they require storage and insurance. In addition, the investor loses the interest on the money invested.

Factors Affecting the Price of Gold

The market price at which gold sells depends upon many factors. Factors such as the vagaries of politics, economics, and supply and demand are listed above. But another important factor that affects the price of gold is the emotions of gold aficionados.

These are the people who purchase gold because they anticipate world crises, uncontrolled inflation, monetary deflation, and all kinds of world-wide economic uncertainties. The gold aficionados believe that these types of unsettling events might cause many people to purchase gold as a haven or as protection against weak currencies. Further, they believe that the increased demand will decrease the supply causing the value of their gold to increase. Another factor that could cause gold to increase in value is heavy world debt. This was a major factor during 1986 and 1987.

When gold prices drop, investors become discouraged, and the price of gold drops still further. When the economy seems to be on the rise and the dollar is increasing in value, the price of gold usually drops. Thus, those aficionados who usually buy gold as a hedge against a bad economy become sellers. The reaction is a drop in the price of gold. Gold sales depress the gold market still further and despair feeds upon itself.

On the other hand, when the economy appears weak and the dollar seems to be losing value, gold aficionados react by increasing their purchases. This reduces the available supply and tends to increase the price. Publicity concerning the increased demand emphasizes the weakening of the economy and/or the dollar and creates an atmosphere of fear. Automatically, frightened investors look for a haven, which increases demand and further increases the price of gold.

When the price of gold is too low, some of the well-heeled gold producers might take steps to protect themselves. They may either curb production or buy gold in the market. They buy gold themselves whenever the cost of producing gold is more than its market price.

When investors are led to believe that the government will print money to pay off the deficit, the value of gold will probably increase. Conflicting economic and financial factors make it difficult for the experts to predict the future value of gold. For instance, gold usually increases in price as the value of the dollar declines. However, the dollar declined in early 1986 and the value of gold remained low. Another factor that reduces the price of gold is the promise of high interest rates. But again, during 1986 and 1987 interest rates were low.

Investor Alerts

Investors must be alerted to a few additional factors that can affect the future prices of gold and create insecurity.

First to be considered is the precarious political situation that exists in South Africa, a major source of gold. Many political economists fear major anti-apartheid uprisings, which would certainly affect production and prices. Worker dissatisfaction can also produce strikes without an uprising. In the event of a strike, the respective mining companies will not be able to pay dividends to their shareholders. This will reduce the value of the involved gold shares, which in turn will reduce the value of some of the mutual funds that hold these shares in their portfolios. Also, the Republic of South Africa reportedly is in debt for more than half of its reserves (from its trade surplus, gold, and foreign reserves). No one knows what action the government might take that could either increase or decrease the value of gold.

The second item to consider is that a new, tested process for gold extraction is materially reducing the cost of producing gold. This new technique is called "heap leaching" or "cyanide leaching." The technique enables the operators to process ore for approximately $100 a ton instead of the previous cost of about $400 a ton. With the new system, stacked ore is soaked with diluted sodium cyanide. This dissolves and releases the gold for recovery at a total cost of about $200 a troy ounce.

The third item to consider is the belief by some investors that the Federal Reserve Board will force them to cash in their interest-bearing securities and buy gold. Yet, in May of 1985, when the discount rate was lowered, investors turned to stocks and bonds instead of gold. (Presumably, because of the prior 2-month slump and the opportunity for profit-buying by investors, gold futures price rebounded, only to slump again by the end of the month.)

The fourth item to consider is that many conservative investors mistakenly believe that gold protects them against inflation. It usually does not. It is only a hedge against inflation if you can purchase it so that it can be redeemed for a fixed dollar amount. Otherwise, you have no protection against a loss in the value of your investment. Moreover, complete protection means compensation for any losses incurred from the fluctuating value of gold itself. This is in addition to being compensated for inflationary losses.

The fifth item to consider is that analysts and promoters increase the demand for gold. This increases the price. They disseminate pessimistic statements like the following one published in 1984: "The strength of the dollar has eroded. If the inflation I foresee occurs, gold could reach $2,000 to $3,000 an ounce during 1986 and 1987." In fact, during 1986 gold was bearish, then bullish, and closed bearish under $400 an ounce. This was in spite of the fact that the value of the dollar had eroded. As the dollar weakened towards the end of 1987, gold became bullish and its domestic price rose to $491.

The sixth item to consider is the performance of gold compared to alternate investments. At the end of 1987 a number of analysts recognized that gold had performed exceptionally well (it hit a low of $285 in 1985). They also observed that for the same period, gold investors could have done better if they had changed from dollars to other major currencies.

Conclusion

You now have a basic background in gold investments. This chapter discussed its production and how its market value is established. It revealed gold investment methods and gave some reasons why people invest in gold. And it described many of the advantages and disadvantages that accompany gold investments. If you want to consider gold investments, please review the chapters on economics in Section 2. The factors discussed in the chapters of Section 2 also affect the price of gold.

Hopefully, if you decide to invest in gold, you will have learned enough to prevent avoidable mistakes. Don't be stampeded by a "once-in-a-lifetime" promotion. Take the necessary time to investigate before investing.

Chapter 30: Oil and Gas Exploration and Development

Oil and Gas Exploration and Development

Like precious metals, oil and gas investments have enjoyed an intriguing mystique. After all, there is only a finite supply. And alternate energy sources may never materialize. Just consider the many millionaires spawned by the burgeoning oil and gas industry? Who wouldn't like to get rich from petroleum products gushing out of the ground. And think of the benefits from both depletion and depreciation tax breaks. Those fabulous oil revenues that have been accumulated by the oil-producing OPEC countries are still building. Every country and person has been affected by the supply and price of oil and gas. And yet, in recent years, many investors have lost fortunes in energy investments. Many learned that wiser investments could have been made outside of the energy field. Unfortunately, most of them invested before considering the unavoidable risks. Many did not know how to protect themselves from inevitable downturns.

The major unavoidable risks are:

- Unexpected dry wells
- An oversupply of oil or gas reserves
- A drastic drop in prices
- An unexpected request from the developer for additional capital.

These risks are indigenous to the oil and gas business. Risks are to be expected. Other than to acquaint you with them, no one can help you avoid them. There are, however, many avoidable risks. This book is designed to alert you and show you how to protect yourself.

First, however, you should understand the mechanics of oil and gas exploration and development practices and procedures. This will help you understand the unavoidable risks. Next, this chapter acquaints you with:

- Fraudulent practices
- Distribution facilities
- Imaginative accounting
- The agreement
- Legal risks or hazards
- Who profits and who loses
- Evaluating reserves
- Economic considerations
- Inflation
- Tax advantages

Exploration and Development Projects and Procedures

Not including stocks, there are two types of projects offered to oil and gas investors: the exploration project and the development project.

Exploration projects are much riskier than the development projects. Also, they are usually much costlier. These programs are often geared for deep, expensive drilling, possibly in untested or unproven areas. The exploration developments usually experience many more dry holes than are encountered by the development projects. Exploration is customarily based on geophysical information and the hope that the result will be a big gusher.

The development project, on the other hand, usually proceeds on one of two basic plans. The first plan is based on geophysical studies that indicate that oil is close by, not too deep, and therefore not too expensive to find. The second plan is based on information available from prior well-drilling in the immediate area that indicates that finding oil or gas may not be too expensive. It will possibly have a steady flow, although it may not be in huge amounts.

Large oil companies shun the second plan because of the small revenue that can be anticipated even if oil is found. They favor potential windfall gushers. Because of their heavy overhead, large oil companies need the big gushers.

Thus, the smaller development projects remain available for development by the smaller, more conservative developers. They are usually satisfied with earning smaller amounts of money, provided there is less risk. The smaller developer has no difficulty in securing capital; there are many investors who have the same investment philosophy—they are happy to invest in less-risky oil ventures. However, there are no guarantees that these wells will continue to produce even after oil or gas is discovered.

Oil and gas can come from the same opening in the ground. However, in some areas, wells spew out natural gas without oil while in other areas the wells yield oil without natural gas.

Primarily, the development of oil and gas consists of five operational steps:

1. The first step is to look at records and maps. If the property has already been leased by the operators, different areas are tested for potential drilling sites.
2. If the property is not already leased, the property must be acquired. This usually involves agreeing to pay the property owner a royalty percentage in exchange for a lease to drill and extract the oil and gas.
3. The third step involves drilling the well bore and taking samples of the underground soil. If the results are satisfactory, preparations are begun for the fourth step.
4. The fourth step is to complete and equip the well. This involves purchasing and installing pipe in the well bore.
5. If the prior four steps provide evidence that oil or gas are obtainable at the site, then the fifth step is begun. Plans are made to secure the equipment to produce, collect, store, and transport the oil or gas to a buyer. The buyer is usually a large oil company which is a refiner or a direct user. In some areas, factories are direct users of gas.

Unfortunately, many wells are only encouraging up to step five. At this time, someone must be found who can use or refine the product. Sometimes, they must be willing to run a pipeline from the well to their own collection base. When there is no demand for the product, many proven and potentially profitable oil and gas wells are locked in without distribution facilities or buyers. Renewal of the OPEC quota system can bring prices to the level that will permit some of these wells to become profitable.

Fraudulent Practices

An example of the seriousness of the thefts, frauds, unlawful gifts, kickbacks, and pilferage that occur in the oil business is illustrated by a front page headline and lengthy, detailed article that appeared in the January 15, 1985 issue of *The Wall Street Journal*. It was entitled, "Slick Operators—Oil Field Investigators say Fraud Flourishes, From Wells to Offices."

While legal recourse can be attempted to recover from a bad deal, the wells and operators are usually too far away from their investors. Proving a case usually requires an expensive audit, court costs, witnesses, extensive legal fees, and a large amount of time.

In the interim, the principals may go into bankruptcy without paying back any money to the investors. This is why investors should never let the idea of making huge profits deter them from investigating the background of the operators and agents. These individuals are responsible for receiving and disbursing investment funds and anticipated revenues. Check their expertise, honesty, integrity, and promptness in distributing profits. Talk to other investors who know and conduct business with them.

Not Fraudulent but Risky

Whenever energy prices rise, energy companies start dusting off plans to procure their energy from many unusual sources. These include such sources as bitumen, shale, coal, zeolite, tar sands, and wind farms. These are all expensive, long-range programs; they require sophisticated engineering and processes that cost huge sums of money. No matter how promising these plans sound to you, the energy companies have already spent fortunes on each. Most have proven unprofitable. Accordingly, operations have been discontinued. Today, most are on the the back burner. Thus, they are not a recommended investment for a novice or small investor for at least another ten or more years.

It is possible to get unfair treatment when investing in an oil syndication that is run on an honest, legitimate basis. This can happen when a legitimate oil and gas company, which owns many oil and gas leaseholds, needs additional capital for drilling and for expansion. Thus, the company syndicates limited partnership interests to the general public. Usually, they indicate the ratio of exploration to developmental wells to be drilled using the new funds and in what period of time. They may also discuss possible tax advantages and the potential for finding producing wells. All of this can seem great. But the important question is, "Will they offer the public an interest in their best wells, or will they keep these for themselves?" The answer, of course, depends on whether you still believe in Santa Claus.

Imaginative Accounting

Imaginative accounting poses another problem that arises from investing with other people. The actual operators of the well, who may not be the syndicators or the investment group, may be the culprits. They can pay fictitious expenses that are difficult to disprove. They can also withhold the distribution of profits for an inordinate length of time.

Even if the operators possess an honest background, in order to procure business or operating licenses, they may be compelled to pay kickbacks against their well. Unfortunately, kickbacks and bribes are usually concealed. This leads to improper accounting procedures and opens the door to further chicanery.

The Importance of Distribution Facilities and Contracts

The lack of distribution pipe lines can cause earnings to shrink even from good wells. For instance, a severe winter may cause many people to freeze because of gas shortages. At the same time, operators of the gas wells located in nearby areas may not be able to sell their products to the "shortaged area" because of the lack of pipe lines. This is not an uncommon problem. Many investors are frustrated when they learn that even though their well has plenty of oil or gas, no one will build a pipeline to their wellhead.

Consequently, before investing in what could be a promising well, you must find out how the product will be distributed. If the project requires pipelines, make sure that the developer has sufficient capital to install them. He should have a contract from a reliable firm that wants to buy the oil or gas.

Some experienced oil and gas well investors participate in ventures that have what are referred to as "take or pay contracts." These are used for successful wells that have distribution facilities and ready users. A take or pay contract assures a steady supply of oil or gas to the oil or gas user within a specified time. However, the user may not always be able to consume his allotment of oil or gas on a steady basis. So, to be assured of a guaranteed supply, the user agrees to pay for a specific amount of oil or gas, whether they take it or not. Even then, the investor should investigate the renewability of a "take or pay contract." This can be the most important factor in the long-term profitability of an oil or gas investment.

How to Investigate a Venture

When invited to participate in an oil or gas venture, do not part with any money or sign any documents without taking a few investigative steps. Don't be impressed by the technical language suggesting that certain levels of the proposed well may be extremely productive. And don't be misled by a fancy office, glossy literature, elegant developer, glowing project details, or the amount of taxes you think you can save. Instead, investigate the veracity and integrity of the company or principals. Ask for the names of a few prior investors and for a copy of financial statements for prior projects. Check with the prior investors as to their profits; compare their statements with the financial statements. Call the Better Business Bureau. Then secure a copy of the venture's geological tests and submit them to an independent geologist, preferably in or near the area of the proposed prospect.

The Agreement, Requests for Additional Funds, and Up-Front Fees

The total amount of money that a limited partner is required to contribute to the venture is limited by the amount specified in the partnership agreement. A limited partner cannot be forced to contribute more funds, even if the venture has contracted excessive debts. But, unless the partnership agreement calls for the general partner to advance additional funds, the partnership may fail for lack of funds. However, the general and limited partners may voluntarily add capital to the venture. Some syndication agreements stipulate that the failure of investors to advance additional equal funds when required by certain contingencies may result in their being eliminated from the syndication. However, agreements that authorize the general partner to borrow additional funds usually stipulate that the general partner be repaid before any of the limited partners' contributions are returned from revenues.

Some companies ask for up-front fees. These range from approximately 6 to 20 percent of the amount of the investment. These fees, which can be the equivalent of a commission, are an immediate gross profit to the promoters or developers that receive them. Commission money should be used to pay for promotional expenses. However, it almost always goes into the pockets of the promoters. And it is never used to fund drilling. The promoters also take from 15 to 25 percent from fund revenues. This offers first-year tax write-offs that they claim can exceed 65 percent of the investment. Regardless of how the promoters calculate, do not participate in a venture when:

- The up-front fees or commissions exceed 15 percent
- Less than 85 percent will be used for drilling
- You know you will not receive at least 55 to 60 percent of the net revenues plus the deductions for intangible drilling costs.

Economic and Political Risks—Who Profits and Who Loses

Two groups profited from the oil quota system enacted by the Organization of Petroleum Exporting Countries (OPEC) in the late 1970s. OPEC, itself, accumulated vast wealth and average investors received large returns on their oil-related projects. These investors bought into oil or gas explorations or developments, either as limited partners or as shareholders in major oil companies. They were in an ideal position to make huge profits if their wells continued to produce.

During the oil shortage caused by the OPEC quota system, both Canada and the state of Texas tried to preserve their wells for the future. To do this, they prevented the successful oil companies from withdrawing oil and gas from their wells. Consequently, investors with direct ownership interests in successful Canadian and Texas gas exploration and development companies suffered. They could not capitalize on the oil shortage or be rewarded for their risks.

Subsequently, as people became more energy conscious and used less oil and gas, the OPEC quota system fell apart. The oil shortage disappeared, prices were drastically reduced, and the overabundance of gas and oil in certain areas of the world prevented investors from cashing in on their investments.

Moreover, the oversupply of oil and gas—and the resulting low prices—caused thousands of domestic oil drilling rigs to shut down. This resulted in financial havoc for their owners, who then suffered large financial losses. The losses prevented the owners from paying the banks that had helped finance them.

Thus, the banks suffered double losses! They lost on the loans for the rigs as well as the oil wells. The operators of the oil wells were forced to shut down. They could not compete with $9-a-barrel oil when all of their operations were based on approximately $30 a barrel.

Despite this note of pessimism, investors will always be lured by the romance of oil and gas. They will continue to want information about oil exploration—whether it is put out by large stock companies or smaller, independent companies that take in partners or co-ventures. New investors live with the hope that the recent quota system agreed upon by nearly all of OPEC's oil ministers will continue and eventually restore prices to about $19 a barrel.

Tax Advantages

Oil and gas projects offer many tax advantages. These include the deduction of certain expenses, equipment depreciation, and depletion allowances. (A depletion allowance is a government tax credit that may be applied to a percentage of the oil or gas that is extracted from the ground.) However, the U.S. tax laws are subject to many changes. Therefore, consult first with an accountant who is familiar with oil and gas accounting and taxes. Do this before you invest in oil or gas for tax shelter purposes.

Many people continued to invest in drilling partnerships in spite of a decline in oil prices in 1986 and a reduction in tax incentives in 1987. Despite the price decline, exploratory drilling is still favored by many experts. They believe that oil prices will eventually rebound. This optimism combined with tax write-offs will provide a larger percentage of profits. However, I strongly suggest that no investments be made for tax purposes without first consulting your tax accountant. Ask how the latest amendments to the Alternative Minimum Tax provisions of the Tax Reform Act of 1986 will affect your proposed investment.

Economic Considerations

The supply and price of oil and gas are subject to many economic and political philosophies. If you become interested in investing in oil or gas, you should become aware of how these philosophies can impact your investment.

First, you should beware that OPEC can control local prices. If its members disagree and do not set production quotas and overproduce, prices drop around the world. On the other hand, when OPEC is able to control production and prices, the world and local prices become stable and permit profitable investments.

Regarding supply and demand, the Paris-based International Energy Agency (a 21-nation organization, most of whose members are from western industrialized countries) met in 1984. This group estimated that the demand for oil by the end of the century would not increase past the 1982 level, even though the demand for energy in that period would increase by 32.9 percent.

Meanwhile, Canada, a very large energy-exporter to the U.S., decided to lower the price of gas to the U.S. Conflicts arose on both sides of the border. In Canada, one group favored reducing the price of gas to help Canadian producers and to bring more capital and jobs to Canada. An opposing group strongly disagreed. They maintained that the energy resources of Canada belonged to the citizens of Canada. They protested that selling gas cheaply to the United States was like "shipping off their heritage at bargain basement prices."

At the same time, energy-producers in the U.S. were complaining that they were "looking at a drastic disruption of our market." They believed that the U.S. was tying itself to Canada in the same way that it was tied to the Arab oil-producing countries.

Peculiarly, in the late 1970s when OPEC decided to pressure the world with high oil prices, Canada limited its supply to the U.S. They explained that they were not self-sufficient, wanted to reduce their imports from the OPEC countries, and did not have enough spare oil to ship to the U.S. This restrictive action encouraged oil exploration in the U.S. Eventually, it enabled both U.S. and Canadian petroleum companies to maintain a high price level for their products.

The resulting high oil prices contributed greatly to inflation. In addition to energy uses, petroleum is required in the production of many products. At this writing, the OPEC countries have reduced their prices by about 35 to 40 percent. The lower prices have discouraged investors from speculating in oil and gas wells. This eventually may create another shortage. Consequently, the would-be oil investor should watch both economic and political events with a keen eye. Try to determine if and when a new shortage will create the correct investment atmosphere to become involved in oil and gas ventures. Billions of dollars have been lost by petroleum operators who were driven out of business by reduced demand and lowered oil and gas prices. As previously mentioned, many banks that underwrote these companies also failed from lost billions in loans. In a single twelve-month period in 1987 and 1988, close to 200 banks failed in the states of Texas and Oklahoma.

The Value of Reserves

Finding oil or gas is not enough. After it is found, we only have reserves. Reserves are the amount of petroleum that is estimated to be in the ground. Ordinarily, the cash value of reserves are less than 20 percent of the amount for which they could be sold.

A common mistake made by investors when evaluating oil and gas investments relates to the value they place on oil or gas reserves. Evaluating reserves creates problems because there is more than one method that is used. Each method produces a different answer. For example, a well contains an estimated one billion barrels of oil and the price of a barrel of oil is worth $25. However, you can't determine the asset value by multiplying one billion barrels by $25 a barrel ($25 billion) and then deducting the costs of extraction and administration. Many promoters and stockbrokers use this simplistic approach to cite the value of a particular petroleum-based venture. But other factors must be considered. Read on for a more accurate explanation.

It is a fact that many brokers who sell oil stocks are deplorably unfamiliar with the oil and gas business. For one thing, they don't understand the true value of reserves. Therefore, they establish the value of the reserves by multiplying the estimated volume of oil or gas in the ground by the current price.

Reserve assets are only worth what someone will pay for them. In order for prospective purchasers of reserve assets to calculate a fair purchase price, they must first determine for how many years their cash must be invested before they get it back. Then they must consider how many years they will be compelled to wait until their investment shows a profit. Lastly, they must consider whether the profit will be worth the cash outlay and long wait.

Moreover, for various reasons endemic to the oil and gas industry, reserves may suddenly become difficult to extract. This often happens without prior warning. Because of this, prospective purchasers of reserves must always calculate in advance what their investment will cost them in lost interest or in potential profits should extraction of the reserve become problematic.

Consequently, it is possible that the estimated $25 billion in reserve assets cited earlier may only sell for 10 or 20 percent of its estimated value. In this case the value could range from $2.5 billion to $5 billion instead of $25 billion.

Note
For comparative purposes, the U.S. benchmark price for crude oil is determined by the current price of what is called *West Texas Intermediate*.

The advantages and disadvantages of oil and gas exploration and development have been presented. Now you might be interested in my opinion about your making an investment. I would tell you to invest in an oil and gas venture if you are able to meet the following qualifications.

1. If you lose all the money that you invest, it will not affect your family or life style.
2. Do not proceed without your accountant's unqualified approval after getting all the facts and discussing the tax consequences.
3. Acquire and investigate all of the details of the investment as suggested in "How to Investigate a Venture" paragraphs of this chapter. If you cannot verify successful operations and financial performances for the past few years, look for another investment. If you are satisfied with the information you have acquired, ask for a copy of the agreement.
4. Check the agreement as suggested in "The Agreement, Requests for Additional Funds, and Up-front Fees" paragraphs of this chapter. If it still meets with your approval, take it to your attorney. Tell him about any portion of the agreement that is unclear to you. After he reads it and you are both satisfied with it, and if you still feel you can afford to lose the entire investment, then go for it. I wish you good luck.

Conclusion

Contrary to implications that might at times be assumed in this book, I am strongly in favor of investors opening or buying established businesses or investing in potentially profitable ventures. Unfortunately, looking for and finding a potentially profitable business opportunity or investment, as you have come to realize by now, is fraught with peril.

Evaluating the merits of the opportunities offered to you and then deciding whether you should become involved in one or more of them is frequently a nerve-wearing process. Then, if you decide on one and it fails, taking with it your hard-earned capital, the experience could be emotionally shattering!

After the shock, any business or investment loss invariably prompts these questions: "What went wrong? Was it me? Was it avoidable or was chicanery involved?" Whatever the answer, some people become aware of the fact that there was too much they did not take the time to find out, become discouraged, and never invest again. Others adjust by comforting themselves with, "Well, I guess I will have to chalk it up to experience." But did they, perchance, derive any experience from which they could profit?

Other than injuring their pride, unsettling their nerves and losing time and money, the experience has not taught them much. This is because, other than being a little more careful the next time, they still will not know how to protect themselves from a reoccurrence. Like most of us, they follow their established habit patterns and repeat their mistakes. Ever too often they fail to learn the underlying basics of the business or investment in which they are to become involved. Usually they are unaware of the avoidable and unavoidable risks. They ignore a wide variety of available vital information that could affect the success of any business or investment. This includes the various types of fraud, basic investment and business principles, the economy and its affects, financing, how to analyze a business, how to deal with people, and the latest tax information.

Based on a lifetime of legal, business, practical, and personal experience, the author of this book has focused on trying to prevent avoidable, unnecessary business losses. He addresses the dilemma of uninformed investors and tries to help wherever he can. He discusses the advantages and disadvantages of many popular types of investment and business opportunities and offers suggestions. Those that are discussed have universal appeal to all types of investors, even though their goals might be different. *INVESTOR BEWARE* encourages participation in them for those who are qualified and explains how to get started with a minimum of risk.

One final word of caution. Business and economic conditions are not static and can change suddenly without your being aware that a change has occurred. Management may not be keeping up with the times either. Therefore, if you plan right and find a successful investment that consistently performs well without your supervision, don't take the risk of forgetting to check on it regularly. This advice applies whether you are in stocks, syndications, or your own business. Hopefully, your attention to the status of your investment may help you preserve your investment. Perhaps you can't do anything about these matters, but if you spot problems that cannot be corrected, get out before the value of your investment disappears completely.

Index

Accountant, 17, 232, 324, 326, 395, 400
Accounting, creative, 55
Accounting procedures, 247
Accounts receivable, 405
Accumulated retained earnings, 252
Ad valorum tax, 204
Advertising, 400-401
Age, related to time, 106
Agreements, 14
Alternative Minimum Tax, 374, 430
Ambivalent investors, 96, 101
American Eagle, 415
American Stock Exchange, 358
Amortized payments, 347
Analysis and comparison chart, 254
Annuity, 397
Apartment houses, 249, 347
Appraisal methods, 405
Appraisers, 22, 342
Articles of Incorporation, 132
Assessments, 351
Assets, 50, 108-109, 206, 343, 403
Assistance, 390, 402
At-risk rules, 130
Attorney, 17, 324, 326, 394
Attorneys General, 32
Australia, 211

Background check, 92
Bait, 62-63
Balance Sheet, 252
Balance of goods and services, 202
Balance of trade, 147-148, 200
Balance of trade problems, 211
Bank grarantees, 49
Bank of Montreal, 34
BankAmerica Corp., 48
Bankruptcy, 34, 425
Basic values, 342
Basis points, 216
Bearer bonds, 37, 77
Better Business Bureau, 15, 64, 66, 415-416, 428
Black Monday, 165, 167, 169, 182-183, 185-186, 193, 199, 212, 361
Blank investment analysis chart, 251
Blind Ads, 62
Blue chip, 359
Board of Directors, 393
Boiler room, 415
Bondholders, 356
Bonds, 47-48, 220, 355, 357, 373, 398
Book sections, contents, 5
Book value, 397

Bookkeeping reserves, 231
Borrowed stock, 362
Broker, 71-72, 345, 359
Brokerage commissions, 312
Budget deficit, 180, 183, 189
Budget surplus, 189, 191
Budgets, 398
Builders, 341
Bulk Sales Act, 405
Bullion, 411
Business, 385
Business brokers, 394
Business conditions digest, 155
Business experience, 398
Business guide lines, 402
Business location, 399
Business opportunity brokers, 75
Business partner, 125
Business tips, 402
Business-related statistics, 386
Buy and sell agreements, 248
Buyer beware, 28
Buy-in charges, 365
Buying a business, 396
Buying and operating a franchise, 323
Buying techniques, 393
Buy-out clause, 126

California. Rev. Ltd. Part. Act, 131
Canada, 64, 181, 211, 391, 429, 431
Canadian government, 235
Canadian lumber, 206
Canadian stock exchange, 415
Canvassing, 395, 401
Capital, 423
Capital appreciation, 366, 372, 381
Capital budget, 399
Capital expense, 233
Capital funds, 355
Capital gains, 227, 230
Capital gains taxes, 402
Capital growth investments, 177
Capital market, 161
Capitalization, 387, 404, 407
Capitalizing expenses, 57
Carry-over losses, 233
Caveat emptor, 28
Central bank, 167
Certificates of deposit, 237
Certification statements, 249
Certified Public Accountant, 66
Certified financial planner, 369
Character, 27, 35
Character and reputation, 79

Chart, 43
Chemical Bank and Trust Co., 47
Chinese panda, 415
Churning accounts, 73-74
Civil cases, 32
Claims of creditors, 252
Clean audit, 249
Clean opinion, 249
Closer, 12, 64
Co-conspirators, 32
Coincident indicators, 155
Coins, 411
Commercial Attorney, 35
Commercial buildings, 317
Commission, 362, 428
Commodities, 350, 355, 363, 378
Commodities pool, 25
Commodity futures, 378
Commodity Futures Trade Commission, 32
Commodity prices, 221
Common stocks, 219-220
Community property, 344
Competition, 399-400
Con artists, 11, 21, 321
Con man, 21, 23, 25
Concurrent ownership, 343
Condensed balance sheet, 251-252
Condominiums, 342
Confidence games, 31
Confidence men, 15
Conflict of interest, 317
Congress, 74, 184, 227
Congressional Budget Office, 193
Consolidated balance sheet, 251
Conservative investor, 96, 98-99
Conversion premium, 373-374
Conversion ratio, 373
Conversion value, 373
Convertible preferred, 373
Convertible securities, 372, 374
Corporate stocks, 219
Corporation, 131, 179, 219, 355
Corporations and S corporations, 309
Cost of living index, 313
Cost-push, 178
County clerk's office 126, 128
Crashes, 185
Creative accounting, 57
Credit, 11, 389
Credit business, 404
Credit rating, 316
Creditors, 406
Crime, 22
Crisis Response team, 75
Cumulative, 372-373
Cumulative bonds, 373
Cumulative preferred stock, 356
Current accounts measure, 202
Current accounts receivable, 405

Customer satisfaction, 400

Debentures, 357
Debt, 113
Debtor Nations, 217
Deductions, 24, 313
Default, 51
Deficiency judgment, 99, 115
Deficit-reduction theories, 195
Deflation, 173-174, 183, 412, 417
Demand-pull, 178
Department of Commerce, 164
Department of Labor, 391
Depletion allowance, 430
Deposit, 348
Depreciation, 231-232, 351
Depression, 173-174, 182-183
Desert land, 350
Developers, 341
Developing countries, 203
Disclaimer, 249
Discount rate, 167, 418
Distortion by banks, 56
Distribution facilities, 427
Distributorships 42-43
Dividends, 219, 356, 373
Dow Jones Industrial Average, 212
Drilling, 429
Drilling equipment, 229
Drilling partnerships, 430
Dry wells, 423
Dun & Bradstreet, 386
Dun & Bradstreet's Investment Guide, 380

Earnest money, 35
Earnings, 252
Earnings report, 252
Economic analysts, 173
Economic climate, 153, 157
Economic contradictions, 141
Economic cycles, 223
Economic indicators, 146, 153-156
Economic monetarists, 163
Economic risks, 429
Economics, 141
Embezzlement, 33
Employment discrimination, 402
Employment laws, 402
Energy producers, 431
Equity, 337
Equity financing, 219
Equity sharing, 344
Escrow, 17, 35, 49, 343, 405-406
Escrow companies, 343
ESM, 55-56
Established income, 392
Evaluating businesses, 397
Exchange rates, 55
Explanations of the 56 questions, 261-269

Index 439

Exploration, 429
Export regulations, 412
Export-market, 218

Failure rates, 386
Fannie Mae (FNMA), 380
Farmer, 114, 207, 378
Fast food franchises, 313
Faulty accounting, 184
Faulty budgeting, 184
FBI, 25, 55
FDIC, 49, 89
Federal Budget, 189
Federal Open Market Committee, 163, 165
Federal Reserve, 166-169
Federal Reserve Board, 89, 143, 175, 181, 218, 220, 222, 418
Federal Reserve Central Bank, 146
Federal Reserve System, 161-163, 185
Federal Trade Commission, 31, 321
Fees, 366-367
Fictitious firm name, 121-122
FIFO, 249
Financial analysts, 221
Financial contingencies, 109
Financial documents, 247
Financial guidelines, 393
Financial planning, 72
Financial reserves, 108
Financial statements, 58, 245, 403
Financial waiting power, 100
Financing, 346-347
Fiscal Policy, 190
FMOC, 216
Foreign capital, 222
Foreign exchange, 147
Foreign investment, 207
Foreign investors, 157, 218
Forest fires, 210
Franchise, 315-316, 385
Franchise booklet, 321
Franchise difficulties, 324-325
Franchise fees, 321
Franchise information and books, 329
Franchise questions, 327-328
Franchise salesmen, 324
Franchisee, 316
Franchises, 321-322
Franchising, 394
Franchisor, 316, 394
Franchisor's guidance, 322
Fraud, 24, 33-34, 55, 75
Fraudulent, 31
Fraudulent practices, 424-425
Friends, 21, 25
FSLIC, 50
Fundamentals, 381
Futures contracts, 355, 363
Futures market, 73

GAAP, 184
Gadgets, 128
Gambler, 95-96
Gambling, 83, 88, 90, 378
Gas, 423
Gas exploration, 433
General partners, 24, 327
General partnerships, 124, 309
Gephart Amendment, 200, 203
Germany, 194, 205-206
Get-rich-quick, 39, 411
Ginnie Mae, 311
GNP, 193, 217
Gold, 177, 179, 411-419
Gold bullion, 416
Gold coins, 415
Gold content, 416
Gold standard, 212
Goodwill, 322, 324, 393-394, 402
Government bonds, 87
Government securities, 55
Greed factor, 16
Gross National Product, 147-148, 175, 180-181, 184
Gross Domestic Product, 147-148
Gross rental, 348
Guaranteed, 47
Guaranteed income, 62
Guaranteed municipal bonds, 89
Guaranteed profits, 66
Guaranty, 48-51

Hedge, 412
Hedging, 378
High risk, 98, 333
High sailing, 74
High-yield investments, 96
Homeowners, 231
Homestake Mining, 412
Hot tip, 355
House Banking Committee, 89
Hucksters, 31

Imaginative accounting, 424, 427
Imports, 204
Income deferment, 236
Income property, 98, 341, 345, 351
Income shelters, 227
Income statements, 252-253
Index of leading indicators, 143
Individual ownership, 309
Industrial complexes, 342
Industrial Revolution, 141
Industrial wine, 41
Inflation, 31, 173-174, 179, 183, 190, 194, 221-223, 343, 412, 417, 419, 424
Inflation, double-digit, 176-177
Inflation protection, 398
Inside information, 379

Installment sales, 232
Insurance, 390
Insurance brokers, 77
Insurance companies, 47-49
Insured, 315
Intangible assets, 247, 405
Intangible drilling costs, 429
Intelligent Investors, 91
Interest, 219-220, 231, 346-347, 372-373
Interest payments, 100
Interest rate, 87, 98, 157, 161, 163, 168, 183-184, 194, 203, 215-219, 222, 342, 376, 412
Interest-sensitive, 357
International Energy Agency, 431
International Monetary Fund Benchmark, 222
Investigate, 428
Investigate franchises, 323
Investigations, 34
Investing, 83
Investment advisers, 376
Investment capital, 338
Investment climate, 153
Investment counselors, 98, 108
Investment disposition, 95, 97
Investment earnings, 230
Investment goals, 105, 110
Investment lesson, 388
Investment mistakes, 91
Investment property, 345
Investment reasons, 105
Investment signals, 212
Investment tips, 379
Investment trusts, 364
Investor alerts, 418
Investor categories, 95-96, 98-99
Investors, 154
IRAs, 123, 237-239, 364
IRS, 227, 229, 233-235, 316, 342

Japan, 185, 194, 205-206
Japanese, 218-219
Jewelry, 412
Joint ownership, 309
Joint tenancy, 124, 344
Jointly and Severally liable, 51, 124, 130-131
Junk bonds, 377

Keogh Plan, 364
Keynesian economics, 175
Keynesians, 190
Kiln-dried wood, 209
Korean conflict, 391
Krugerrand, 415-416

Lagging indicators, 155
Laissez-Faire theories, 175
Land, 107, 350

Landlord, 342
Leading indicators, 175
Lease, 389, 393
Legal pitfalls, 389
Leverage, 113, 115, 347, 371
Licensing, 403, 406
Liens, 406
LIFO, 249
Limited partners, 24, 428,
Limited Partnership Agreement, 130
Limited partnerships, 127-128, 309, 334
Liquid Assets, 165
Load funds, 365
Loan-loss reserve ratio, 167
Location, 389, 399-400, 403
Long-term bonds, 177
Long-term capital gains, 230

M-1, M-2, M-3, & L indexes, 163-167, 169, 175
Mail, 11, 403
Management, 381, 390, 404
Management fees, 335, 365
Management skills, 407
Marcia Stigum, 165
Margin 108, 185, 231, 371-372
Margin accounts, 369-370
Market price, 360
Marketing techniques, 399
Marks, 61
Maximum tax rate, 230
Mechanically investing, 367-368
Medium of exchange, 413
Middle East, 206
Milton Friedman, 145-146
Minimum percentage of gross income, 313
Mining company stocks, 415
Minor economic theories, 146
Misrepresentations, 396
Mistakes, 403
Mobility, 31
Moderate investor, 95
Modus operandi, 39
Monetarist economics, 175
Monetarists, 144
Monetary trends, 166, 216
Monetary currency, 413
Monetary indexes, 164
Monetary-debasement, 178
Money market, 161
Money supply, 161, 163, 167, 182
Monthly payments, 349-350
Moody's, 357
Mortgage companies, 50
Mortgages, 346
Multilevel distributorship, 43
Municipal bonds, 232, 237, 374-376
Municipalities, 47
Mutual companies, 413

Index

Mutual funds, 364-368

N.Y. Stock Exchange, 358-360
NASA, 71, 78
National Assoc. of Securities Dealers, 370
Negative psychology, 64
Net asset value, 405
Net basis, 313
Net income, 393
No-loads, 365-366
Non-recourse, 115
North American Securities Assoc., 321

Oil, 87, 423
Oil and gas, 227
Oil development, 424
Oil exploration, 424, 433
Oil shortage, 429
Oil wells, 429
Oliver, Daniel, 31
OPEC, 412, 429-431
Operating budget, 400
Operating entity, 393
Options, 34, 355, 363
Options Clearing Corp., 363
Osmond family defrauded, 26
Over the Counter, 358

P/E ratio, 392
Paper currency, 157
Parental support, 237
Partnership agreement, 125
Partnerships, 25-26, 317, 430
Passive income, 324
Payments on capital accounts, 202
Payroll taxes, 390
Pension funds, 367
Percentage of profit, 113-114
Petroleum companies, 431
Pigeon, finding a, 16
Pilferage, 389
Pitch, 13, 62-64
Pitchmen 31-32, 61
Political refugees, 412-413
Political risks, 429
Ponzi, Charles A., 39
Ponzi-type schemes, 2, 27, 39-41
Pork barrel clauses, 203
Power to sell, 108, 115
Precious gems, 61
Preferred stocks, 356, 372-373
Preview of the 56 questions, 254-259
Price, stock, 361
Prime rate, 216
Producer, 378
Professional advice, 379, 398
Profit, 32-33, 360
Profit and loss statements, 251-252
Profitability, 404

Program trading, 73
Programmed trading, 362
Promissory notes, 41
Promoter, 11, 129
Promotion, 400
Promotional literature, 415
Property ownership, 342
Prosecution, high cost of, 33
Prospectus, 313, 315
Protection, 64
Protectionist bills and tariffs, 203-204
Protective clauses, 246
Prudent risk-takers, 86
Pump priming, 193
Purchasing power, 177, 180
Put and call options, 412
Put option, 363
Pyramid chart, 43
Pyramid schemes, 27, 39, 41-42

Qualified opinions, 249
Qualified statements, 57
Qualifying prospects, 12
Questions, investment, 1, 254
Quick tips, 66
Quick-flip, 235

Ranches, 342
Ratios, 260
Real estate, 179, 227, 311, 317, 341-343
Real estate brokers, 75
Real estate deductions, 237
Real estate fraud, 75
Real estate investment trusts, 309
Recession, 90, 173-174, 183, 194, 342
Recklessly negligent, 57
Record-keeping, 390
Records, 390
Redemption clauses, 375
Referrals, 13
Registered bonds, 377
Registered Investment Advisers, 369
Regulation T, 370
Rent concessions, 347
Rental schedule, 393
Reserve assets, 432
Reserve funds, 98
Reserves, 432
Residential retreats, 27
Retail business, 395
Retail sales, 321
Risk, 313, 423
Risk capital, 334
Risk-free, 1, 28
Risk-taking, 83, 88-91
Risks and problems, 336

Sales closers, 99-100
Sales pitch, 12

Sales tactics, 15
Sales tax records, 396, 405
Salesmanship, 399
Sample balance sheet, 253-254
Sample house, 13
Savings and loan, 76
SBA, 390
SBICs, 334
Scams, 21, 32, 61, 63
Schemes, 40, 42, 64
SEC, 369, 371, 415
Secured Note, 76-77
Securities, 231-232, 355
Securities & Exchange Commission, 32, 40-41, 74, 58, 311
Securities fraud, 32
Self-employment tax, 130
Self-serving brokers, 72
Selling short, 378, 380
Sensitive economic factors, 156
Separate ownerships, 343
Service, 389
Service businesses, 404
Shareholders, 219, 356
Shell corporation, 50
Shills, 397
Shoplifters, 404
Short selling, 362
Short-term capital gains, 230
Short-term losses, 96, 233
Signatures, 343
Silver, 32, 179
Small Business Administration, 334, 386
Small investment, 318
Sole proprietor, 121-123
Solicitations, telephone, 11
Sophisticated investors, 41, 247
South Africa, 412, 418
South African Exchange, 416
Soviet Union, 210, 414
Speculating, 378
Speculator, 90, 95-96, 99-100, 313, 380
Spotting investment con games and swindles, 7
Spouse, 97, 100, 107-108
Stakeholder, 405
Standard & Poor, 49, 356
Start-up capitalization, 337
Start-up companies, 334
Starting a business, 328
State laws, 406
Statement of Accumulated Retained Earnings, 251
Statement of Financial Condition, 251
Statement of Income, Expenses, and Profits, 345
Statements, financial, 58
Statements, qualified, 57
Statements, unaudited, 57

Statistics, 174
Stock Exchanges, 357
Stock Indexes, 363, 367
Stock market, 194
Stockbroker, 71-72
Stocks, 355, 374
Student Loan Program, 391
Subchapter S Corporations, 121, 134
Subscription warrants, 356
Sucker list, 11
Sugar, 32, 203
Supply and Demand, 361
Supply-side economics, 145, 175
Supply-side economists, 180
Supply-siders, 190
Swindled, 25, 32, 35
Swindler, 12, 14, 21-22, 33, 39, 61
Syndication, 309, 311-313, 316-318

Take or pay contracts, 47-48, 427
Tangible assets, 247
Tax advantages, 430
Tax audits, 229
Tax benefits, 121
Tax breaks, 23, 235
Tax exempt securities, 375
Tax exemptions, 232
Tax fraud, 24
Tax incentives, 430
Tax rates, 122
Tax records, 406
Tax reduction, 145
Tax Reform Act, 115, 120, 227-228, 230, 233, 313, 317, 351-352, 372, 374, 380
Tax shelters, 23, 229, 234-236, 351
Tax traps, 227, 234
Tax-free income, 229
Taxes, 132, 134, 351
Taxing, 192
Ted Turner, 113
Tenancies in common, 343
Tenancy in Partnership, 344
Tenant, 344, 348
Termination, 327, 389
The 56-question test, 254
The Investment Analysis Chart, 299-303
The triple witching hour, 362
Third World debt, 207
Total Assets, 252
Total Liabilities, 252
Total of Stockholders' Equity, 252
Trade cycle, 206
Trade deficit, 183, 191, 195-196, 199, 206
Trade fixtures, 352
Trade imbalances, 206
Trade of goods, 201
Trade of services, 201
Trademarked names, 322
Trading program, 32

Index 443

Trading techniques, 362
Training service, 391
Traps, 351
Treasury Department, 161-162, 169
Treasury bill, 161, 216
Treasury bonds, 376
Treasury Dept., 161-162
Treasury notes, 221
Tricky accounting, 55
Trust deed, 101
Trusts, 123
Types of ownership, 309

U.S. banking system, 182
U.S. banks, 207
U.S. Benchmark, 433
U.S. Bureau of Economic Analysis, 155
U.S. Department of Commerce, 143
U.S. dollar, 179, 203, 206, 208, 219, 222
U.S. economy, 220
U.S. Government Printing Office, 398
U.S. Int. Trade Comm., 210
U.S. rate of exchange, 209
U.S. Supreme Court, 47
U.S. Treasury bonds, 232
Ultra-conservative investors, 88, 96, 99
Unanticipated events, 389
Unaudited reports, 248
Unaudited statements, 57
Undercapitalized, 316
Undeveloped land, 349
Undisclosed charges, 367
Unsecured note, 76-77
Up-front fees, 428, 433

Vacant land, 341
Value of the dollar, 215
Vancouvre Sun, 27
Vending machines, 62, 64
Venture capital, 333, 337
Venture capital ltd., partnerships, 335
Veterans program, 402
Victim, 23, 35, 40, 63-64
Vital data, 248

Wall Steet Journal, 24, 33, 50, 113, 133, 141, 147, 167, 182
Warrants, 356
Washington Public Power (WPPSS), 47
Washington state, 50
West Texas Intermediate, 433
Wheat subsidy, 210
Wheat, 208
White collar crimes, 21-22, 31, 33-34
Window dressing, 56-57
Wine, industrial, 41
Worthless guaranteed bonds, 47
Written agreement, 14, 17

Yen, 219
Yield, 87
Young couple, 108

Zero coupon bonds, 78, 377
Zoning, 399, 406

BUSINESS AND PROFESSIONAL BOOKS

MegaTraits $17.95
Dr. Doris Lee McCoy 1-55622-056-1

Dr. McCoy traveled extensively to interview over 1,000 "successful" people. Interviews with such people as Charlton Heston, Malcolm Forbes, and Ronald Reagan led Dr. McCoy to discover 12 traits of success. She sought consistencies and success patterns from which you can benefit. Are there specific points to help all of us become more successful? The answer is a resounding YES! There are traits consistently found in the lives of successful people. Read *MegaTraits* to discover how you too can develop and utilize these unique attributes.

Business Emotions $14.95
Richard Contino 1-55622-058-8

Revolutionize your thinking, conditioning, and approach. Learn why emotions are a controlling factor in every success and failure situation. This practical book will guide you through the maze of hidden psychological issues in a simple and straightforward manner. Achieve predictable, positive, and immediate results.

Innovation, Inc. $12.95
Stephen Grossman, Bruce Rodgers, 1-55622-054-5
Beverly Moore

Unlock your hidden potential to reach a new plane of creative thinking. Seek out new avenues of problem-solving by elevating your ability to conceive ideas. Techniques and exercises in this book expand your creativity. The authors take you on a journey designed to spark confidence by reorganizing your thinking processes and patterns. Learn to use innovative thinking to inspire fresh ideas and formulate imaginative concepts.

Investor Beware $14.95
Henry Rothenberg 1-55622-055-3

Create your own luck with this book detailing the essentials for safe investments. Avoid shady, risky, and unsuccessful investments. Learn how to anticipate and interpret various investment climates and analyze a business from financial statements. The average investor will find what he needs to know about economics, financing, taxes, operating entities, and types of investments. Discover the ramifications of diversified investments such as real estate, franchises, oil and gas, gold, tax shelters, and syndications.

Steps to Strategic Management $13.95
Rick Molz 1-55622-050-2

This book is the story of one individual. . .YOU. Put yourself in the shoes of Joe Clancy, the imaginary entrepreneur in this book. By following the clear, ongoing example of Joe, you will discover how strategic management works. A series of nine steps will help you develop a systematic approach to strategic management. With honesty and hard work, you can use this book to help shape your future.

Call Wordware Publishing, Inc. for names of the bookstores in your area.
(214) 423-0090